The PRACTICAL VEDANTA of Swami Rama Tirtha

Edited by Brandt Dayton

www.HimalayanInstitute.in

Himalayan Institute India
Near Nageshwar Mandir
Chatnag, Jhunsi
Allahabad – 211019 (U.P.)

Email: info@HimalayanInstitute.in
Web: www.HimalayanInstitute.in

Tenth printing, 2015, Printed in India

ISBN 10: 0-89389-038-3
ISBN 13: 978-089389-038-4

Library of Congress Cataloging-in-Publication Data:
Rama Tirtha, Swami, 1873-1906
1. Vedanta—Collected works. I. Dayton Brandt
II. Title.
B132.V3R34125 1978 181.48 78-10567

Swami Rama Tirtha

Rama guarantees that anybody in this world,
who reads or hears all of Rama's speeches,
would get his doubts removed
and is sure to come
to the conviction
of his own divinity.

Contents

Editor's Note

The purpose of the following volume is to present to the English reader both representative and remarkable writings of Swami Rama Tirtha. Those of us who inhabit the narrow world of this one language are unfortunate in not being able to follow the wisdom of a great man into Urdu or Persian in which forms he is said to have expressed himself the most masterfully. Yet in these many lectures and letters, Rama's genius seems to have led him intuitively to English words equivalently direct and sublime. Certainly few true sages of India before him have combined such thorough scholarship of both Eastern and Western thought.

Most of the lectures in Section I chosen for this volume were delivered in English during Swami Rama Tirtha's American tour of 1902-4 and were transcribed on each occasion by an American disciple. Several articles of India origin, however, have been translated from the Urdu as noted. To conserve space and limit the overlap of idea, all of the lectures have been abridged somewhat. Within the main sections of lectures which have been presented, certain lines have been deleted or transposed in order to render repetitious rhetoric more readable. The article entitled "Non-Duality" presented here in its entirety, was published originally in the Urdu magazine *Alif* whose first issue appeared in January, 1900.

The quotations in Section II were culled from a wide collection of original thoughts and universal aphorisms compiled by Swami Rama Tirtha in thirteen notebooks. From these seed bins of perception into philosophy and nature, science and religion, ideas were gathered by the sage into lectures and articles. These few selections reflect the range of Rama's heart and intellect.

Swami Rama was known in his day as a philosopher-poet and was best loved by many for the playfully, wildly lyrical side of his nature. The poems of Section III were most often transcribed as immediate records of deeply joyful moods. While his efforts in Urdu were pursued with more art, Rama lacked literary ambition and rarely returned to polish the lines he wrote. Nonetheless, his simple, even awkward, English versions are carried high on spontaneous waves of pure inspiration.

Swami Rama Tirtha's letters give brief glimpses into the personal life which he disdained. In Section IV, excerpts of those letters have been chosen and presented in biographical sequence which give insight into Rama's spiritual development at crucial junctures in his life. The date, place of origin, and recipient of each letter has been noted to the extent that they could be established accurately. Most of these fragments were addressed in Urdu to Rama's first spiritual teacher, Dhanna Bhakta Rama, with whom he maintained a devoted correspondence. Besides two American letters, only those few which originated from Darjeeling in 1905 were written in English. Several of the longer essays which describe Rama's spiritual experiences deep in the Himalayas formed part of a personal journal and were not necessarily directed to any individual. These transcripts of a pure and passionate relationship with nature constitute perhaps the most uniquely beautiful literature left by Swami Rama Tirtha.

We express our gratitude to the Shri Rama Tirtha Pratisthan, Lucknow, India, for allowing us to use their material in this book.

Brandt Dayton
June 16, 1978

Introduction

Swami Rama Tirtha was one of the greatest seers, not only of India, but of the whole world. He was a sage, poet, philosopher and spiritual leader of our times. To give an exhaustive list of his many attainments from early youth onward would be a difficult task—for his was a towering personality. Philosophy, mathematics, the Persian language, these were only a few of the subjects at his command.

As a student Swami Rama Tirtha was fond of keeping journals. Over a thousand of his letters, mostly written to his Guru while he was a student, and later to his friends and followers, are still available. They reflect his unique personality at every stage as in a mirror. Swami Rama Tirtha spoke ex tempore. He writes: "Poverty is blessed: it constructs a ladder of tear drops to the throne of God." His father felt that Rama Tirtha should be earning bread for the family, but destiny seemed to have willed otherwise.

Both as a student and as a professor, Swami Rama Tirtha placed great emphasis on the value of work. "We are abundantly reaping the fruits of the labors of others. Let us not forget that we ought to do something for others in return." He felt that we owe a heavy debt to humanity and that we ought to leave the world better than we found it. "Work with all your heart and might remembering that work is worship. Genuine work will be found to be its own reward." Work is the normal state of man. The natural way to enlightenment is the faithful use of what we have. Practice alone makes us perfect. It is not enough to know theory; man must practice the art if he wants to swim across the river.

After a few years, Rama Tirtha retired to the Himalayas to build a little sacred shrine for God in his heart. "In this network of life, evolution is simply orderly change. Some fruits stick onto the tree even after they are ripe while others fall when they are ripe." Rama Tirtha loved the Himalayan Mountains. For him, retreating into the Himalayas was necessary for Self-realization. Before he could work in the world he had to accumulate a vast store of energy. Filled with the flames of divine fire he boldly and fearlessly taught the practical Vedanta which one should practice even in the face of persecution and opposition.

The Vedas are the most ancient books in the library of man. They are considered by those who study them to be an infinite source of knowledge. The latter part of these texts are called Upanishads or *sruti*. The Upanishads are the finest part of the Vedas and are called Vedanta because in them Vedic wisdom reaches its culmination or *anta*. Vedanta shows the seeker the way to liberation and the Summum Bonum of life. To Swami Rama Tirtha goes the credit for reviving Vedanta in the modern world. He revived India's spiritual heritage and called his philosophy Practical Vedanta.

From the prime of his manhood onward he traveled from country to country lecturing in the leading universities of the world. Deep insight and spiritual inspiration were his magic wands, by whose power he roamed from the Himalayan Mountains to the east and west coasts of the United States. He did not, as many Easterners had, dismiss the West with a supercilious sneer. He respected the West for its science, its strength, freedom, justice, and activities for human rights. He did not identify himself with any caste, creed, sex, or color. He was of the cosmos. He did not believe in a God or a religion of disparity. While denouncing nationalism, he propagated the ideals of universal consciousness and became a chief proponent of practical Vedanta. His internationalism was enveloped with practical Vedanta. He believed that India has a message and a mission, special work entrusted to her by providence.

Both Swami Rama Tirtha's poetry and prose embody his universal and practical philosophy. The music of his works which fills the outer ear is but an echo of the inner harmony of humanity and the universe, which exists at the heart of things and which he has caught and made manifest by his works. In his works, Eastern literature has outgrown its character and has become fit to fraternize with world literature. Universal currents of thoughts and spirituality have flowed into modern life through his writings. His poems and lectures on practical Vedanta lead the readers into the secret of his access to the court of the Lord of Life and of his communion with Him. His writings in a spiritual vein have brought solace and healing to many a troubled soul. How wonderfully full of real life, devotion and inspiration they are!

"His body was a lake which trembled seeing the sun enter into its depths. He confounds logic by his divine ecstasy, enchants the very air around himself with his brilliant speech that was all poetry, all music . . . a truly eloquent apostle of the life of the spirit." Puran Singh

Swami Rama Tirtha said that the highest of all prayers is to remember one's own Self which is the Self of all. You have not to become pure; you are pure already. You are not to be perfect; you are that already.

Brandt Dayton, the compiler and editor of this book, undertook this task to make the book available for Western readers. A great service has been done especially for those who are prepared to listen to the music of the silence, follow it, and improve and enlighten themselves. The practical Vedanta of Swami Rama Tirtha will benefit readers philosophically, devotionally, intellectually and spiritually. It is an inspirational book which can help lead one to fearlessness and Self-realization.

Sri Swami Rama of the Himalayas

Biography

With the irony which often inaugurates great spiritual lives, Swami Rama Tirtha was born on October 22, 1873 to humble Brahmin parents in the village of Muraliwala in the Gujranwala district of the Punjab. Though fallen into poverty and obscurity, the family of Tirtha Rama, as he was first called, claimed high and ancient descent as members of the Goswami caste from the sage Vashishtha and the mystic saint Tulsidas. A narrow-minded man of little education and less temper, Rama's father struggled for a living as a local priest; his mother was known to be a quietly religious woman. The astrologer who investigated the horoscope of the newborn child was said to laugh and weep. He wept because the child would die or lose its mother and laughed for if the child lived the world would celebrate the career of a great scholar and man of God. It was foretold that between the thirtieth and fortieth years of his life he would die in water.

Indeed when Tirtha Rama was only a year old his mother died, and the sickly child was entrusted to an old aunt in whose devout arms he daily visited the village temples. Rama's father tells of a serious little son that showed a strong fascination for the sound of the conch and often insisted upon being carried to the *katha* where religious stories were recited.

At the unknowing age of ten Tirtha Rama was bound in marriage to the small daughter of a neighboring Brahmin. He was later to rebuke his father that "you condemned me to the servitude of a householder's life at a very early age." The young boy was sent to school in a distant village where he was placed under the tutelage of one Dhanna Bhakta Rama, a simple, religious man of some local reputation. Far more remarkable than the spiritual attainments of this strange *sadhu* was the complete devotion with which Tirtha Rama accepted his guidance. Within this relationship Rama's ardent love for God first found direction. Although Dhanna Bhakta was eventually to lose his own path and long pester his disciple with complaints, Rama never forsook his original reverence. He looked after his old guru until the end of his life.

From an early age, Tirtha Rama encountered study and books with a singleminded diligence. Resolved to acquire an "English" education against his father's opposition, he joined Mission College in Lahore in 1888. Stories of his brilliant determination as a scholar at Forman Christian and Government Colleges in Lahore are renowned. So zealously did he pursue his favorite subject of mathematics that he vowed one night to take his life rather than fail to solve four extremely formidable problems. Under the circumstances the answers obliged.

Tirtha Rama's academic honors were gained against great obstacles of poverty and poor health. His modest scholarships never met the demands for support of his family, master, and young wife with whom he was finally billeted by a spiteful father. In miserable quarters Rama kept late night company with snakes and thieves, and with classic dedication, he was more likely to buy oil for his lamp than food for his faded body. Fellow students and college officials conspired frequently to improve the plight of the austere scholar who had won their unanimous esteem.

Fate denied Rama a scholarship for study in England which he deserved as first student of the university. Having passed his M.A. examination in 1895, he defied the stifling pressure upon every educated Indian of his day to serve the British bureaucracy. To those who encouraged a petty but profitable government career Rama replied, "I have not toiled so much for selling my harvest but for distributing it. I would prefer being a teacher to being an executive officer." First at the Mission School and later at Forman Christian College, increasing crowds of students were drawn to the conscientious professor of mathematics who in his selfless motive to serve shared with them his salary as well as his learning. Any needy student could purchase milk for himself against Rama's meagre credit.

It was during these days in Lahore that from Rama's early openness to God emerged the spiritual passion which was to overwhelm his life. By nature inclined toward *bhakti*, an attitude of love toward God, Rama became absorbed in the spirit of the Bhagavad Gita and lost in reveries of Lord Krishna. Friends reported often overhearing his wandering cries, "Lord! Another day has passed away, and I have not seen Thee. Will my life be wasted thus? I have not knowingly transgressed Thy commandments–why do I suffer the pangs of separation?" This first fervor met its object in a vision of Krishna which overcame Rama on a visit to holy shrines in the summer of 1896. The inspired devotee began to pour forth lectures which spellbound large audiences.

Tirtha Rama's spiritual ambitions were converted by a visit of His Holiness the Jagadguru Shankaracharya to Lahore. This august representative of orthodox Vedanta was impressed by the intent young man assigned to attend him and instructed Rama privately in the rigorous philosophies of yoga. Henceforth Rama was to take up the ancient quest for Self-realization. His timely meeting with Swami Vivekananda in November, 1897 must have spurred him on toward this ideal. A towering example of renunciation, Ramakrishna's brilliant disciple had invigorated India and intrigued the West by translating Vedanta into practical terms. Tirtha Rama's own career would soon pursue a parallel course.

Rama's letters in the ensuing year describe a life of intensifying focus within. With solitary resolution he headed in the summer of 1898 toward the upper reaches of the Ganges at Hardwar and Rishikesh. Discarding all possessions, he vowed upon the wild banks of the river to restore his soul to its Self or abandon his life. Finally reduced to desperation, he tossed himself into a dangerous current. The holy river, with which he would commune for the rest of his life, carried Rama to a rock. Upon it he was enlightened. For days afterwards he remained in a state of ecstasy. Essays written with rare rapture record this first experience of Reality.

Upon his return to Lahore Tirtha Rama's outer life was rapidly transformed by the burning force of his Realization. Seekers from all the districts of Western India came to witness his clear vision at the *satsangs*, or religious assemblies, organized by him in these days. Narayana, his most intimate and lifelong disciple, sat among them. With his aid Rama soon launched the periodical *Alif* which was to inspire the intelligentsia of India. University officials were alarmed by these religious activities and requested Rama to resign his professorship in January, 1899.

Welcoming the sole serivce of God, Rama decided shortly after the birth of his second son to withdraw from civilization with his family and disciples. As a member of the hesitant party which Rama led into the forest, Narayana relates that Rama charged them, "Let us resign ourselves completely to Him and live as He desires." He instructed them to demonstrate this faith by consigning their entire belongings to the Ganges at Gangotri. All followed his bidding but were equally emboldened and relieved when within a few hours a local baba had arranged for their provisions. Rama's liberated spirit soared in the mountains around Tehri, but his wife could not bear the austerity of their new existence. With her smaller son she returned to the plains.

Now the path of renunciation had opened inevitably. One day early in 1901, with special privilege granted him by the Shankaracharya, Rama entered the Ganges, performed ancient rites and emerged a *sannyasi*. To mark his formal initiation into spiritual life he reversed the order of his names and thereafter called himself Swami Rama Tirtha. For many months he roamed remote peaks of the Himalayas, alone and intoxicated in the soul of nature. With winter he descended to Muttra, where in December 1901 he created a sensation at a Conference of Religions; but by May Rama Tirtha had wound his way back to Tehri whose lofty solitude invited him irresistibly. The local Maharaja sought out the sage who ranged his forest mountains, and this spiritual and this temporal lord became famous friends. His Highness received word of an All-Religions Conference to be held in Japan and persuaded the unassuming swami to attend. Sailing with Narayana from Calcutta in August 1902, Rama Tirtha was launched upon his far-flung worldly mission.

In Japan, as in other nations of the new century, Swami Rama drew original force from his intuitive identification with common Truth, however it emerged in human life. Upon arrival in Nagasaki, he remarked, "Rama has nothing to teach these peoples. They are all Vedantins. They are all Ramas. How cheerful, how happy, how quiet, how laborious. This is all that Rama calls life." He soon discovered that he had followed a false rumor to Tokyo—no religious conference was planned. An obliging fool to fate, he rejoiced at his mistake and proposed to conduct his own parliament of religions. All Japan responded with the admiration expressed by a great and learned Professor of Tokyo Imperial University who declared of his new acquaintance, "I have met many pandits and philosophers at the house of Professor Max Muller in England and other places, but I have never seen a personality like Swami Rama, who is so living and so significant an illustration of his whole philosophy. In him Vedanta and Buddhism meet. He is true religion. He is a true poet and philosopher."

Surprised at first sight of a "Hindoo" swami, America soon rose in honor also. The following story is told of Rama Tirtha in 1902 as he disembarked from a steamer in San Francisco: "A curious American, wonderstruck as to why he (Rama) was not in the usual haste of getting down, asked, "Where is your luggage, Sir?"

"I carry no luggage," said the Swami, "but what I have about me."

"Where do you keep your money?"

"I keep no money."

"How do you live?"

"I only live by loving all. When I am thirsty there is always one with a cup of water for me, and when I am hungry there is always one with a loaf of bread."

"But have you then any friends in America?"

"Ah, yes, I know but one American–you," said the Swami, touching his shoulder, and by his touch the American realized, so to say, his old forgotten acquaintance with him and became his ardent admirer."[1]

Within two years Rama Tirtha lectured widely across the United States, touring eastward from San Francisco to Portland, Denver, Minneapolis, Chicago, Buffalo, Boston, New York, Philadelphia and Washington, D.C. In the land of rude materialism Rama won respect for his ruggedness as well as his rareness of soul. He made headlines as the first man to climb Mt. Shasta in Oregon. Pitching a tent along the Sacramento River, he lived roughly for many months on the ranch of a California friend. Rama introduced Americans to universal principles of spirituality which he called the "Common Path." He spoke directly to the Western intellect by transposing the alien ideals of Vedanta philosophy into concrete codes for personal success. An honest ambassador, he brought before the Great Democracy the fallen fate of his homeland and delivered to President Roosevelt in May of 1903 his famous "Appeal on Behalf of India."

1 Shargo, P. Brijnath. *Life of Swami Rama Tirtha*, The Rama Tirtha Pratishthan, Lucknow, pages 260-261.

The charm of Swami Rama, to which thousands of Americans succumbed, is suggested in an excerpt from a San Francisco newspaper article of the time: "This remarkable sage of the Himalayas is a slender, intellectual young man with the ascetic mould of a priest and the light complexion of a high caste Brahmin. His forehead is broad and high; his head, splendidly developed; his nose, thin and delicate as a woman's, while his chin reveals great firmness of will without stubbornness. A wide, kindly almost tender mouth parts freely over dazzlingly white, perfect teeth in a smile that seems to light up all surrounding space and wins instantaneous confidence and the good will of all who come within the circle of its radiance.

" 'How do I live?' he said yesterday. 'This is simple. I do not try. I believe; I attune my soul to the harmony of love for all men. That makes all men love me, and where love is, there is no want, no suffering. This state of mind and faith bring influences to me that supply my needs without asking. If I am hungry there is always someone to feed me. I am forbidden to receive money or to ask for anything, yet I have everything, and more than most, for I live largely in a world that few can attain.' "

Before completing the world circle of his journey, Rama demonstrated his spiritual affinity with all great religions by stirring the hearts of Moslem audiences in Egypt. When he arrived at last in Bombay in December 1904 a grand reception awaited him. The Indian people revered Rama as a symbol of self-reliant patriotism. The British government, however, did not appreciate his straightforward views on social reform and national freedom and placed him under surveillance immediately upon his return to the country. Unintimidated and amused,

Swami Rama exposed two British spies by telling them, "My countrymen, you have come to detect Rama. Rama opens his heart to you. The best thing in the world is to detect Rama. Detect him; find him; the world is under your feet."

Rama rejected suggestions that he assemble religious and political influence through a society organized in his name. He resumed instead the independent path which he called "balanced recklessness." Often surrounded by students Rama wandered in the summer of 1905 from Pushkar Lake to the mountain district of Darjeeling. By the end of the year he had returned to his old haunts around Hardwar, hoping to restore his physical health which had begun to falter after long and strenuous neglect. Retiring to ever remote ashrams along the Ganges, Rama ascended once again the silent heights of God-consciousness. His bodily strength continued to dwindle; his disciples grew distraught, but Rama Tirtha, unperturbed, applied his remaining energies to the study of the Vedas. According to the description of his disciple Puran Singh, at this late stage of Rama's life "he was nearing the Hindu ideal of a Vedantic philosopher and would sit crosslegged for days and days unaffected by the opposites and unconcerned with his body." To this disciple's lament that Rama had lost his laughter and vitality, he replied, "Puranji, the world is concerned only with my blossoms, and they taste me when I appear before them in my flowers. But they do not know how much I have to labor underground in the dark recesses, in my roots that gather the food for the flowers and the fruits. I am now in my roots. Silence is greater work than the fireworks of preaching and giving off our thoughts to the world."

The Maharaja of Tehri had ordered that a hut be constructed for Rama at a sacred spot on the banks of the Ganges. This was to be the great sage's last abode. In September, 1906 he parted from his disciple Narayana with forewarning words, "My son, Ram shall soon be silent. His pen and tongue will fail him. Ram's body is growing weaker day by day; his mind has gotten so tired of the world that nothing interests him now. He feels as if he will no more go down to the plains. No wonder if Ram's body soon becomes inactive. Never shall he leave his dear Ganga's bosom. Therefore go to your cave; practice seclusion, dive deep every moment into Ram and come out as the embodiment of Vedanta. Have no griefs, no worries, no sorrows. Feel Ram with you, within you. He is your body. He is your mind. He is your all in all. He is your own self. Emerge from your seclusion and be as Ram himself."

One week later on the holy day known as Diwali, October 17, 1906, Swami Rama Tirtha left his body while bathing in the Ganges. All India grieved at the official report that the young saint had drowned, but the philosophy which Rama personifed knew no defeat in death. Written moments before he gave up his life, his last words affirm the fearless freedom of his soul: "O Death, certainly blow up this one body. I have enough bodies to me. I can wear those divine silver threads, the beams of the moon, and live. I can roam as divine minstrel in the guise of hilly streams and mountain brooks. I can dance in the waves of the sea. I am the breeze that proudly walks, and I am the wind inebriated. All these shapes of mine are wandering shapes of change. I came down from yonder hills, raised the dead, awakened the sleeping, unveiled the fair faces of some and wiped the tears of a few weeping ones. The nightingale and the rose bush both I saw, and I comforted them. I touched this, touched that. I doff my hat and off I am. Here I go and there I go; none can find me."

Lectures

FOREST TALKS

When great ideas have once been born into the world and formulated they may be misrepresented, thwarted or even defeated and made to retire for a time into the background, but they are destined not to perish, and they continue to live a life of their own till in the fullness of time the advance of human thought and morality reaches a stage of evolution when it becomes possible to realize them in the social order.

The little seed set now must lie quiet before it will germinate, and many alternations of sunshine and shower fall upon it before it becomes a plant. Come thou again ere long, and behold! a mighty tree that no storm can shake.

> Call these thoughts Utopian, but they are Truth, and
> Truth crushed to Earth shall rise again;
> The eternal Years of God are hers.

This is the fiery lava sprouting from the volcano on human breast.

This is the upheaval of the heaven-kissing summits whose streams shall feed the farthest generations.

CIVILIZATION

Stretched beneath the cedars and pines, a cool stone serving for pillow, the soft sand for bed, one leg resting carelessly on the other, drinking fresh air with the whole heart, kissing the glorious light with fullness of joy, singing Om, letting the murmuring stream to keep time, Rama is questioned, half in joke, by a visitor—some upstart of civilization.

"Why do you import Asiatic laziness into America? Go out; do some good."

Rama—"O my dear Self! As to doing good, is not that profession already choked, overcrowded? Leave me alone, me and my Rama. Laziness, did you say? Oriental laziness? Why? What is laziness?"

Is it not laziness to keep floundering in the quagmire of conventionality and let oneself flow down the current of custom and fashion and sink like a dead weight in the well of appearances and be caught in the pond of possession and spend the time which should be God's in making gold and call it 'doing good?' Is is not laziness to practically let others live your life and have no freedom in dress, eating, walking, sleeping, laughing and weeping, not to say anything of talking? Is it not laziness to lose your Godhead? What for is this hurry and worry, this break-neck hot haste and feverish rush? To accumulate the almighty dollar like others, and what then? To enjoy as others? No. There is no enjoyment in running after enjoyment. O dear dupes of opinions, why postpone your enjoyment? Why don't you sit down here in this natural garden on the banks of this beautiful mountain stream and enjoy the company of your real blood relations—free air, silvery light, playful water and green earth—relations of which your blood is really formed? Hide-bound in caste are the civilized nations. They separate themselves from fellow-beings and exile themselves from free open nature and fresh fragrant natural life into close drawing rooms, dens and dungeons. They banish themselves from the wide world, excommunicate themselves from all creation, ostracize themselves from plants and animals. By arrogating to themselves airs of superiority, prestige, respectability, honor, they cut themselves into isolated stagnation. Have mercy, my friends, have mercy on yourselves.

The wealth swept out of possession of the more needy and added to your property by organized craft will enable you simply to have sickening dinners of hotels and taverns and furnish you with pallid countenances and conventional looks, will imprison you in boxes called rooms, choked with the stink of artificiality, will keep you all the time in the restlessness of mind excited by all sorts of unnatural stimulants, physical and mental. Why all such fuss for mere self-delusion? In the name of such supposed pleasures lose not your hold on real joy, no need of beating about the bush. Come, enjoy it now and here. Come, lie with me on the grass.

Don't you waste away your life in soliciting the favor of silver or gold to insure your life. Can your life be insured by becoming rich in money and paying in time? Don't you believe it, O deluded immortal! Why seek excuses for existence in rush and push about dainty trifles?

> The world is much with us; late and soon,
> Getting and spending, we lay waste our powers;
> Little we see in Nature that is ours;
> We have given our hearts away, a sordid boon!
> This sea that bears her bosom to the moon;

The winds that would be howling at all hours
And are up-gathered now like sleeping flowers;
For this, for everything, we are out of tune;
It moves us not—Great God! I'd rather be
A pagan suckled in a creed outworn,
So might I, standing on this pleasant lea,
Have glimpses that would make me less forlorn,
Have sight of Proteus rising from the sea;
Or hear old Triton blow his wreathed horn.
—*Wordsworth*

The so-called advanced nations of Europe and America are only in advanced stages of mortification. Advancement means spiritual or intellectual advancement. True progress must touch the real man and not waste itself on his mere shadow. Progress has nothing to do with material riches or with the multiplying of unnecessary necessities. The ancient Aryans, writing magnificent works, living unsophisticated, free lives and owning nothing in the world, led a mode of life to be repeated by history again with proper modifications. Present civilization is side-tracked from its main end. Man is talked of just as they speak of corn and wheat, with prices rising and falling. Rise above it. Nothing can set a price on you.

Beloved devotees of show, to you the Ayran ideal of *sannyasa*, renunciation, appears as idle dreaming. Be on your guard, please, the time is ripe to shake you and wake you up and make you realize what a terrible nightmare you were under. The civilized man without renunciation through love is only a more experienced and wiser savage.

Be not charmed by glamor, artificiality, conventionality, money-madness of the civilized world. These have proved a failure. These were tried in the fire and found wanting like wood, hay or stubble. Half the population is dying of starvation; the other half is buried under conspicuous waste, superfluous furniture, scent, bottles, affectations, galvanized manners, all sorts of precious trifles, squalid riches and unhealthy show.

Neither mental nor manual labor is incompatible with health and longevity except that the one is maintained at the expense of the other. But in the present day world some are living on (rather dying of) manual labor; others are perishing from the luxury of intellectual dissipation (mental strain). This is like dry bread being divided among some members of the family, and mere butter (or garnishing) distributed among some others.

The self-condemned slums of the universe are those who possess anything; the real *Shudras** are those who claim anything; the self-impeached prisoners in dingy dungeons are those who own anything, the pitiable atoms are those who are for accumulation. These suicides, choking and strangling themselves in the dirty dust of riches call themselves kings and presidents; some drowning themselves in the depth of darkness call themselves doctors and philosophers. Some befoundered in the quagmire of weakness and nervousness call it strength; some at bottom taking airs of superiority at their very ludicrous condition, self-hypnotized to fish on dry floor, helplessly suffering from the nightmare of possession and property, these self-persecuting strange ascetics need emancipation and waking up. Down with the prerogatives and presumptions of wealth, knowledge, titles and authority. Equality is the law of happiness. Savage greed, the animal instinct of clutching, grasping and the worse than animal tendency to possess and accumulate keeps them hurried, worried and flurried. Let the typhoid fever of arrogance and vain

* Members of the lowest or untouchable caste.

ambition be allayed. Let the inexorable Truth be instilled and drilled into every ear: "Just in as much as thou hast possessed anything, thou has been possessed and obsessed."

Be not oppressed by the pressure of civilization or the ways of the world around you, O aspirer after truth! Be not handicapped by the show and display of the so-called advancing nations. Their "facts and figures" are mere trickery of the senses, fables and fictions; and their "hard cash or stern reality" is mere gossamer and wil-o'-the-wisp. In the twentieth century the day is not far off when the progressing nations must change their forms of government or ways of living and fashion them on the principles of freedom and Vedanta. In renouncing the sense of possession and adopting the spirit of Vedantic renunciation lies the salvation of nation as well as of individuals. There is no other way.

In all the civilized Western countries, suffering from the fever of thirst to accumulate, indigenous forces are strongly at work which soon, very soon, must wake up the self-stifled grubs from the nightmare of possession. The reign of renunciation is to bless the world, the Kingdom of Freedom.

THE SECRET OF SUCCESS

January 26, 1903
Golden Gate Hall, San Francisco

My own Self in the form of ladies and gentlemen,

Three boys were given one five cent piece by their master to share equally among themselves. They decided to purchase something with the money. One of the boys was an Englishman, the other a Hindu, and the third a Persian. None of them fully understood the language of the other, so they had some difficulty in deciding what to buy. The English boy insisted on purchasing a watermelon. The Hindu boy said, "No, no, I would like to have a *handwana.*" The third boy, the Persian, said, "No, no, we must have a *tarbooz.*" Thus they could not decide what to buy. Each insisted upon purchasing the thing which he preferred, disregarding the inclinations of the others. There was quite a wrangle among them. They were quarrelling and walking through the streets. They happened to pass a man who understood these three languages, English, Persian and Hindustani. That man was amused over their quarrel. He said he could decide the matter for them. All the three referred to him and were willing to abide by his decision. This man took the five cent piece from them and asked them to wait at the corner. He himself went out to the shop of a fruit seller and purchased one big watermelon for the five cent piece. He kept it concealed from them and called them one by one. He asked first the English boy to come, and not allowing the young boy to know what he was doing, he cut the watermelon into three equal slices, took out one part, handed it to the English boy and said, "Is not that what you wanted?"

The boy was highly pleased; he accepted it cheerfully, gratefully, and went away frisking and jumping, saying that it was what he wanted. Then the gentleman called the Persian boy to approach him and handed him the second piece and asked him if that was what he desired. Oh, the Persian boy was highly elated and said, "This is my *tarbooz*! This is what I wanted!" He went away very merry. Then the Hindu boy was called; the third piece was handed to him, and he was asked if that was the object of his desire. The Hindu boy was well satisfied. He said, "This is what I wanted; this is my *hindwana.*" Why was the quarrel or quibble caused? What is it that brought about the misunderstanding among the lads? The mere names, the mere names, nothing else. Take off the names; see behind the veil of names. Oh! there you find that the three different names, *watermelon, tarbooz* and *hindwana*, imply one and the same thing.

Just so is Rama highly amused at the quibbles, quarrels, misunderstandings and controversies between different religions, Christians fighting Jews, Jews conflicting with Mohammadans, Mohammadans combating the Brahmanas, Brahmanas finding fault with the Buddhists and the Buddhists returning the compliment in a similar manner. The cause of those quarrels and misunderstandings is chiefly in names. Take off the veil of names; see behind them; look at what they imply, and there you will not find much difference.

Rama oftentimes uses the word "Vedanta," a name. It is this name which makes some people prejudiced against hearing anything from Rama. One man comes and he preaches in the name of Buddha; many people do not like to hear him, because he brings to them a name which is not agreeable to their ears. Be not confounded by names, be not misled by names. Examine everything by itself, see if it works.

Accept not a religion because it is the oldest; its being the oldest is no proof of its being the true one. Sometimes the oldest houses ought to be pulled down, and the oldest clothes must be changed. The latest innovation, if it can stand the test of reason, is as good as the fresh rose bedecked with sparkling dew. Accept not a religion because it is the latest. The latest things are not always the best, not having stood the test of time. Accept not a religion on the ground of its being believed in by a vast majority of mankind because the vast majority of mankind believes practically in the religion of Satan, in the religion of ignorance. There was a time when the vast majority of mankind believed in slavery, but that could be no proof of slavery's being a proper institution. Believe not in a religion on the ground of its being believed in by the chosen few. Sometimes the small minority that accepts a religion is in darkness, misled. Accept not a religion because it comes from a great ascetic, from a man who has renounced everything, because we see that there are many ascetics, men who have renounced everything, and yet they know nothing; they are veritable fanatics. Accept not a religion because it comes from princes or kings; kings are often enough spiritually poor. Accept not a religion because it comes from a person whose character was the highest; oftentimes people of the grandest character have failed in expounding the truth. A man's digestive power may be exceptionally strong, and yet he may not know anything about the process of assimilation. Here is a painter. He gives you a lovely, exquisite, splendid work of art, and yet the painter may be the ugliest man in the world. There are people who are very ugly, and yet they promulgate beautiful truths. Socrates was such a man. There was Sir Francis Bacon, not a very moral man, not of over-fine character, and yet he gave to the world *Novum Organum* and was the first to teach inductive logic; his philosophy was sublime. Believe not in a religion because it comes from a very famous man. Sir Isaac Newton is very famous, and yet his emissory theory of light is wrong; his rate or proportion at which a flowing quantity increases its magnitude, the method of fluxions (Newtonian calculas), does not come up to the Differential System of Liebnitz. Accept a thing and believe in a religion on its own merits. Examine it yourself. Sift it. Sell not your liberty to Buddha, Jesus, Mohammad or Krishna. If Buddha taught that way, or if Christ taught this way, or if Mohammad taught in some other way, it was all good and all right for them; they lived in other times. They mastered their problems; they judged by their own intellects; it was so grand of them. But you are living today; you shall have to judge and criticize and examine matters for yourselves. Be free, free to look at everything by your own light. If your ancestors believed in a particular religion, it was perhaps very good for them to believe in that, but now your salvation is your own business, your redemption is not the business of your ancestors. They believed in a particular religion which may, or may not, have saved them, but you have to work out your own emancipation. Whatever comes before you, examine it per se; examine it by yourself, not giving up your freedom. To your ancestors only one particular religion may have been shown; to you all sorts of truths, all sorts of religions, all sorts of philosophies, all sorts of sciences are being demonstrated. If the religion of your ancestors is yours on the ground of its being laid before you, so is the religion of Buddhism yours on the ground of its being placed before you; so is Vedanta yours on the ground of its being put before you.

Truth is nobody's property. Truth is not the property of Jesus; we ought not to preach it in the name of Jesus. Truth is not the property of Buddha; we need not preach it in the name of Buddha. It is not the property of Mohammad; it is not the property of Krishna or anybody. It is everybody's property. If anybody basked in the sun's rays before, you can bask in the sun today. If one man drinks the fresh waters of the spring, you can drink the same fresh water. Such should your attitude be towards all religions. Nobody in his heart of hearts would hesitate to divest his neighbors of his worldly possessions, but is it not strange that when our neighbors offer us most willingly their spiritual or religious treasures which are admittedly far superior to worldly riches, we instead of cheerfully accepting stand up in arms against them? Rama brings Vedanta to you, not with the intention of nicknaming you Vedantins. No. You may call it Christianity—names are nothing to us. Rama brings to you a religion which is not only found in the Bible and in the most ancient Scriptures but also in the latest works on philosophy and science. Rama brings you a religion which is found in the streets, which is written upon the leaves, which is murmured by the brooks, which is whispered in the winds, which is throbbing in your own veins and arteries, a religion which concerns your business and bosom, a religion which you have not to practice by going into a particular church only, a religion which you have to practice and live in your everyday life, about your hearth, in your dining room; everywhere you have to live that religion. We might not call it Vedanta; we might call it by some other name. The term Vedanta simply means the fundamental truth. The Truth is your own; it is not Rama's more than yours. It does not belong to the Hindu more than to you. It belongs to nobody and everybody, and everything belongs to it.

We will see now how it is that this Vedanta makes our way smooth and our undertakings so pleasant in this life. We shall take up practical Vedanta today, in other words, the secret of success. The secret of success is Vedanta put into practice. Practical Vedanta is the secret of success. Every science has its corresponding art, and we shall take up today that phase of Vedanta which is more art than science—the practical Vedanta.

Some people say that Vedanta teaches pessimism, Vedanta teaches hopelessness; it teaches idleness, laziness. Rama requests those people to keep their logic with them and not to sell their intellect to others, to keep it to themselves and see whether the teachings of Vedanta lead to life, energy, power, success or something else. Ask not whether the Indians live it or not. Rama tells plainly that it is not the exclusive property of the Indians; it is everybody's property. It is your own birthright. The Americans in business life live it more, and thus they are successful in the line. The Indians in practice do not live it to the same extent as the Americans do; thus they are backward from the material standpoint.

Rama brings you no perverted Vedanta, but the real Vedanta from the fountainheads of nature. Apply your logic and bring your reason to bear upon the subject and you will see how wonderful Vedanta is and how it leads us to success in every department, how everybody despite himself must drift along the line of Vedanta and obey its dictates.

The secret of success is manifold. There are phases of the secret. We shall take these principles one by one and find out their relation to Vedanta as expounded in the Hindu scriptures.

First Principle—Work

It is an open secret that work, attack, persistent application is the secret of success.

"Hammer on! hammer on!" is the first principle of success. Without work you can never succeed. A lazy man is bound to perish in the "struggle for existence"; he cannot live; he must die. Here presents a question most commonly raised against Vedanta. How can you reconcile continuous labor with the unaffected, impersonal, pure nature of Self or *Atman* as demonstrated by Vedanta? Does not Vedanta lead to laziness and inaction by inculcating the realization of rest and peace of Divine Self and by preaching renunciation? This objection is due to the terrible misunderstanding of the nature of work or renunciation.

What is work? Intense work, according to Vedanta, is rest. Here is a paradoxical statement, a startling statement, "Work is rest." The greatest worker, when he is at the height of his work, when he is doing his best, mark him. In the eyes of others he is engaged in strenuous efforts, but examine him from his own standpoint; he is no doer. Just as in the eyes of distant observers the rainbow contains beautiful colors, but when one examines it on the spot, there are no colors of any kind present therein. The hero in war, say Napoleon or Washington or anybody, when he is fighting, doing his best, look at him. The body works automatically, as it were; the mind is absorbed in the work to such a degree that "I am working" is entirely gone. The small enjoying ego is absolutely lost; the credit-seeking little self is absent. This incessant work unwittingly leads you to the highest yoga.

Vedanta wants you to rise above the little self, the small ego, through intense work. Let the body and mind be continuously at work to such a degree that the labor may not be felt at all. A poet is inspired when he is above the idea of the little self or ego, when he has no thought of "I am writing poetry." Ask anybody who has had the experience of solving difficult problems in mathematics, and he will tell you that only then are problems solved and difficulties removed when the idea "I am doing this" is entirely absent; and the more a man can rise above the little ego or the small self, the more glorious works come out of him.

Thus does Vedanta teach rising above the little ego by dint of earnest work and losing everything in the real indescribable principle which, according to Vedanta, is the real Self, *Atman* or God. When a thinker, philosopher, poet, scientist or any worker attunes himself to a state of abstraction and rises to the heights of resignation to such a degree that no trace of personality is left in him, and Vedanta is practically realized, then and then only does God, the master musician, take up in His own hands the organ or instrument of his body and mind and send forth grand vibrations, sweet notes, exquisite symphonies out of him. People say, "Oh, he is inspired!" whereas there is no

I or me in him, no doing, no enjoying traceable from his standpoint. This is realizing Vedanta in practical life. Thus all success flows from Vedanta being unknowingly put into practice.

There is no necessity of your retiring into the forests and pursuing abnormal practices to realize Vedantic yoga. You are the father of yoga, Shiva himself, when you are lost in activity or merged in work. According to Vedanta the body is not your Self. Do you not see that you are at the height of glory, at your very best, only when in practice you realize this truth, and the body and mind become to you non-existent by virtue of intense exertion?

What work is will be explained by a lamp or light. Take a gas or oil lamp. The light is so glorious, so dazzling, so splendid, brilliant and bright. What is it that lends glory and lustre to the lamp? It is denying the ego through constant work. Let the lamp try to spare its wick and oil and the lamp will be dark, all failure, no success. In order that there may be success the lamp must burn, must not spare its wick and oil. That is what Vedanta preaches. In order that you may have success, in order that you may prosper you must through your acts, by your own everyday life, burn your own body and muscles, cremate them in the fire of use. You must use them. You must consume your body and mind, put them in a burning state. Crucify your body and mind. Work and work and then will light shine through you. All work is nothing else but the burning of your wick and oil. In other words, all work is nothing else but making your body and mind illusions, practically nothing from the standpoint of your own consciousness. Rise above them and that is work.

Once there came two brave Hindu brothers to the

court of Akbar the Great, an emperor of India. They requested to be employed by the king. The king inquired about their qualifications. They said they were heroes. The king asked them to give a proof of their heroism. So in Akbar's court they stood face to face. Off flashed their shining daggers, sharp-pointed daggers. Each of them placed the sharp end of his dagger against the breast of his brother. Cheerfully and smilingly they ran to each other. Their hands were steady, and the daggers were piercing through the bodies, but unflinchingly and calmly they approached each other, no swerving, no hesitating. Their souls united in heaven; their bodies met on earth and fell bleeding on the ground. A very queer proof of their heroism was given to the king. That is an illustration of the fact that true work is accomplished only when the self-asserting worker is sacrificed. Bees have to put their lives into the sting they give. "The man who is his own master knocks in vain at the doors of poetry," says Plato.

Thus all prosperity and success come by living Vedanta in practice. Incessant work, incessant labor is the greatest yoga for a man of the world. You are the greatest worker to the world when to yourself you are no worker.

Again in what mood and mode does successful work become natural for us? It is very easy to say, "Work, to become the greatest painter; everybody wants to become a great musician, but everybody does not become what he wants. What is it that disposes you to inaction? What is it that makes you enjoy labor? Have you not found that oftentimes when you wished to work, you could not? Have you not observed that sometimes you did not like to labor, and yet was splendid work done? Have you not marked that there is something higher which governs your working capacity? How often a man wakes up in the morning and finds himself in a peculiar mood, a mood which is indescribable, in perfect harmony with nature. He takes up his pen, and from his pen flows magnificent poetry or philosophy. A painter tries to paint a beautiful picture, but he cannot, despite all his struggles. He rises one morning and finds himself inspired, as it were, and there he draws beautiful works of art. Is is not so?

Thus we see that there is something higher which puts all your working powers at their best. If you avail yourself of that higher mood, you can always keep yourself at your best, and the work through your hands will be perfect, most beautiful. That higher mood or that higher secret Vedanta lays before you; it is nothing else but being in perfect harmony with the universe, being in tune with the divinity, practically living in the true *Atman* or God within you and being raised above the little ego or selfish desires. Thus can work become wonderful by availing yourselves of the secret of all light or power within you.

The more your work becomes impersonal, and the more you rise above "I am doing," the more you renounce the proprietary, copyrighting spirit, and the more you leave behind the accumulating, favor-carrying spirit, the more you deny your unreal apparent self, the better will your work be. Vedanta requires you to work for its own sake. In order that your work should be success, you should not mind the end; you should not care for the consequences or the result. Let the means and the end be brought together; let the very work be your end. Vedanta wants you to be at rest in your inner Self. Let the inner soul be at rest, and the body be continually at work; let the body be subject to the laws of dynamics and in action, and let the inner Self be always at statical rest. It is our selfish restlessness that spoils all our work. Follow work for the sake of peace of *nirvana* connected with it.

Second Principle—Unselfish Sacrifice

There was a quarrel between a pond and a river. The pond addressed the river thus: "O river, you are very foolish to give all your water and all your wealth to the ocean. Do not squander your water and wealth on the ocean. The ocean is ungrateful; the ocean needs it not. If you go on pouring into the ocean all your accumulated treasures, the ocean will remain as salty as it is today; the ocean will remain as bitter as it is today; the brine of the sea will not be altered. 'Do not throw pearls before swine.' Keep all your treasures with you." This was worldly wisdom. Here was the river told to consider the end, to care for the result and regard the consequences. However, the river was a Vedantin. After hearing this worldly wisdom the river replied, "No, the consequence and the result are nothing to me; failure and success are nothing to me. I must work because I love work. I must work for its own sake. To work is my aim; to keep in activity is my life. My soul, my real *Atman* is energy itself." The river went on working; the river went on pouring into the ocean millions upon millions of gallons of water. The miserly economic pond became dry in three or four months; it became putrid, stagnant, full of festering filth, but the river remained fresh and pure; its perennial springs did not dry up. Silently and slowly was water taken from the surface of the ocean to replenish the fountainheads of the river. Monsoons and trade winds invisibly, silently and slowly carried water from the ocean and kept the river source fresh forever.

Just so Vedanta requires you not to follow the sophistic policy of the pond. It is the small, selfish pond that cares for the result, "What will become of me and my work?" Let your work be for work's sake. You must work. Your work should be your goal, and thus Vedanta frees you from fretting and worrying desires. This is the meaning of freedom from desires which Vedanta preaches. Worry not about the consequences; expect nothing from the people; bother not about favourable reviews of your work or severe criticism thereon. Care not whether what you are doing will tell or not. Do the work for its own sake. This way you have to free yourself from desire. You have not to free yourself from work, but you have to free yourself from yearning restlessness. In this way how splendid does your work become. The most effective and best cure for all sorts of distracting passions and temptations is work. However, that would be only a negative recommendation. The positive joy that accompanies faithful work is a spark of salvation, unconscious Self-realization. It keeps you pure, untainted, and one with Divinity.

Everybody wants to be white, dazzling, brilliant, bright. How can you become glorious? Why are objects white? Just look at the white objects. What makes them so white? Science tells you that the secret of whiteness is renunciation, nothing less. The seven colors in the rays of the sun impinge upon different objects. Some objects absorb and retain most of these colors and project back only one. Such objects are known by the very color they throw back or deny to themselves. You call that rose pink, but that is the very color which does not belong to the rose. The colors it has absorbed, which are really in it, are the colors you do not attribute to the rose. How strange! The black objects absorb all the colors in the rays of the sun. They give out no color; they renounce nothing; they throw back nothing, and they are dark, black. The white objects absorb nothing; they claim nothing; they renounce everything. They do not try to keep selfish possession. They have not a proprietary spirit, and thus they are white, dazzling, brilliant, bright.

Similarly if you want to become glorious and prosperous, you shall have to rise in your heart of hearts above the selfish, proprietary spirit. Be always a giver, a free worker; never throw your heart in a begging, expecting attitude. Get rid of the monopolizing habit. Why should you lay exclusive claim to the air in your lungs? That air is everybody's property. On the other hand when you cease to appropriate the small quantity of air in your lungs, you find yourself heir to all the atmosphere; unlimited become your resources. Breathe in the oxygen of the universe. Be not vain; be not proud. Never feel that anything belongs to your little self. It is God's, your real *Atman's*. Take the case of Sir Isaac Newton. How was it that he became so bright, brilliant, glorious in the eyes of the world? At the time of his death, the spirit in which he had worked was made known. When complimented on being the greatest man in the world, he replied, "Oh, no! this intellect or this small personality of mine is simply like a little child gathering pebbles on the vast, immense seashore of knowledge." He was yet lying upon the sands, gathering pebbles. Thus we see that the unassuming spirit which appropriates or claims nothing, which does not aggrandize the little self, is the spirit which puts your capacity and working powers at their best, and this is the characteristic spirit of Vedanta.

You have all kinds of desires, and you wish that your desires should be fulfilled; but learn the secret of the fulfillment of desires. It is only when you let go the desire that it fructifies. How are arrows shot? We take up the bow and bend it. As long as we are stretching the string, the arrow does not reach the enemy. You may stretch it ever so hard; the arrow will be with you still. It is only when you let it go that bang flies the arrow to pierce the bosom of your foe. Similarly so long as you keep your desire stretched or go on desiring, willing, wishing and yearning, it will not reach the bosom of the other party. It is only when you let it go that it penetrates the soul of the party concerned. "It is only when you leave me and lose me that you find me by your side." It is only when you cast yourself in a strange, indescribable sentiment which is higher than both of us, that you find me. This is what Vedanta tells you.

Two monks were traveling together. One of them maintained in practice the spirit of accumulation. The other was a man of renunciation. They discussed the subject of possession versus renunciation till they reached the bank of a river. It was late in the evening. The man who preached renunciation had no money with him, but the other had. The man of renunciation said, "What do we care for the body? We have no money to pay the boatman. We can pass away the night even on this bank singing the name of God."

The monied monk replied, "If we stay on this side of the river, we can find no village, no hamlet or hut, no company. Wolves will devour us; snakes will bite us; cold will chill us. We had better ferry to the other side. I have money with which to pay the boatman to ferry us over to the other bank. On that side there is a village. We will live there comfortably." Well, the boatman came over, and both of them were ferried across the river to the opposite shore. At night the man who had paid the fare remonstrated with the man of renunciation: "Do you not see the advantage of keeping money? I kept money and two lives were saved. Henceforth you should never preach renunciation. Had I also been a man of renunciation like you, we would have both starved or been chilled and killed on that side of the river."

The man of renunciation answered, "Had you kept the money with you, had you not parted with the money and renounced it to the boatman, we would have died on the other bank. Thus it was the giving up of money, or renunciation, that brought us safety. Again," he continued, "if I kept no money in my pocket, your pocket became my pocket. My faith kept money for me in that pocket. I never suffer. Whenever I am in need, I am provided for." This story indicates that so long as you keep your desires in your pocket, there is no safety or rest for you. Renounce your desires, rise above them, and you find double peace—immediate rest and eventual fruition of desires. Remember that your desires will be realized only when you rise above them into the Supreme Reality. When you consciously or unconsciously lose yourself in the Divinity, then, and then only, will the time be ripe for the fulfilment of desires.

Third Principle—Love

The third principle of success is love, harmony with

the universe, adaptation to circumstances. What does love mean? Practically, love means realizing your oneness and identity with your neighbors, with all those who come in contact with you. If you are a shopkeeper, unless you realize the interests of your customers to be one with your own, you will make no progress; your work will suffer. If the hand wants to be selfish and assert itself as different from the other members of the body and begins to argue this way, "Look here, I am the right hand. I do all sorts of labor. Why should the whole body partake of what is earned by my sweating drugdery! Should the food earned by my toil be given to the stomach and thence to all other organs? No. no. I will have everything to myself." Then, in order to carry into effect this selfish idea, there is no other way for the hand but to take that food and inject it into skin. Will that be beneficial to the hand? Will the hand succeed that way? Impossible! Never!

Similarly remember that all the world is one body. Your body is simply like the hand, one organ, simply like the finger or nail. In order that you may succeed, you should not look upon yourself as separate and distinct from the Self of the whole world. In order that the hand may prosper, it must realize that its interests are identical with those of the whole. Feeding the Self of the whole is feeding the Self of the hand. Unless you realize this fact, live this truth, that you are one with the universe, that you and God are one, you cannot succeed. Deprived of ease, afflicted by disease you are when you stagnate in the slough of separation and division. You are perfect and whole when you realize yourself to be the whole and the All. By feeling this oneness you practically live Vedanta. Infringe upon this divine and sublime truth, break this sacred law in practice, and you are bound to suffer for your sacrilege like the silly, selfish hand. Coleridge in his *Ancient Mariner* very beautifully brings out this truth. So does Byron in his *Prisoner of Chillon*. It is proved in these poems that whenever a man falls out of harmony with nature he suffers. The very moment you realize your unity with fellow beings, all prosperity is yours:

He prayeth best who loveth best,
Both man, and bird and beast.
He prayeth well who loveth well,
All things both great and small.

A king went into a forest on a hunting expedition. In the heat of chase the king became separated from his companions. Under the scorching rays of the burning sun he felt very thirsty. He found in the woods a small garden. The king went into the garden, but, being in sportsman's dress, the gardener could not recognize him. The poor village gardener had never seen the king's person before. The king asked the gardener to bring him something to drink because he felt so very thirsty. The gardener went straight into the garden, took some pomegranates, squeezed out the juice and brought a big cup full of it to the king. The king gulped it down, but it did not quench his parching thirst entirely. The king asked him to bring another cup of the pomegranate juice. The gardener went for it. When the gardener had left the king's presence, the latter began to reflect within himself, "This garden seems to be very rich; in a few minutes the man could bring me a large cup full of the fresh juice. A heavy income tax ought to be levied on the owner of such a flourishing concern, etc., etc." On the other hand the gardener delayed and delayed, and did not return to the king even in an hour. The king began to wonder, "How is it that when I first asked him to bring me something to drink, he brought that pomegranate juice in only a few minutes, and now he has been squeezing out the juice of pomegranates for about an hour and the cup is not full yet? How is that?" After one hour the cup was brought to the king, but not brimful. The king asked the reason why the cup was somewhat empty whereas he filled the cup so soon at first. The gardener, who was a sage, replied, "Our king had very good intentions when I went out to bring you the first cup of pomegranate juice but when I went out to bring you the second cup, our king's kind, benevolent nature must have changed. I can give no other explanation for such a sudden change in the rich nature of my pomegranates." The king reflected within himself, and lo! The statement was perfectly right. When the king had first stepped into the garden, he was very charitably disposed to and full of love for the people there, thinking in his mind that they were very poor and needed help; but when the old man had brought him one cup of pomegranate juice in so short a time, the king's mind had changed, and his views altered. The falling out of tune with nature on the king's part affected the pomegranates in the garden. The moment the Law of Love was violated by the king, that very moment the trees held back the juice from him.

The story may be true or false. We have nothing to do with it; but the truth is undeniable that so long as you are in perfect harmony with nature, so long as your mind is in tune with the universe and you are feeling and realizing your oneness with each and all, all the circumstances and surroundings, even winds and waves, will be in your favor. The very moment you are at discord with the All, that very moment your friends and relatives will turn against you, that very moment you will make the whole world stand up in arms against you. Understand this divine Law of Love and practice it. Love is a vital principle of success.

Fourth Principle—Cheerfulness

The fourth principle of success is self-possession or cheerfulness. How is self-possession or cheerfulness kept up? It is very easy to say, "Be cheerful, be calm, be collected." But how difficult it is to remain cheerful, calm and collected under all circumstances! By simply laying down the law you cannot be cheerful. You cannot do anything by artificial rules. How are we then to keep ourselves cheerful? What is it that governs your mood? Vedanta points out that we become moody, cheerless or "in the blues"; we become sad and melancholic when we descend to the plane of the body, the little self and craving desires. Then only are we unbalanced. We feel our stomach only when it is sick. We feel our nose only when we are suffering from cold. We feel our arm only when it is aching. So we feel our personal ego, little self, or body only when we are spiritually out of order. The engrossing regard for the body and care-creating attention to the personal little ego involves sad spiritual illness. We fall from Eden the moment our bodily weakness makes itself felt. Hurled are we from heaven the instant we taste of the tree of distinction and difference. We can regain the paradise lost by suffering the flesh to be crucified. You can recover your balance and be cheerful the moment you rise above the body, above the little selfish, sordid, paltry, petting clingings.

Thus in order to secure cheerfulness and self-possession you will have to put into practice the central teaching of Vedanta, the eternal Truth that your true *Atman,* your real Self is the only rigid Reality. The phenomenal, worldly circumstances become mobile, malleable and volatile for you when you are soaked in the stern fact of your true *Atman*. I am not the body. All the bodily concerns, connections and ties are mere playthings. They are simply the relations or offices in a theatrical performance. I, as an actor, have one man for my enemy and one man for my friend; another man is my father; someone else my son; but in reality I am neither the son nor the father; the foes and friends are no foes and friends. I am Absolute Divinity. The worldly ties and connections do not concern me. All relations are mere illusions. Every actor should well perform his role in the play but he who takes to heart and applies to his real Self the dramatic part of love or hatred is nothing short of insane. Again the world is but a dramatic show, so why should I attach undue importance to the outside forms of duty? If one man is king, why envy him; another a beggar, why despise him?

> Honor and disgrace from no condition rise;
> Act well your part, there all the honor lies.

Vedanta inculcates that you should not bother yourself about your surroundings and circumstances. Know the law and shake off all fear. Suppose here is a magistrate. He comes into his court and takes his seat. He finds the parties, clerks, lawyers, servants and other people already waiting for him. The magistrate had not to send for the witnesses to invite the lawyers or to go and call the plaintiffs and others. He had not to dust the room, to sweep the floor and fix the table. The very influence of the magistrate puts everything in order just as the very presence of the sun wakes up all nature, enlivens rivers, plants, birds, beasts and men. Similarly when you plant yourself firmly in the Truth, when you install yourself in the position of the disinterested Supreme Judge, your very *Atman*, when your glorious Self shines in its full splendor, all the circumstances, all your surroundings will take care of themselves, everything will be enlivened and put in order in the genial light of your presence. It is related of Rama, the greatest hero of India, that when he started to regain Sita, which represents Divine Knowledge, all nature offered services to him. Monkeys, geese, squirrels and even stones, air and water vied with one another to enlist on his side. Shine in the glory and majesty of your Self. Away with grovelling attachment and degrading hatred, and woe unto the gods and angels if they do not serve you as abject slaves. Why does everybody lackey a child? The little tyrant rides on the strongest shoulders and pulls the hair of laurelled heads. How is that? Why, because the child lives above the circumstances in divinity unconsciously.

If you go on doing your duty, if you are faithful to your work, bother not yourself about the outside aids and helps. They are bound to come to you, must come to you. When you make a speech and have anything worth being preserved, bother not yourself about who will come and take it down or who will publish it, etc. Take the seat of a magistrate, be firm in your pristine dignity, never mar your cheerfulness by scruples about the outside matters and external aids.

If there be felt an itching sensation in any part of the body, the hand automatically reaches that region to scratch. The power or Self which underlies the hand is evidently the same as the power or Self which underlies the place of irritation. Just so, bear in mind that the Self in you is the same as the Self in all surroundings or environments and when your mind is in harmonious vibration with this underlying Self Supreme and your body has become the whole world, outside aids and helps must fly to you as naturally and spontaneously as the hand runs to the place of sensation.

When we run after our shadow to catch it, the shadow will never be caught; the shadow will always outrun us. However, if we run towards the sun, turning our back on the shadow, it will dog us. Similarly the moment you turn towards these outside matters and want to grasp them and keep them, they will elude your grasp, will outrun you. The very moment you turn your back upon them and face the Light of lights, your inner Self, that very moment favorable circumstances will seek you. This is the law.

Most people are turned pale, are driven into the corner by the word "duty." Duty, like a bugbear, haunts them, goes on thrashing them, leaves them no rest or time, is always upon them. Such hurrying slaves, nay, machines of duty, lose in power what they gain in speed. Allow not the sense of duty to throw you off the balance or dampen your spirits. Remember that all duty is after all imposed on you by yourself. Ultimately you are your own master. You yourself chose your position, offered your services and created your superiors. Again, if you need their money, they require your services just as much. The terms are of equality, the action and reaction being equal. You serve your own will and that of nobody else.

Your present surroundings are created by yourself; the little world of relations is your own workmanship; your future will be your own doing. You are the master of your own destiny. Know that and rejoice, be cheerful.

> We build our future thought by thought
> For good or bad and know it not.
> Thoughts is another name for fate;
> Choose, then, thy destiny, and wait.
> Mind is the master of its sphere;
> Be calm, be steadfast and sincere;
> Fear is the only foe to fear
> Let the God in thee rise and say
> To adverse circumstance—'Obey'
> And thy dear wish shall have its way.

Take to your work, not as a plodding laborer but like a noble prince for pleasure's sake, as useful exercise, as happy play or merry game. Never approach a task in a scared spirit. Be yourself. Realize that kings and presidents are simply your servants. Work as stars work—

> Undismayed at all the things about them.
> Unaffrighted at the things they see.
> These demand not that the things without them
> Yield them love, amusement, sympathy.
> The exquisite reward of song
> Was sung—the self-same thrill and glow
> Which to unfolding flowers belong.
> And wrens and thrushes know.

Feel no responsibility, ask for no reward. All authority should be subservient to you. You are your own authority. No sense of duty or outside authority should be to you an overshadowing cloud. The order wrought by outside authority may at best be geometrical, but the order which you create yourself will be organic.

Fifth Principle—Fearlessness

We come next to the fifth principle of success,

fearlessness. What is fearlessness—not faith in *maya*, but a living knowledge and a true faith in the real Self. Fear comes to us when we feel ourselves to be the body or the abode of fear. The body is always liable to be eaten by worms of anguish; it is vulnerable and pregnable to all kinds of suffering. The very moment that we rise above the little body, we are free from fear. Live as divinity; live Vedanta, and who can harm you? Who can inflict injury upon you? Fearlessness and Vedanta are inseparable.

How is fearlessness essential to success? This will be illustrated by a fact of personal experience. There came five bears at one time in the Himalayan forests face to face with Rama, but they did not molest him at all. Why was it so? Simply on account of fearlessness. Rama was filled with that spirit, "I am not the body; I am not the mind; the Supreme Divinity I am; I am God. No fire can burn me; no weapon can wound me." They were looked straight in the eyes, and they ran away. At one time a wild wolf was outstared; at another time a tiger likewise fled. When a cat comes, pigeons close their eyes. They think the cat does not see them because they do not see the cat; nevertheless the cat eats them up. If you are afraid, the cat will eat you up. Have you not noticed that while walking in the suburban quarters, if we betray the least sign of fear, even dogs rush at us and molest us? However, if we are fearless, we can overcome and tame lions and tigers. When we are pouring liquid from one vessel into another, if our hands waver ever so little, the liquid is sure to be spilt. Pour the fluid unhesitatingly, confidently, fearlessly into the receptacle and no drop will be lost.

It is by hesitation and fear that you bring yourself into sad plights. Let nothing disconcert you or take you by surprise. You are the All. Dispel the fear-inducing attachment to the body. Is it not a pity that the noise of a trivial firecracker or even a small mouse, a rustling leaf, nay, a trembling shadow should startle a full hundred and fifty pounds avoirdupois of wool-clad flesh? No calamity is ever worse than the dread of the calamity. You would rather suffer death than harbor fear of death.

Someone says "No one ever found the walking fern who did not have the walking fern in his mind." If you have love in your mind, you will find love; if you entertain hate, you will meet hate. If you are afraid of detectives and defrauders, you will not miss them. If you expect selfishness and deceit, you shall not be disappointed; from all sides will selfishness and deceit confront you. Fear not then. Have holiness and purity in you. You will never come across anything unclean. Life success and spiritual success must go together. Deluded are they who divorce one from the other.

Thieves break into a house only when it is unguarded. If the house is kept lighted all the time, they dare not steal into it. Keep in your mind the light of Truth ever ablaze and no devil of fear or temptation will approach you. Believe in the law divine. Please make not your life wretched by hanging on worldly wisdom. Timid prudence makes a downright atheist out of you. Why allow the mists and fogs of circumstances to cloud you? Are you not the sun of suns? Are you not the Lord of the Universe? What vagaries of circumstances are there which you cannot disperse, dispel and evaporate? Far be it from you to consider any menacing surroundings as real in the least. Fearless, fearless, fearless you are.

Sixth Principle—Self-Reliance

The sixth secret of success is Self-reliance. You know the elephant is a much larger animal than the lion. The elephant's body seems to be much stronger than the body of a lion, and yet a single lion can put to flight a whole herd of elephants. What is the secret of the lion's power? The only secret is that the lion is a practical Vedantin, and the elephants are dualists. The elephants believe in the body; the lion believes not in the body, but in something higher than the body, the spirit. Even though the body of the lion is comparatively very small, the lion believes his power to be infinite, his inner force illimitable. The elephants live in groups of forty or fifty, sometimes one hundred or two hundred, and when the elephants go to rest, they always keep one strong elephant as watch and guard. They fear that their enemies may attack and devour them. They know not that a single one of them is capable of destroying thousands of lions only if he has faith in himself, but the poor tuskers lack faith in the inner Self and the consequent courage.

Thus is self-trust a fundamental principle of bliss. Vedanta teaches you not to call yourself a grovelling, sneaking, miserable sinner or wretch. Vedanta wants you to believe in your innate power. You are infinite; God almighty you are; infinite God you are. Believe that. What an inspiring truth! Believe in the outside and you fail. That is the law.

Two brothers involved in litigation appeared before a magistrate. One of them was a millionaire; the other, a pauper. The magistrate asked the millionaire how it was that he became so rich and his brother so poor. He said,

"Five years ago we inherited equal property from our parents. Fifty thousand dollars fell to his share, and fifty thousand dollars to me. This man, regarding himself as wealthy, became lazy (you know some rich people think it beneath their dignity to labor) and whatever work was to be done he entrusted to his servants. If he received a letter, he would give it to his servants and say, 'Go, attend to this business.' Anything that was to be accomplished he told his servants to do. He lolled away his time in ease and comfort—'Eat, drink and be merry.' He would always bid his servants, 'Go, go, attend to this business or that.' " Speaking of himself, the rich man said, "When I got my fifty thousand dollars, I never committed my work to anybody. When anything was to be done, I would always run to do it myself, and I always told the servants, 'Come, come, follow me.' The words on my lips were always 'Come, come,' and the words on the lips of my brother were 'Go, go.' Everything he possessed obeyed his motto; his servants, friends, property and wealth went away, entirely left him. My maxim was 'Come.' Friends came to me, property increased, everything multiplied."

When we depend upon others, we say "Go, go." Everything will go away, and when we rely upon Self and trust nothing but the *Atman*, all things flock to us. If you think yourself a poor sneaking vermin, that you become; and if you honor yourself and rely on your Self, grandeur you win. What you think the same you must become.

So long as you go on relying and depending upon outside powers, failure will be the result. Trusting upon God within, put the body in action and success is assured. If the mountain does not come to Mohammad, Mohammad will go to the mountain. There was a man who was hungry, and, in order that he might appease his hunger, he sat down at a certain place, closed his eyes and began to eat imaginary curry. After a while he was seen with his mouth open, endeavoring to cool his burnt tongue. Somebody asked him what the matter was. He said that in his food there was a very hot chilli. The name is cool, but the thing itself is very hot. Thereupon the bystander remarked, "Oh poor fellow, if you had to live on imaginary food, then why not select something far sweeter than hot chilli? As it was your own creation, your own doing, your own imagination, why did you not make a better choice?"

Since according to Vedanta, all the world is but your own creation, your own idea, why think yourself a low, miserable sinner? Why not think yourself a fearless, self-reliant incarnation of divinity?

Have a living faith in the Truth, a right knowledge of things around you. Take all your circumstances at their own worth, and realize the spirit to such a degree that this world becomes unreal to you. In astronomy, while calculating the distances of the fixed stars, this world is looked upon as a mathematical point, as nothing in relation to those stars and planets, a mere cypher. If so, can this earth be anything in contrast with the supreme infinite power, the *Atman*? Realize that; feel that. The Light of lights you are, all glory is yours. Feel that, and realize it to such a degree that this earth and name and fame, the earthly relations and popularity and unpopularity, worldly honor and disgrace, criticism of your foes and flattery of your friends may become meaningless to you. This is the secret of success.

Two men were being carried down by the swift current of the Niagara. One of them found a big log, and he caught hold of it with the desire to be saved. The other man found a tiny rope thrown down for their rescue by the people on the bank. Happily he caught hold of this rope which was not heavy like the log of wood, and, though the rope was apparently very wavering and frail, he was saved, but the man who caught hold of the big log of wood was carried off with the log by the rapid current into the yawning grave of surging waters beneath the roaring falls.

Similarly, O people of the world, you trust in these outward names, fame, riches, wealth, land and prosperity. These seem to be big like the log of wood; but the saving principle they are not. The saving principle is like the fine thread. It is not material; you cannot feel and handle it; you cannot touch it. The subtle principle, the subtle truth is very fine, but that is the rope which will save you. All these worldly things on which you depend will simply work your ruin and throw you into a deep abyss of hopelessness, anxiety and pain. Beware, beware. Have a strong hold of the Truth. Believe more in the Truth than in outside objects. The law of nature is that whenever a man believes practically in the outside objects and wealth he must fail. That is the law. Trust in the divinity and you are safe. Be not dupes of senses.

Rise above hypnotism and suggestions of your neighbors. All your worldly ties and connections hypnotize you into misery and anxiety. Rise above that. Believe in the truth; realize your oneness with the divinity, and saved you are. Nay, salvation itself ye are.

Far be it from you to regard the world more seriously than the real Self. Do not keep yourself a sensitive, pitiable, limited ego. Let nothing pique you. Attend to business as doctors attend their patients without contacting the disease. Work in the spirit of an unaffected witness, free from all entanglements. Remain immune.

Seventh Principle—Purity

The last, but not the least, point which guarantees success is purity. It is true that "Thought is another name for fate." What a man thinks, that he becomes. If you begin to think impure thoughts and harbor debasing immorality, with the fulfilment of these selfish desires, heart-breaking affliction, excruciating suffering and distracting sorrow shall be forced upon you in the bargain. Grief shall prey upon your soul. The fool thinks he enjoys sensuous pleasures, but knows not that in an impure thought or deed his very vitality is bought, sold and consumed. The law of karma retaliates and baffles you when you want to abuse it for selfish ends. Do not dictate your will to God. Let God's will be done regarding bodily wants. In earthly requirements let God's will become your will. Feel, feel that you are the very power supreme, whose will has shaped the circumstances in the forms they have. Enjoy your poverty as your own work. If you find yourself led astray by the flesh and caught in the quagmire of carnality, there is the occasion to assert and exert strenuously your giant will to secure and retain God-consciousness. In this country cupidity is glazed under the holy name of love. What a mockery! People don't live whole. Abnormal affections and inordinate passions cut and divide their days into patches. It is very seldom that an entire young man speaks. It is always a disabled proper fraction, more correctly a most improper portion of him, that appears in public. One part of him lies with his sweetheart; another, with some other object. Love your labor; keep your heart where your hand is. While the feet and hands are warm and working, let your head be cool and collected. Keep your thoughts always at home, centered in the real Self, and never mind the circumstances. Let not the thought of doing good to humanity vex you. Why should the world be so poor as to be constantly begging your attention? Let the body go on working for your own salvation's sake. Ignorant folk keep vainly yearning and praying for light. Why should you desire even that? The craving for the light keeps you in the dark. For one minute cast overboard all desire. Chant Om. No attachment, no repulsion, perfect poise; there your whole being is Light personified. Banish all worldly motives of work. Cast off, exorcise the demons of desires. Make all your work sacred. Rid yourself of the disease of attachment or clinging. Attachment to one object detaches you from the All. It is the selfish, swinish motives that make your business and life secular. Attend your labor; to taste renunciation unconsciously entails work, because work keeps you with God above the body or little self. Work minus desire is a synonym for the highest renunciation or worship. Why should you have any motive for work? Ignorant wretches believe that objects accomplished bring more happiness than the work itself. The blind know not that no result can bring more happiness than the work itself. Happiness lives clothed in the garb of work. You can have your success always with you. This way does the wide world become your holy temple and your whole life one continuous hymn! What care have you for the effect? Far be it from you to worry about salary or pay.

If you get no proud position, let not glaring vanity prevent you from sweeping the streets. Hesitate not to do the duty that lies next to your hand. It is no self-respect to shun the work not sanctioned by fashion. True self-respect is respect for the real Self, the God within. Body-respect is the opposite pole of virtue, the shortest cut to perdition. When you are ready to extend your hands to any labor, the noblest offices and the most respectable occupations will stretch their hands to receive you cordially. That is the law. If you do not shrink and curl up from God indwelling in labor, God will not be outdone in courtesy. Light will shine through you despite yourself. Believe not in the applause or censure of mankind. All that simply misleads and deceives you. Your heaven is within you. You play the part of an impure, unchaste adulterer when you stoop down to indulge in so-called outside objects of pleasure. Tell to the external enjoyments, "Get behind me, Satan; I'll take nothing at thy hands." Are you not really the source of all joy?

> For him in vain the envious seasons roll
> Who bears eternal summer in his soul.

Perch the Indian dove or the nightingale on top of a pine tree, and delicious songs naturally flow from it. Let your mind be seated at home, and the sweetest melodies spring from it naturally, spontaneously, without effort. Your Godhead is not a thing to be accomplished. Realization is not a thing to be achieved. You have not to do anything to gain God-vision; you have simply to undo what you have already done in the way of forming dark cocoons of desires around you. Fear not, you are free. Even your seeming bondage is imposed by your freedom. To you no harm can accrue unless you invite it. No sword can cut unless you think that it cuts. No need of loving your shackles and chains as ornaments. Shake off vain fancies; burn up all crookedness, and what power is there under the sun which will not be only too thankful to get the privilege of unloosing your shoes? Assert your Godhead; fling into utter oblivion the little self, as if it had never existed. When the little bubble bursts, it finds itself the whole ocean. You are the whole, the infinite, the All. Shine in your pristine glory. For you, O perfect one, there is no duty, no action, nothing to be done. All nature waits on you with bated breath. The world thanks her stars to have the good fortune of paying you homage, adoring you. Please, would you mind the powers of nature kneeling and bowing before you!

BALANCED MIND
February 15, 1903
San Francisco

My own Self in all these forms,

The question put the other day was "Can a man realize Vedanta in this age?" It was suggested by someone that a man must leave this or that in order to realize Vedanta and retire to the forest of the Himalayas. However, Rama says, "No, no. You need not retire into the forests."

In these days the common complaint is lack of time. They say, "We have got no time; we have to attend to all sorts of business; our relatives and friends take up our time." There is a prayer, "O God! Save me from my enemies," but the prayer which modern man should offer more properly would be, "O God! Save me from my friends." Friends rob us of all our time. Then anxieties, worries, troubles take away our time. Then we have to attend to our children and our helpmates; we have to receive visits and pay visits; we have to read things. How can we spare time for spiritual advancement? Oh duties! They take away our time. We cannot spare time even to take dinner easily. In the name of duties all your life is being frittered away. Let us ask wherefrom these duties come. Who imposes these duties upon you? You yourselves. In fact it is you who make your duties. Duties should not come upon you as a cruel master. You regard it your duty to attend to the office work, but who put that office work on you? It is you yourself. So if you ultimately realize the nature of duties, you will see that you are your own master and that all these duties which absolutely enslave you are created by yourself. If you once feel that, there is nothing in this world that binds you. Everything originally comes from you. You can be very happy, and you can adjust your position most smoothly.

Once a man came to Samuel Johnson and said, "Doctor, I am undone, undone. I am unfit for any work; I cannot do anything. What can a man do in this world?"

Dr. Johnson inquired what the matter was with him, what reasons he lay down for his complaint. So this man began to state his argument in this way: "Man lives in this world for a period of a hundred years at the utmost, and what are a hundred years compared with infinity, eternity? Half of this age is passed in sleep. You know, we sleep every day, and our period of childhood is one long sleep, and our period of old age is also a time of debility and helplessness, when we can do nothing. Again our period of youth is mis-spent, ill-spent in evil thoughts, in all sorts of temptations. Again what is left to us is spent in sporting about. We play a great deal, and what is left out of that is wasted away in attending to nature's calls, and in eating, drinking, etc.; and what is left out of that goes in anger, envy, anxiety, troubles and worries. These are also natural for every man. What remains still, what little is left to us, is taken up by attending to our children, to our friends and relatives. What can a man do in this world? We must weep for those that die, and we must rejoice at the birth of new arrivals. All our time must be wasted in this way. How can a man do anything solid, anything real? How can a man spare time for realizing his Godhead? We cannot. Away with these churches, away with these religious teachers and preachers. Tell them that people in this world cannot spare time for religion; they have no time for realizing their

Godhead. That is too much for us." Dr. Johnson did not smile at these words; he did not reprimand this man nor reproach him, but only began to weep and began to sympathize with him. He said, "Men ought to commit suicide because they have no time for godly professions. Brother! To this complaint of yours, I have another complaint to add. I have a worse complaint to add." This man asked Dr. Johnson to state his complaint. Dr. Johnson began a mock cry and said, "Look here! There is left no soil or earth for me. There is left no soil or earth which will grow corn enough to feed me. I am undone, undone." "Well, " he said, "Doctor, how could that be? I admit that you eat too much—you eat as much as ten men do—yet there is soil enough on the earth to produce corn or vegetable for your body. Why do you complain?" Dr. Johnson said, "Look here, what is this earth of yours? This earth is nothing; this earth is looked upon as a mathematical point in astronomical calculations. When we are calculating the distances of stars and suns, we regard this earth as nil, as a cipher; and three-fourths of this cipher, or world, is occupied by water; and what is left out of that? Mark. A great deal is taken up by barren sands, and a considerable part is taken up by barren hills and stones, and a considerable part of this earth is occupied by sites of big cities like London. Again roads, railroads, streets take up a great deal of this earth. What is there in this earth left for man? We will suppose that there is something left for man out of all that, but how many living beings are there who want to take advantage of the insignificant part of the soil that is left? There are so many birds, so many ants, so many horses, so many elephants—all of these want to keep themselves on the earth that is left and is capable of producing anything. Very little falls to the lot of man! How many men are there in this world? Look at London, full of millions and millions of men. Look at this enormous population. All these want to feed upon the insignificant part of this big cipher of this world. How can the earth produce food enough for my satisfaction? My logic leads me to this desperation, to this sad conclusion that I should die, because I can find no earth which can produce food to feed me." Now the man said, "Doctor, your argument is not right. Your logic seems to be all right, but still despite this logic of yours, this earth can keep you." Dr. Johnson said, "Sir, if this complaint of mine is groundless, your complaint that you have no time to supply yourself with spiritual food is also groundless. If the earth is sufficient to supply me with material food, time also is sufficient for your purpose. It can also supply you with spiritual food." Thus Rama makes the same answer to this question that the present civilization does not allow us time to get any spiritual food. This question Rama answers in the same way as Dr. Johnson answered that question many years ago. You have time enough even under these circumstances to advance spiritually; you have time enough, if you make proper use of it.

There was a man on horseback going to a distant place. He happened to pass by a Persian wheel in India. You know that in India water is drawn out of a well by a kind of arrangement which we call a Persian wheel. When water is pumped out of a well by a Persian wheel, there is a noise. Now this man brought his mare or horse to drink the water that was coming out of the well with the Persian wheel. The horse, not being accustomed to hearing that kind of noise, was startled a little and would not drink that water. The horseman asked the peasants who were working the Persian wheel to stop that noise. The peasants stopped that noise by stopping the Persian wheel. The noise was stopped, but the stopping of the noise stopped also the coming of the water. Now the horse had no water to drink. The horse advanced towards the cistern, where the water was to be found, but there was no water at all. Now this horseman turned to the farmers and complained to them, "O queer farmers! I asked you to stop the noise; I did not ask you to stop the water. Strange fellows you are. You will not show kindness to a stranger to allow his horse a drink of water." The farmers said, "Sir, we wish from the bottom of our hearts to serve you, to treat you and to serve your horse with water, but your request is beyond our power to comply. If you want to have water, if you want your horse to drink water, you ought to coax him to drink when the noise is going on, because when we stop the noise, no water will be supplied. Water comes always alongside of this noise." Similarly Rama says, "If you want to realize Vedanta, realize it even in the midst of all sorts of noise, even in the heart of all sorts of troubles. In this world you can never, never get yourself in a state where there will be no noise, no botherations from without. Live on the heights of the Himalayas; there also you will have troubles around. Live as savages; there also you will have botherations around you. Go wherever you please; botherations and troubles will never leave you. They are always with you. If you want to realize Vedanta, realize it when the noise of the Persian wheel is going on all around you. All the great men have been produced despite discouraging environments and circumstances. In fact the harder these circumstances, and the more trying the environment, the stronger are the men who come out of those circumstances. So welcome all these outside troubles and anxieties. Live Vedanta even in these surroundings, and when you live Vedanta, you will see that the surroundings and circumstances will succumb to you, will yield to you. They will become subservient to you; you will become their master. Is it society that weighs us down? Is it this world that keeps us down? You do not live in this world. Everybody lives in a tiny, little world of his own creation. You have made your worlds around your small selves. There are people who do not know anything beyond the small domestic circle; there are people who do not know anything beyond the small world of their own caste. There are people who do not know anything beyond the small world formed by their wives, husbands or children. Live in this wide world at least. Rise above the little petty worlds. It is not the broad world that keeps you down. It is the small world of your own creation that keeps you down. If you can rise above it, the whole world will yield to you.

How can a man in the present circumstances achieve realization of the Spirit? The answer will depend upon the nature of the man himself. Men in this world may be broadly divided as possessing three kinds of temperament, three kinds of mind. There are some whose minds are of the nature of unstable equilibrium; there are others whose concentration or peace of mind may be of the nature of stable equilibrium; there are others who are always in neutral equilibrium. What is unstable equilibrium? Place a pencil vertically upon the palm of the hand. It never stays. For a second or so it may be at rest, but every whiff of wind will throw it down. This is called unstable equilibrium. Hold the pencil by one end and keep it hanging like a pendulum. It is at rest, but being a pendulum, it will go on oscillating for some time. After a while it will stop again. The equilibrium may be disturbed, but it will be regained soon. In the first position of the pencil, however, the equilibrium may not be regained. There is a third kind of equilibrium. Place the pencil horizontally. It is at rest. In this position, wherever you place the pencil, it is at rest; it is in equilibrium all the time. Just so there are some people whose minds are all the time disturbed, all the time distracted; they cannot be in equilibrium; they cannot be at rest. External circumstances bring them rest, but they are distracted again. There are other people whose minds are usually calm, collected and quiet, but being once disturbed they go on oscillating for a long, long time. The majority of men in this world are of that nature. You are walking through the streets; somebody comes and shakes hands with you and makes some remark which is not complimentary. He goes away, but the act is done. The effect of that disturbance continues for hours, sometimes for days, for weeks, for months, sometimes even for years. The mind keeps on oscillating; once disturbed, it goes on oscillating, goes on moving up and down. This oscillating state of mind ruins your life. It takes away all your time. Now just mark. The acts did not take much time, but the after-effects or say the oscillations of your mind take away most of your life. If you could prevent those peculiar oscillations, if you could overcome that inner disturbance, if you could resist or bring under control that hesitation or that continuous vibration of the mind and palpitation, if you could overcome it, your life would be the life of millions of men. Even your thirty years of life may be equivalent to hundreds and hundreds of years. Mark the disease of your mind, the psychological disease from which you are suffering. Know that disease and cure it. The disease of your mind is the oscillating tendency. When the thing is done the mind keeps on oscillating between a tear and a smile. These are only pendulum men. Now the third kind of men are the heroes, the liberated souls. These are men whose minds cannot be disturbed by any circumstances. Let anything come to pass and they are undisturbed; they are at rest. Place them in the surging waves of the rolling ocean; place them in war, and the mind is as fresh and as pure as ever. Remain with a free man for a thousand years; go away, and you have left no disturbance there. The mirror shows your face back to you. You know the mirror does not exactly portray your face. If you have an earring in the left ear, you will find the earring in the right ear of the mirror; and so the right becomes the left and the left becomes the right. You remain before the mirror for a hundred years and for a hundred years the mirror goes on answering you. Leave the mirror; the mirror is just the same. So is the case with a liberated soul or a man of wisdom. He is one upon whom the outside stain can leave no tainting spot, whom nothing can pollute and who remains as free as ever. You may come and praise him all the time. Go away, and his mind will not afterwards be chewing the cud of your praise. You come and pass critical, cynical remarks; you go away, and he will not be ruminating over your criticisms. Free, free—he believes in his divinity.

Now Rama says that if you really study Vedanta and keep the Vedantic teachings continually before you, and by self-suggestions in the right direction, you remember your Godhead and keep the reality before you, your mind, if originally of unstable equilibrium, will become of stable equilibrium, and if it is of stable equilibrium, it will acquire neutral equilibrium by degrees. This Vedanta, this truth, you have to keep before you all the time. Rama will now tell you some outside aids and helps to keep you continually in that state. Try it and you will see that even though this is not preached by people, yet it is a wonderful advice. You will mark it. When people come and have a talk with Rama, sometimes remarks, cynical, critical remarks, are made; then they go away. Do you know how Rama keeps himself safe from their suggestions? Different ways there are. One way is this. You see that small book before you? This is a marvelous book. It was written by a man whose equal is not to be found. This man is not famous, he is not worshipped in India. This book is not a famous book like the *Bhagavad Gita*; it was not written by Krishna. It was written by a man who was unknown to name and fame. But here is a man who gives you all the Christs, Krishnas, Buddhas. Rama takes up this book.* It is in Sanskrit, and when Rama reads one verse out of this book, that is enough to wipe out and wash away all pollution of lives and lives. It throws Rama at once into a state of ecstasy. One verse of this small book appeals to the heart and uplifts, reasserts the Godhead in Rama. It destroys the low nature and rends asunder the veil of *maya* at once. So Rama tells you, you may keep a book of that kind. You may have some psalms which lift you up, inspire you; you may have some songs which inspire you immediately; you may have some poems which appeal to

* It seems Rama refers to *Avadhut Gita* here.

you. You may have the Bible; you may have the Sermon on the Mount. You may mark the passages of your favorite authors, the passages which inspire you. You may have a small notebook in which you keep collected all those sayings which inspire you, which fill you with prayer. Keep that always right at hand, and after you have mixed with your friends or left any uncongenial company instead of allowing your mind to keep on oscillating, instead of allowing your mind to remain in a disturbed state, at once take up this inspiring passage and make the mind steady.

Now you see Rama has told you the cause, the mental disease. Rama has laid before you the general malady of the human soul. The general malady is this oscillating tendency, and Rama has told you how you can keep the mind steady.

Om! Om! Om!

THE GOAL OF RELIGION

December 6, 1902

Hermetic Brotherhood Hall, San Francisco

My Alter Egos, my other Selves,

According to the Hindus, everybody is God, the most precious jewel, the whole treasure, the supreme bliss and source of all happiness in himself. Everybody is God and All in himself. If so, how is it that people suffer? They suffer not because they have not the remedy, not because they do not possess the infinite joy in themselves, not because they have not the priceless jewel within themselves, but because they do not know how to untie the knot which holds it, how to open the casket which contains it. In other words, people do not know how to enter their own spirits and realize their own Self. All religion is simply an attempt to unveil ourselves and to explain our Self. We have placed a curtain before the precious jewel within us with our own hands, by our own efforts, and have made ourselves miserable, poor wretches; as Emerson puts it, "Every man is God playing the fool."

All creeds are simply efforts to strike out, to rend asunder the veil which covers our eyes. There are some creeds which have succeeded in making the veil much thinner than other creeds, but in all creeds there are people who have the true spirit in them, and wherever the true spirit comes, whether the curtain be thick or thin, it is pushed aside for the time being, and a glimpse into the reality is had. It will be illustrated by this example. Here is a curtain or veil. (Here Rama placed a handkerchief before his eyes.) It is before the eyes. We can push aside the curtain and see, but the curtain again comes up before the eyes. The curtain is made thinner (here some of the folds of the handkerchief were taken down), and when the curtain is very thin it can still be shoved aside, but it comes up before the eyes again. It does not leave the eyes permanently. We will make it thinner still. In this state also it can be slid aside for a while, but it comes before the eyes again. When the veil is made extremely thin, even though it be not thrust aside, the veil does not stand in the way of our vision. We can see through it, and even now as before, we can also remove it at times. When the curtain is made extremely thin, it is practically no curtain, and we enjoy supreme happiness in spite of it. We are face to face with God; nay, we are God. Nothing in this world can disturb us or mar our happiness; nothing can stand in our way. This is the advantage of Vedanta over other creeds, that it reduces the curtain of ignorance *(maya)* to its thinnest and enables a *jnani* to enjoy blissful vision even in business life.

All the sects in this world, including those of India, may be branched under three principal headings. In Sanskrit we call these *Tassyaivaham, Tavaivaham, Twamevaham*. The meaning of the first, *Tassyaivaham*, is "I am His." This form of a creed keeps the curtain in its thickest form. The second stage of religious creeds is *Tavaivaham*, which means "I am thine." You will notice the difference between the first phase of creeds or dogmas and the second. In the first attempts in the religious direction, the devotee, the worshipper, looks upon God as away from him, as invisible, and he speaks of God in the third person as if he were absent, "I am His." This is the beginning of religion. It is like mother's milk to every child of religion. Without having once fed upon this milk, a man is incapable of making further progress in religion. "I am His." Is it not sweet when a man realizes even this idea perfectly, awakes early in the morning and thinks, "My master wakes me"; goes to his official duties and looks upon those duties as imposed upon him by his dear, sweet master, God; looks upon the whole world as God's and regards his house, his relatives, his friends as God's, as vouchsafed unto him by God? Oh, is not the world turned into a veritable heaven; is not the world converted into a paradise? Let the man be sincere, let him earnestly and with his whole heart feel and realize that everything about him is his master's, his God's, and this body is His. When realized perfectly, even this idea brings exquisite joy, indescribable happiness, supreme bliss; it is sublime. This is sweet enough when realized and put into practice, but as a creed it is only the beginning.

Compare with it the second phase of creeds, the second stage of religious life and devotion called *Tavaivaham*, "I am Thine. I need thee every hour; I am Thine, Thine." The first was sweet, but this is sweeter. The first state was very lovely and very dear, but this is more lovely and much dearer. Just mark the difference. The difference is illustrated by the veil having become thinner. You know that in "I am Thine" God is no longer spoken of in the third person. He is no longer looked upon as absent, as behind the curtain, but comes face to face with us. He is near and dear to us, very close to us. He comes closer to us; we become more familiar with Him. As a creed this is higher. However, it often happens that people believe in this creed and address God as very familiar, very near to them, but they lack the true earnest spirit, the living faith.

Since living faith is conjoined to the first state of religious development, the curtain, though very thick, is for the time being removed. While a man is feeling with his whole heart and soul, with every drop of his blood, the idea that he is God's, "I am His," as it were, being poured forth from every pore of his body, the sincerity, the earnestness, the ardour and the zeal for the time being remove the curtain from before his eyes; and he is lost, merged in God, in the All. He becomes God for that time. Sometimes the man who believes in the high principle "I am Thine" lacks that true living faith and does not enjoy full well the sweets of God's presence, but the living faith and earnestness can be conjoined to the second stage of religious creed as well.

The third form of creed is called *Twamevaham* and means "I am Thou." You see how near it brings us to God. In the first form, "I am His," God is away, off. In the second form, "I am Thine," God is face to face with us; he has become closer to us. But in the final stage of religious development the two become one, and the lover and the beloved are lost in love. Thus is Vedanta realized. The moth neared and neared the light till it burned its body and became light. The word "Upanishad" (Vedanta) means literally approaching so close (upa) to the Light of lights that most certainly (ni) the moth of separating and dividing consciousness may be destroyed (shad). The true lover of God becomes one with Him, and unconsciously, spontaneously, involuntarily such expressions find utterance through his lips: "I am He"; "I am He"; "I am He"; "I am Thou"; "Thou and I are one." "I am God; I am God. Nothing less can I be." This is the final stage of religious development. That is the highest devotion. This is called Vedanta, which means the end of knowledge. Here does all knowledge find its end; here is the goal reached. Even in this creed, where the curtain is so thin that we can see the whole reality, there are some who lack earnestness, sincerity or single-mindedness and do not slide away the curtain entirely to taste full realization. There are those also who, after arriving intellectually at this conviction, begin to realize the idea through feeling to such a degree that they remove the curtain and enjoy heavenly bliss, they become heaven itself. These are called "liberated" even in this life—*jivanmuktas.*

The refining of the creed or the thinning of the curtain comes chiefly through the intellect, and the lifting of the veil is effected through feeling. The three forms of the creed have been described. Now let us see how far it is possible for men in the different creeds to shift the curtain between whiles. A few Hindu stories will serve as illustrations.

In a religious book of the Hindus, *Yoga Vashishtha*, we are told of a lady who was thrown into fire. The people saw that the fire did not burn her. Her lover was thrown into the fire, but it also did not burn him. How was it? They were thrown into the river, but it did not carry them off. They were thrown down from tops of mountains, and not a bone was broken. How was it? At that time they could not give any explanation; they were beyond themselves; they were in that state where no questions could reach them. Long afterwards the reason was asked, and they said that to each of them the beloved one was all in all. The fire was no fire; it appeared to that lady to be her lover, and to the man the same fire appeared to be his beloved one. The water was no water to them; it was all the beloved one. The stones were no stones to them; the body was no body to them; it was all the beloved one. How could the beloved one harm them?

Some time ago a Hindu monk was sitting on the bank of the Ganga in the deep Himalayan forests near Rishikesh. On the opposite bank some other monks were observing him while he was chanting to himself, "*Shivoham! Shivoham! Shivoham!*" which means "I am God." There appeared a tiger on the scene. The tiger came and got him in his claws, and though in the fangs of the tiger, the same chant was coming out from him in the same tone, in the same fearless strain, "*Shivoham! Shivoham! Shivoham!*" The tiger tore off his hands and legs, and there was the same sound, unabated in intensity. What do you think of that? What do you think of this truth, "I am God?" Could you call it agnosticism? Far from it, far from it. This is the final realization. Do not lovers on reaching that summit of love, feel themselves to be one with their beloved one? Does not the mother call her child the flesh of her flesh, the blood of her blood, the bones of her bones? Does not the mother regard the child as her other ego, as her other self? Are not the interests of the child identical with the interests of the mother? Indeed they are.

Embracing God, accepting Him, wedding Him, becoming one with Him to such a degree and so intensely that there may be left no trace of separation. Instead of praying, "Thy will be done, O Lord," let your joy be "My will is being done."

The above stories illustrate the third kind of love. The following will illustrate the second state of religious development, "I am Thine, I am Thine." Two boys came to a master and wanted him to instruct them in religion. He said that he would not teach them unless he had examined them. Well, he gave them two pigeons, one to each, and asked them to go out and kill the pigeons at some retired place where nobody might see them. One of them went straight into the crowded thoroughfare. Turning his back to the people who were passing through the street and putting a piece of cloth over his head, he took up the pigeon, wrenched its neck and came back straightway to the teacher and said, "Master, master, here is your order carried out." The Swami inquired, "Did you strangle the pigeon when no one was seeing you?" He said, "Yes." "All right; let us see now what your companion has done."

The other boy went out into a deep, dense forest and was about to twist the neck of the pigeon, and lo! there were the gentle, soft and glittering eyes of the pigeon looking him straight in the face. He met those eyes, and in his attempt to break the neck of the pigeon he was frightened. The idea struck him that the condition laid upon him by the master was a very trying, hard one. Here the witness, the observer is present even in this pigeon. "O, I am not alone! I am not in the place where no one will see me; I am being observed. Well, what shall I do? Where shall I go?" He went on and on and retired into some other forest. There also when he was about to commit the act he met the eyes of the pigeon, and the pigeon saw him. The observer was in the pigeon itself.

Again and again he tried to kill the pigeon; over and over again he tried but did not succeed in fulfilling the condition imposed upon him by the master. Broken hearted, he came back reluctantly to the master and laid the pigeon alive at the feet of the Swami and wept and wept and cried, "Master, master, I cannot fulfill this condition. Be kind enough to impart the knowledge of God to me. This examination is too trying for me. I cannot bear this examination. Please be merciful, have mercy on me and impart to me divine knowledge. I want that, I surely need it." The master took up the child, raised him in his arms, caressed and patted him and lovingly spoke to him: "O dear one, O dear one, even as you have seen the observer in the eyes of the bird that you were going to slay, even so, wherever you may happen to go, and whenever you are moved by a temptation to perpetrate a crime, realize the presence of God. Realize the observer, the witness, in the flesh and in the eyes of the woman for whom you crave. Realize that your master sees you even in her eyes. My master sees me. Act as if you are always in the presence of the Great Master, even face to face with the divinity, all the time in the sight of the beloved."

They say that in a grand museum in Naples there is a beautiful angelic face on the roof, and at whatever part of the museum you may happen to be, whatever part you may happen to visit—you may go to the roof; you may go to the basement—wherever you may be, the bright, dazzling, pure eyes of the angel look you straight in the eyes. People who are in the second state of spiritual development, if true to themselves, live constantly under the eyes of the Master. They feel and realize that wherever they may go, in the innermost chamber of the house, in the most secluded caves of the forest, they find themselves under the eyes of God, seen by Him, fed by His light, nourished by His grace.

Now we come to the primary stage of spiritual

development. "I am His! I am His! I am God's !" This seems to be an elementary stage. Oh! How difficult it is for people to realize the elementary stage of religious development. If a man really sincere, really single-minded, really devout, puts into practice what he believes, makes this idea course with the blood through his veins, feels it with every drop of his blood, gets himself saturated with this elementary creed, he may become an angel in this world.

A highly revered saint in India, Guru Nanak, was in his early youth working in a place where it was his duty to give away alms, to distribute food and treasure to the people. Some poor men were brought before him with an order from his Master to give unto them thirteen bushels of flour. He gave them one bushel, he gave them the second, the third, the fourth, the fifth, the sixth, until he came to the number thirteen. He was counting the number of bushels audibly while dealing out the flour. The number thirteen is called *tera* in the Indian language. This is a very remarkable word. It has two meanings. One is thirteen—ten plus three, and the other meaning of the word is "I am God's!" "I am a part of Him. I am His!"

Well, he counted twelve, and then came the turn of the number *tera*. When he had given them the thirteenth bushel and was pronouncing *tera*, such holy associations were aroused in him that he actually gave up his body and all to God. He forgot everything about the world; he was beyond himself. No, he was in Himself. In this state of ecstasy he went on saying, "*tera, tera, tera, tera,*" and went on unconsciously giving to the people bushel after bushel, until he fell down in a state of superconsciousness, in a state of transcendental bliss.

Thus we see that people who are in the elementary stages can often rise to the greatest heights, if they are as good as their word, if they are sincere and earnest, if they do not want to throw dust into the eyes of God, if they do not want to make promises with God and then break them. When once in the temple or church they say, "I am Thine," let them feel it. Let them live it. Let them realize it. This is true religion.

The different sects throughout the world can be classed under these three heads: "I am His!'.; "I am Thine!"; "I am Thou." So far as the forms are concerned, the second form, "I am Thine" is higher than the first, "I am His" and the third form, "I am Thou," is the highest. Into any of these three forms we may infuse the true religious spirit.

According to the Hindus, those who bring a true religious spirit to bear upon the elementary state of the creed will, in this birth or in the next, rise to the higher creed; they will rise to the second creed and with the second creed, again associating the true religious spirit in this life or the next, will by and by rise to the next higher religious creed which is "I am He," "I am Thou." When this state is reached, there are no births. The man is free, free, free! Man is God, Lord! He has reached the end! OM!

THE PATH OF TRUTH

March 1, 1903

U.S.A.

My own Self in the form of ladies and gentlemen,

The subject of tonight's discourse, as announced in the papers, is "The Path of Truth." This is a heading which might have some meaning to the Western ears but from the standpoint of Vedanta this is an erroneous title. The path to truth or the path of truth is a contradiction in terms. Truth is not distant. How can there be a path to it then? Truth is with you already; it is your Self already. You are in it already; nay, you are truth. You are that. So it is wrong to make use of the words "path of truth." Your realization of God consciousness, realization of divinity, is not a thing to be accomplished; it is not a thing to be achieved. It is not a thing to be done; it is done already. You are that already. You have simply to break through the cocoons of desires which imprison you; you have simply to undo what you have done.

This undoing of what has been done is to some a very hard task, and thus with reference to the path to truth we shall discuss the process of undoing. There is some effort to be made in undoing your snares. What are these snares, these chains and shackles which bind you? Your ears may today appreciate it or not; the Americans and Europeans may today mark the beauty of this statement or not; the truth remains there all the same. The truth is that all your attachments, all your loves and hatreds, all your desires are shackles and chains. These bind you. These do not allow you to see God. You cannot serve two masters. You cannot serve mammon and God at the same time. You cannot be a slave of the flesh and at the same time the master of the universe. To realize the truth is to become the master of the universe, and to entertain desires is to acknowledge bondage, thraldom and slavery of the things of this world. Everybody desires to become Christ; everybody wants to realize the truth, to become a prophet, but very few, if any, are ready to pay the price.

There was in Bharat a great wrestler and athlete. He wanted a barber to tattoo him, to engrave on his arm the picture of a lion. He told the barber to paint a great, magnificent lion on both his arms. He said he was born under the influence of the sign of the zodiac, Leo, and he was supposed to be a very brave man. The barber took up the needle to paint or tattoo him, and just when he was pricking a little the athlete could not bear it. He began to pant for breath and addressed the barber, "Wait, wait, what are you going to do?" The barber said that he was going to draw the tail of the lion. This fellow in reality could not stand the pricking sensation, but made a very queer pretence and said, "You don't know that fashionable people cut off the tails of their dogs and horses, and so the lion which has no tail is considered a very strong lion. Why are you drawing the tail of the lion? The tail is not needed." "All right, " said the barber, "I won't draw the tail. I will draw the other parts of the lion." The barber took up the needle again, and just pricked it through his skin. This too the fellow could not bear. He remonstrated and said, "What are you going to do next?" The barber said, "I am going to draw the ears of the lion." The man said again, "O barber, you are very foolish. Don't you know the people cut off the ears of their dogs? They don't need dogs with long ears. Don't you know that the lion which is without ears is the best?" The barber desisted. After a while the barber took up his needle and was again pricking him. The man could not bear it and remonstrated saying, "What are you going to do now, O barber?" The barber said, "I am going to paint now the waist of the lion." There the man said, "Haven't you read the descriptions given by Indian poets? Lions are always painted as having a very small, thin, nominal waist. You need not draw the waist of the lion." The barber now threw aside his colors and his painting needle and asked the fellow to go away from his presence.

Here is a man who asserts that he is born under the influence of the sign of the zodiac called Leo. Here is a man who pretends to be a great wrestler, a great athlete. Here is a man who calls himself a lion. He wants to have lions tattooed all over his body, but he cannot bear the sting of a needle. Such are the majority of people who want to see God, who want to realize Vedanta, who want to know the whole truth this moment, who want to accomplish everything, to become Christ in half a minute. When the time comes to get that lion, truth, painted in their souls, to get that lion of righteousness printed or tattooed in their being, they cannot bear the sting; there they hesitate. "The thing I want, but the price I will not pay."

In order that you may reach the truth and realize the divinity, your dearest wants and desires will be pricked through and through; your dearest wants and attachments will have to be severed; all your favorite superstitions and prejudices will have to be wiped out; all your preconceived notions will have to be torn aside. Free you will have to become of all the debasing and degrading yearnings; pure you will have to make yourself. Purity. Without paying the price you cannot reach God; you cannot regain your own birthright. "Blessed are the pure in heart, for they shall see God." What is purity of heart? Purity of heart does not mean only abstaining from conjugal sins; it means that, but it means a great deal more. Whether you relish these words today or not, you will have to relish them one day; you will have to come to the same conclusion today or tomorrow. The conclusion is that all attachment, whether it be the attachment to your house, your clock or your dog, the attachment to father, mother or child, for a man who aspires to the realization of truth, for a man who wants to gain possession of the whole truth this moment, for a man of noble aspirations, is just as degrading and weakening as adultery. Purity of heart means making yourself free of all clingings to the objects of this world. Renunciation, nothing short of it—purity of heart means that. Blessed are the pure in heart for they shall see God. Gain this purity and you see God.

There is a very beautiful story of Atlanta in the old mythology. They say that every man who wanted to wed her had to run a race with her. Nobody could get ahead of her, but one person consulted his god Jupiter and asked the advice of his favorite god as to the way of outrunning Atlanta and winning her. The god gave him very queer advice. He told this man to bestrew the path along which they had to run with gold bricks. You know, the god Jupiter could not help this devotee of his to outrun Atlanta in any other way. This Atlanta had received from the highest deity a boon which made her the strongest and swiftest being in the whole universe. So this devotee of

Jupiter threw gold bricks all along the race course and challenged Atlanta to run a race with him. Both began to run. This man was naturally much weaker than Atlanta. She outran him in one second, but as she lost sight of him, she saw gold bricks lying along the path and stopped to pick them up. While she was picking up the gold bricks, that devotee went ahead of her. After a minute or so she overtook him again but again saw to the left of the race course another brick. She went to pick it up and that devotee of Jupiter went ahead of her. After a while she got him again, but then she found some more gold bricks. She stopped to pick up those. In the meantime that fellow outran her and so on. Towards the close of the race, Atlanta had collected a very heavy load of gold. It was very difficult for her to carry it and also outrun him. Finally that man got the better of Atlanta, who was won. All the gold that Atlanta had collected also fell to the share of the man who outran her and she herself went over to that man. He got everything.

Such is the way with most people who want to tread the path of righteousness and the path of truth. When you commence to tread the path of truth, you find all sorts of base lucre and worldly temptations around you. You stoop to pick them up, but the moment you do so and enjoy these worldly temptations and entertainments you find you are lagging behind. You are losing the race, procrastinating, making your path dreary and losing everything. Beware of worldly attachments and materiality. You cannot reach the truth and also enjoy worldly pleasures. The saying goes that if you enjoy the truth you will no longer be able to enjoy worldly pleasures. Enjoy worldly pleasure and truth will elude your grasp, get ahead of you. Rama is telling you the truth today. So many people come to Rama and say to him over and over again that they want realization. You may gain realization this moment. Get rid of attachments, and at the same time shake off all hatred and jealousy. What is jealousy; what is hatred? It is inverted attachment. When we hate somebody it is because we are attached to something else. Here you will ask how you are to get rid of your sons, brothers and husbands, etc. Well, this is your own outlook. The truth is, let truth or God become your father, let God or truth become your mother, let God or truth be your wife, let God or truth be to you your grandfather, your teacher, your house, your property, your everything. Have all your attachments severed from every object, and concentrate yourself on one thing, the one fact, the one truth, viz., your divinity. Immediately on the spot you gain realization.

There is a beautiful song in the Indian language, which need not be sung here. The purport of the song is that if your father stands in the way of your realizing the truth, tread over him, go beyond him, just as Prahlad, a hero in India, forsook his father because the latter stood in the way of his realizing the truth. If your mother stands in the way of your realizing the truth, forsake her. This is what the New Testament says. The Hindu Bible also says the same. Love truth for the sake of your parents. Love and honor parents as far as they do not retard your progress towards the truth. If your brother stands in the way of your realizing the truth, shake him off just as Vibhishan did. If your wife stands in the way of your realizing the truth, cast her aside just as Bhartirihari did. If your husband stands in the way of your realizing the truth, throw him off just as Mira did. If your preceptor, your religious guide, stands in the way of your realizing the truth, shake him off, cast him overboard just as Bali did, because your real relative, your truest friend, is truth and truth alone. All other relations and companions are only fleeting, for a day only, but truth is with you always. Truth is your real Self. Truth is nearer to you than your parents. Truth is nearer to you than your wife, children, friends, etc. Respect truth more than kings, parents, children, father, mother, anyone.

There is a fine illustration given by the life of a king in India. He trod the path of truth. It is said that he was going up the Himalayas to let his body melt down in the snows. There is a long story about it. Rama need not relate to you the whole. For some reason, for a great reason, he was going with his parents, with his wife and her brothers and his four brothers toward the summits of the Himalayas. It is said that he was treading the path of righteousness; he was going to seek truth. He was going ahead, marching on. His younger brother was following him, and after his younger brother came his other brother, and so on in the right order; and after the brothers was the wife of this king. He went ahead, his face towards the goal, and his eyes set upon the truth. He found that his wife was wailing behind him, tottering down as she could not follow him; she was fatigued and about to die. Here the king did not turn his face back. He asked his wife to run up to him a few feet, saying he would carry her with him, "Come up to me, come up to me." But she could not go up to him those three feet. She was lagging behind; she could not manage to go up to him, and he did not turn back. To turn back one step from the truth is not allowable. Never will King Yudhishthira turn back one step. The wife totters down, but for her the king is not to turn back from the truth. Thousands of wives you have had in your previous births, and if you have any future births, you do not know how many times you will be married again; how many relatives you have had, and how many relatives you will have in the future. For the sake of these ties and relations you have not to turn back from the truth. Go ahead; go ahead. Let nothing draw you back. Have more respect for truth, have more respect for divinity than for your wife. The truth concerns the whole human race. Divinity or truth concerns all time, is eternal, and your worldly ties are not so. They are momentary. Bear in mind the law that what is really good for you must be really good for your wife or your companions. If you see that for you it is really beneficial to live apart from your wife, remember that it is also really good for her to live apart from you. This is the rule. The same divinity or truth that underlies your personality underlies the personality or being of your wife also. The wife of King Yudhishthira fell down, but the king went straight on and asked his brothers to follow him. They ran on with him for some time, but the youngest brother could not keep pace any longer. He was tottering down, overtaken with fatigue and about to fall when he cried, "Brother, brother Yudhishthira, I am going to die; save me." King Yudhishthira did not turn his eyes away from the goal, from the truth. On he went; he went ahead. He simply called out to his younger brother to gather courage enough to run up to him those two or three feet, saying he would take him with himself on that condition; but for nothing whatsoever could he go one step behind to give him even a pull.

On he goes. The youngest brother dies. After a while the second brother, who was at the end of the chain, cried and was about to totter down. He called for help, "Brother, brother Yudhishthira, help me; help me. I am going to fall down." Brother Yudhishthira did not turn back. On he went. This way all the brothers died, but King Yudhishthira did not swerve or turn back a single step. Away he went; on he went on the path of righteousness.

The story runs that when King Yudhishthira reached the pinnacle of truth, when he reached the goal, God Himself, truth personified, appeared to him. Just as we read in the Bible that God appeared in the shape of a dove, so in the Hindu scriptures we read about God appearing to certain persons in the body of an angel or in the shape of the king of heaven. So the story goes that when King Yudhishthira reached the pinnacle of truth, truth personified approached and asked him to go in person to heaven, to ascend to heaven. As you read in the Bible about certain people being raised alive to heaven, so here King Yudhishthira is being asked to ascend to heaven alive. When he looked at his right hand side, he found a dog with him. King Yudhishthira said, "O God, O truth, if you want to raise me to the highest heaven, you will have to take this dog also with me. Let this dog also ascend to the highest heaven with me." The story says that God or truth personified said, "King Yudhishthira, that cannot be. The dog is not worthy of being taken to the highest heaven; the dog has yet to pass through many transmigrations; the dog has yet to come into the body of man and live the right life and live as a pure, immaculate person. How then can it be raised to the highest heaven? You are worthy of being taken to the highest heaven in body, but not the dog." Then King Yudhishthira said, "O Truth, O God, I come here for your sake and not for the sake of heaven or paradise. If you want to raise me to the highest paradise and to enthrone me there, you will have to take this dog also with me. My wife did not keep pace with me; she staggered on the path of righteousness. My youngest brother did not keep pace with me; he staggered on the path of truth. My other brothers did not keep company with me; they forsook me; they yielded themselves to weakness; they allowed temptations to get the better of them; they did not keep pace with me. Here is this dog; he alone comes up with me. He shares my pains; he shares my struggles; he shares my fights; he partakes of my anguish, he labors with me. Here is this dog. If he divides with me my difficulties, my hard fights and struggles, why should not he enjoy my paradise or heaven? I will never go to your paradise or heaven if you do not make this dog share equally with me that paradise or heaven. I have no use for your paradise if you do not let in this dog with me."

Then truth personified, or God, said once more to King Yudhishthira, "Please do not ask this favor of me; do not ask me to take this dog with you." But King Yudhishthira said, "Away, ye Brahman; you are no truth or God personified. You may be some devil; you cannot be God or truth, because if you were truth, then why should you allow any injustice in your presence; Don't you mark that if you give me the exclusive enjoyment of heaven and don't allow the dog to share my happiness, then you are unjust to the dog which shared my troubles? This is not worthy of God or truth personified." The story says that thereupon truth personified, or God, appeared in His true colors and that very dog was immediately found to be no longer the dog but to be in full glory the Lord Almighty Himself. That king had been examined and tried, and in the final examination, in the final trial, he came out successful.

This is the way you have to tread the path of truth. Even if your dearest and nearest companions, those who are next of kin to you, do not keep pace with you on the path of righteousness, do not look upon them as your friends; and if a dog accompanies you on the path of righteousness, that dog should be the nearest and dearest being to you. Thus make your friends on the principle of favoring your righteousness; select no friend on the principle of favoring your evil nature. If you select your companions on the principle that they enjoy the same kind of evil propensities that you do, suffering, excruciating pain and anguish will be your lot.

It is related of a Hindu saint that he was once going through the streets hungry. You know in India saints or sages come down from mountains and walk through the streets when they are hungry and beg food for their bodies. On very rare occasions they visit the streets. Usually they live outside the cities in the forests, devoting their time entirely to God-consciousness. The hungry saint was fed. If Rama also takes something you will have good reason to excuse him. A lady brought to him dainty food to eat. He just took that loaf of bread in his handkerchief, left the house and went out into the forest, as is the way with monks in India. There he put the loaf in water and, making it wet, ate it. The next day he came again to the streets at the usual time. Again the lady approached him and gave him something very rich to eat. He went back. The third day also that lady brought him something very good to eat, but while she was giving him this dainty food she made the remark, "I keep waiting for you. My eyes have become sore in waiting for you, in keeping watch at the door. Your eyes have bewitched me." These were the words that escaped the lips of that lady. The sage went away. He went to some other door, and there he got some food. He went out to the forests and threw into the river the food which was offered him by the first lady who expressed her love to him, and the other food that was presented to him by the second lady he ate. The next day do you know what he did? He got very hot irons and poked out his eyes and tied them in his handkerchief. With the aid of a stick, with great difficulty walking the streets, he felt his way to the house of the lady who had expressed her love to him. There he found that the lady was waiting for him very anxiously. His eyes were fixed on the ground. The lady did not notice that he had poked out his eyes, but when she brought something very rich for him to eat, he presented his eyeballs to her saying, "Mother, mother, take up these eyes because the eyes have bewitched you, and have caused you so much trouble. You have every right to possess these eyes. Mother, you wanted these eyes. Have them, keep them, love and enjoy them, do with these eyeballs whatever you wish; but for heaven's sake, for mercy's sake, do not retard my progress onward. Make me not stumble in the path of truth."

Now we see, O people, that if your eyes are the stumbling block in your way, cast them out. It is better for your body to be without light than for your whole being to perish in darkness. If your ears tempt you and keep you backward, cut them out. If your wife, money, property, or anything stands in the way, away with it.

Could you love truth with the same love as you have for your wife and relatives, could you love divinity and *Atman* or realization with the same zest or zeal with which you love your wife, could you love God with even half the love that you show your wife, you would realize the truth this second. When you begin to tread the path of righteousness and overcome some of the temptations which present themselves in the beginning, if you come out victorious over the ordinary temptations, what will you find? You will not find this path all rough and without any beauty; you will not find this path rugged through and through. They say that the path of truth is narrower than a needle's end. In the Vedas it is written that the path of truth is as sharp and narrow as the razor's edge, but this is not the whole truth. In the beginning the path seems to be very narrow and sharp, but when you come out victorious over the ordinary temptations, you will find the path to be wonderfully beautiful and exceedingly easy. You will find that the whole of nature helps you, and everything stands on your side. These difficulties, these temptations, these obstacles, these struggles and oppositions only bully you. They only scare and frighten you but do not really harm you. If you can outstare them and scare them off, you will find that the difficulties and temptations were seeming difficulties and temptations only. You will find all nature standing on your side, the whole of creation ready to lackey you.

It is said in one of the Hindu scriptures, which is the "Iliad" of India and which relates the story of Rama, the greatest hero of India, that when he went to search out truth, to discover or regain truth, all nature offered him her services. It is said that monkeys formed his army, and squirrels helped him in building a bridge over the gulf. It is said that even geese came up on his side to assist him in overcoming his foes. It is said that the stones forgot their nature, and when thrown into water, instead of sinking, said, "We shall float in order that the cause of truth be advanced." It is said that air, the atmosphere, was on his side; fire helped him; winds and storms were on his side. There is a saying in the English language that the wind and wave are always for the brave. All nature stands up on your side when you persist, when you overcome the primitive seeming difficulties. If you overcome the struggles or temptations in the beginning, the whole of nature must serve you. Persist in standing by the truth, and you will find that you live in no ordinary world. The world will be a world of miracles of you, and woe unto the gods if they do not lackey you in your advance onward. Nature is waiting anxiously upon the ruler of the universe. You are the master of the universe, you are the husband of the whole world, if you persist by the truth.

Now Rama will conclude by relating to you the life of one of the greatest men in the world, the life of an Eastern saint. Shams Tabrez is his name. This man was born under peculiar circumstances. The story may be true or false—we have nothing to do with it—but there must be some truth in it. It is related about his father that he was once the poorest man in the country. That poorest man devoted his life entirely to God-consciousness. He forgot that his body was ever born; he entirely forgot that his personality ever existed in this world. For him the world had never been a world. He was God, all divinity. When a man's whole being is saturated with an idea from head to foot, every pore of his body is alive to God-consciousness. It is related that when he walked through the streets the people heard through the pores of his body this song, "Haq, Ahalhaq," which means "God, I am God." The song on his lips was always, "Analhaq; Analhaq; divinity I am; divinity I am." The ordinary people gathered around him. They wanted to murder him. They accused him of heresy. Why is he calling himself God? He was divinity himself; to him the body was no body; the world was no world. When the words "Analhaq" escaped his lips, he was not even conscious of that. Just as a man snores when asleep, similarly from his standpoint he was entirely lost in divinity, and if those words "Analhaq" escaped his lips, they were like the snoring of a man who is asleep.

However the people wanted to kill him. What was that to him whom they would kill? They would kill the body, but that body from his standpoint never existed. To kill his body what pain could it cause him? It is related that this man's body was placed upon a cross. You know that having your body put on a cross is an easy thing, but there they have something worse than a cross. It was a long iron pole, the sharp-pointed end of the iron pole pressing through the solar plexus. This way was a man put to death in those days. You see, this is worse than a cross even! His body was placed upon a cross of that kind; and it is related that while his body was placed there, this man's face was glowing with glory, and through every hair of his body the same sweet song was all the time coming out, "Analhaq; I am God, I am God; divinity I am, divinity I am." The body died. To him it made no difference. There you see that if for the sake of truth you have to give up the body, give it up. This is the last attachment broken. For the sake of truth you have to give up not only worldly attachments, but if there be need to give up the body, give it up. This is how you have to tread the path of truth.

When the man was hanging upon that pointed pole drops of blood fell from his body. The story says that those drops of blood were gathered by a young girl. This young girl who believed the same way as the saint, this young girl who was of the same thought as the preacher, drank up this blood, and they say that she was conceived. It may be true or false; we have nothing to do with that. According to Vedanta, if Christ could be of immaculate conception, this could also be true because here was a man who was not inferior to Christ, really superior to him in many respects. This woman gave birth to a baby who is the sage whose life Rama wants to relate to you. From his beginning, from his very childhood, he was all divinity, even far exceeding his father. There is such a great book; you will believe that; a grand work which came from the lips of this hero. This man did not take up a pen and write it, but it is said that through him always came out poetry; all that he spoke was poetry, all that he said was poetry. What kind of poetry? Not the doggerel of your American poets. It was real poetry in the true sense of the word. It was God-consciousness and nothing else. It was sublime with divine ideas. Every word is worth its weight in gold, if it could be weighed at all.

There is a very remarkable fact related about this man. At one time there appeared to him some people who were connected with some show—a circus. When they performed it in the presence of the king, he was highly pleased with them and offered them a thousand dollars.

Afterwards the king repented. The king did not think it advisable to give away thousands of dollars every night for mere empty shows. So, in order to get back his thousand dollars, he made a pretence and asked those people to appear in the garb of a lion. If the lion's performance was pleasing to the king, he might give them something enormous, something great, otherwise the king would fine them all their property. These people could not give a lion's performance. In India, there are people who put on all sorts of garbs and appear in the shape of some animals and make themselves appear to all intents and purposes the animals they play, but they could not assume the garb of a lion.

These people came to this man and were weeping and crying and shedding tears. The story says that this sage, being in tune with the universe, in harmony with the whole nature, being one with each and all, natural sympathy overtook his heart. All of a sudden he spoke to those people to be of good cheer because he was to appear as a lion and to give the performance of a lion himself. So the story goes that the next day when the king and his courtiers were all standing, waiting to see a man assume the shape and figure of a lion, all of a sudden, as if by magic, a real lion jumped into the pit. This lion at once roared and roared; he took up the child of the king and tore it to pieces. He took up some other boy and threw it out to the sky. You see here was a man who was in reality divinity and God. To this man the idea "I am this little puny body" had become a thing of the past; it had become absolutely meaningless. He was divinity himself; the God that appeared in the shape of a lion, the same was he, and he was in a moment's thought a lion.

Just as you think so you become, and if you have felt and realized your self as God, all your thoughts and desires are bound to fructify, to be realized on the spot. So this man's thought that he could appear as a lion was immediately realized, and a lion he was. The show was over. The sage after killing this boy went away, because he had not to become a lion and respect this body or that. He was no respecter of persons. But the king was exasperated, the king and the courtiers were all rage personified; they wanted to wreak vengeance upon this man. They came to him and said, 'Sir, sir, please bring this boy to life again. If you can kill him, you can bring him to life also. Bring him back to life just as Christ used to bring to life the dead by saying 'Qum Biyzan Allah' which means "Rise in the name of God; glory to God and walk; be alive, come back to life.' " The sage laughed and said, "Qum Biyazn Allah" which means "Come back to life in the name of God," but the boy did not revive. The saint said, "The boy does not come to life in the name of God." He said again, "Come to life in the name of God." Still the boy did not come to life. He said again, "Come to life, get up and walk in the name of God, the Lord," but the boy did not come to life. The sage smiled and said, "Qum Biyazni" which means "Come to life by my order; through my command, come to life," and the boy came to life. This is the truth. The boy came to life, but the people all around him could not bear it. They said, "Here is a heretic. He takes all this credit to himself. He wants to make himself equal to God. He ought to be put to death. He ought to be murdered, flayed alive." To the sage it meant nothing. The people understood him not. He is not calling the body, the little personality, God. He had already killed and crucified his flesh. The people wanted to flay him alive, and the story says that that man immediately applied his nails to his head. Just as the skin of animals is torn and separated from the body, so with his own nails he tore his own skin, cut it off and threw it away. A fine, long poem was written by him on that occasion. The purport of that song is, "O Self, O Self," he is addressing himself, "To whom the poison of the world is nectar and to whom the nectar of the world (that is to say the sensuous enjoyments) is poison. Here are people wanting something. The world is nothing else but a dead carcass; (and here dead carcass means "sensuous enjoyments) the worldly pleasures are nothing else but a dead carcass; and the people who run after them are no better than dogs. Here are these dogs. Give them this flesh to eat." This story may or may not be true. Rama has nothing to do with it, but the spirit of the story, the moral of the story, you have to bear in mind.

Here, in order to realize the truth, to tread the path of righteousness, give up all attachment; rise above worldly desires and selfish clingings. If you free yourself of worldly clingings and selfish desires, what about the truth? Truth you are this moment. Fools pray, "More light, I want more light." You need not pray that way. You need not waste even a prayer on calling for light. If you make yourselves this second divested of all desires, if you free yourselves of all worldly clingings, Light you are. You know that every desire of yours chops out a part of yourself, leaves you only a small fraction of yourself. How seldom it is that we meet a whole man. A whole man is an inspired man; a whole man is the truth. Every wish or clinging makes you a proper fraction, but in reality it makes you an improper portion, insignificant portion, of yourself. The very moment you cast overboard these desires, clingings, loves, hatreds and attachments and also throw off even the desire for light and chant Om for a second, freeing yourself from hatred and attachment, well balanced in equilibrium, nothing of yourself left with that person, with that body or with that object, then think who it is within you. Is it not your own Self that makes the hair grow and the blood flow through your veins? Is it not your own Self who created this body? This wonderful world is also your handiwork. This is your own creation most certainly. Mark it. Who is it that hears through you? Is it not your Self? Who is it that sees through you? Is it not your Self? Who is it that makes the blood flow in your veins? Is it not your Self? And if that Self of yours could work out such marvelous facts, the world is your own creation. Feel that and rejoice in your own divinity, and derive pleasure from within you; enjoy happiness of your own *Atman.* Throw aside all abnormal desires and inordinate wishes. Chant Om, Om. If you do that for a few moments, your whole being from head to foot becomes Light. Why pray for light when light is your own Self? You become Light immediately. Make yourself whole, get rid of desires and attachments, get rid of this repulsion and attraction. It is attachment that detaches. When you reach home, see to what you are attached. If you are attached to name or fame, give up that. If you are attached to the desire for popularity, detach yourself from it; if you are attached even to the wish, to the desire, to help the world, give that up. This seems to be something inordinate. Why should the world be so poor as to be begging help from you all the time?

Rạma says, take up your duty or work with no notice or desire on your part. Do your work; enjoy your work, because your work by itself is pleasure, because work is the other name of realization. Take to your work because work you have to do. Work leads you to realization. Do not take to work on any other ground. Come to your work in an independent spirit; just as a prince is to play football or some other game for pleasure's sake, so come to your work because pleasure or happiness lives in the garb of work. Independent we feel, not bound by a thing.

People say duty, duty, duty. Why should duty lord it over you? Feel no responsibility to anybody; you are your own Lord. Have no fear. We say you will have to work, but when your hands are not employed, when your hands are free and you are sitting in your room, enjoy your godhead, relish your divinity. That is the finest work. There throw aside all attachment you own. People say that attachment is necessary, motives are necessary, to make us work. A false idea. Give up all attachment; free yourself of all desires and the very second you find yourself free, you feel no responsibity or burdens thrown on your shoulders. All the burdens on your shoulders are placed there by yourself. Nobody is required to come and relieve you of the burdens. When you find that there is no burden on your shoulders, when you find all the objects of love are with you, when you live this Vedanta, your whole being is light. Being the Light of lights, to whom are you to pray for light? This is the secret. Free you become. Who puts you in bondage? Who is it that enslaves you? Your own desires, nothing else. All the magnetism of the world, all the powers of the world, flow from you; all the miracles of the world are your abject slaves, nothing more. Get rid of these desires; free you become this moment, and when you get rid of all desires, what immense joy should it not bring you? No responsibility, no fear. Why should you fear? You are afraid lest this thing should be lost. You fear this man; you fear that; you fear ridicule; because you desire this good name, you are attached to good name. All fear and anxiety is the result of desires; headaches and heartaches are the consequences of desires. You cringe and sneak before the president or king because you desire his good grace. You become the Lord of lords, the King of kings when you are free of desires, when one by one these desires are thrown off. How free and happy you become that moment! Thus Rama says that the path of truth is not a thing to be accomplished or brought about. By your exertions and efforts you will have to undo simply the bondage and thraldom which you have already done through your desires.

UNIVERSAL UNITY*

September 22, 1905
Gorakhpur, U.P., India

Dear *Atma*, Own Self

The tongue is the organ of speech while the ears are those of hearing; but from where does the tongue get the power to speak or the ears to hear? You will agree that there is only one original power which moves the tongue to speak and the ears to hear. You may agree or not, but the same power is actually working on both sides. The same power, which moves the tongue to speak and the ear to hear, is at work in the speaker as well as in the hearer.

I sing to hear my own song,
I do not mind if anybody understands it or not.

This is not a lecture for you. It is as if Rama is thinking aloud and lecturing to his own self. You should also listen to it as if you are thinking aloud and lecturing to your own self.

Before Rama begins the lecture, you should merge yourself in the idea that there is only one Force pervading all these bodies. You can call it God, *Allah, Atma, Parmatma* or nature. There is One and only One Omnipotence interpenetrating all the bodies, like a thread passing through the beads of a rosary. In fact, it is He and He alone and nothing else.

For long we have been hearing and reading in the books about unity and universal oneness. We can draw the real benefit from it only when we actually realize it and use it in our practical life. In a way, we can say that

* Translated from the Urdu.

this unity is seen, understood and appreciated through the laws of nature which are universal. As a matter of fact, this unity is intrinsically the soul of the universe.

The nations which have realized this universal unity in actual practice have made wonderful researches in science and developed tremendously. He who practices this in his own life is progressive. The man who violates this law of unity is punished in the same way as the one who ignores the law of gravitation. If you touch the fire, you are sure to burn your fingers. If you jump from the roof of a high building, you are sure to fracture your limbs. Similarly, if you ignore the law of unity, you are sure to be segregated to harm your own self.

You might inquire, "What is unity?" Rama will not answer this question with the old arguments of Vedanta but will try to explain it to you scientifically, though in a simple language, in a modern way of thinking. He will, so to say, serve the old wine in a new bottle. Keep aside for the present the talk about soul and God. It will now be proved to you that there does exist a unity in all the different bodies, minds and the intellects. There is oneness in all, both in matter and spirit. In fact, this unity is all-pervading.

The Indian philosophers divide the human covers in five categories (1) *Annamayee Kosh* or physical cover, (2) *Pranmayee Kosh* or the vital cover, (3) *Manomayee Kosh* or the mental cover, (4) *Vigyanmayee Kosh* or the cover of knowledge, (5) *Anandmayee Kosh* or the blissful cover. The gross cover grows and is sustained by taking material food or nourishment. This is also called *Sthool Sharir* in Sanskrit and *Jisme Kasif* in Persian. In English you can call it the "gross body." With the help of this gross body we transact business in our lives in this world. Its manifestation is more evident in the waking state. The vital cover is maintained through our breathing which produces vitality in us to maintain life. The mental cover and the cover of knowledge or consciousness are concerned with our feeling and thinking faculties.

The *Pranmayee Kosh*, the *Manomayee Kosh* and the *Vigyanmayee Kosh* combine to form the subtle body or *sukshama sharir*, as we call it in Sanskrit. In Persian they call it *Jisme Latif*, or *Alame Malkut*. It is concerned with our dreaming state.

The *Anandmayee Kosh*, or the blissful cover, is called *Karan Sharir* in Sanskrit and *Jisme Illati* in Persian. In English it may be called the "seed" or "causal body." Its manifestation is more evident in the deep sleep state but your *Atma* or the soul is not attached to any of these covers. The outermost cover, the gross body, is like an overcoat. The subtle body is like an undercoat. The seed or the causal body is like your underwear. If your *Atma* or soul is closely examined, it will be found to be the same throughout, not only in your own body but also in all the different bodies.

Rama will further elaborate it. Of these bodies the gross body is the grossest of all. The subtle body, as its name indicates, is subtler than the gross body. It is subtler even than hydrogen or ether. The causal body is subtler still. As you know, the greater the grossness or the density of a body, the smaller the place it would occupy. Its reverse is also true. The subtler the body, the greater the space it occupies. According to this law, a subtle body occupies much greater space than a gross body, and since the causal body is the subtlest of all the bodies, it is much more pervasive than any two of the other bodies, the gross or the subtle body. But *Atma* is neither any body nor any form of matter. It is, therefore, subtler than the subtlest in the universe. It is subtler than even the *Akash*. It, therefore, pervades the entire universe and is all-embracing. It is because of this nature that it is not limited to any one body alone but pervades all the bodies of different names and forms in this universe. It is the same throughout in all the different bodies, as already stated earlier.

Under the influence of this *Atma* the whole universe is working according to the set laws governed by it. The earth, the sun, the moon, the planets, the stars, the elements, etc. all follow the laws quietly and submissively. None can dare oppose or break these laws. It is this *Atma* which is called *Parmatma, Allah, Brahman* or God. It is on account of the all-pervasiveness of the *Atma* that the inner unity is maintained in the diversity of this entire universe. It is this fundamental unity due to *Atma* which is expressed in various ways throughout. Rama will not say any more today, as he already explained *Atma* in detail yesterday. Rama will, however, explain this unity, as seen in different lights in this universe.

Even if we take only the gross bodies, we find that there is unity in all of them. Our gross bodies are closely related with one another, like the different waves of an ocean. Some are small, some big, some low, some high, but though these waves appear differently, yet they are one with the ocean. After all, the different waves are nothing but the sea water. Similarly, the vicious, the virtuous, the rich or the poor are all one, like the waves in which only one *Atma* or nature is permeating. They may appear different by virtue of their different names and forms, but they are all one, because they are nothing but the same, like the sea water which is common to all. Let us look at it more carefully.

You may eat fruits, vegetables, cereals or meat to build your body. Then you excrete them and, in their excreted form, they may be used as manure for the vegetables, fruits, etc. The same matter of your body reappears in the shape of vegetables, fruits or cereals to be taken up again by you or others. Thus you see that the same gross matter which was once yours becomes that of others in no time. It is rather a continuous process showing our physical unity with others.

Then again doctors say that the body of a man is entirely changed after seven years. Every particle of the body is replaced by a new one. The body which I call mine at this moment does not remain there. The body of Rama of seven years ago is now forming the body or bodies of others. The body which you are calling yours belongs to each and all. Thus you see that even on the physical plane there is a continuity of unity.

If a body is healthy, it will spread health. If a body is sickly, it will spread disease. The man who does not care to remain healthy is a danger not only to himself but also to others. Therefore it is very necessary that one must be healthy, not only for one's own sake but also for the sake of society in which one lives and moves about. Such a unity is in respect of *Annamayee Kosh*, or the gross body.

Now let us take *Pranmayee Kosh*, or the vital cover. You are constantly inhaling air which unites us all through the process of breathing. Air contains oxygen, which enters your lungs. The oxygen, as you know, supports combustion and maintains normal heat inside your body. It causes energy to be produced in your body and thus maintains life in all the living beings, acting as a common requisite.

Oxygen purifies the blood and maintains its redness. When oxygen enters the lungs there is gaseous exchange. Oxygen is absorbed by the blood, and carbon dioxide from the blood is thrown out through the lungs with exhalation. This carbon dioxide supplies food to the green vegetation. The plants and the vegetation absorb the carbon dioxide and break it up into carbon and oxygen. They assimilate this carbon as their food for their growth and give back oxygen to the atmosphere. This released oxygen is again utilized by the living beings to produce energy and to sustain their lives. Such a continuous process from the animals to the vegetables and vice versa in cyclic order clearly goes to prove that there is unity, not only among the human bodies, but also between the bodies of other animals and those of the vegetable kingdom. Without the oxygen produced by the vegetation, the animals, including human beings, cannot sustain their lives. And without the carbon dioxide given out by the animal kingdom, the vegetable kingdom cannot survive. They are interdependent.

Just as one organ of a gross body is dependent on the working of the other organs of the same body, so too the animal kingdom is dependent for its life and existence on the vegetable kingdom and vice versa, proving that they are the different organs of the same body (universal body of nature).

Moreover, the plants and the vegetation have also to depend on the mineral kingdom for their life food. Both the vegetable and the animal kingdoms require potassium, phosphorus, minerals, carbon, nitrogen, etc. for their growth and nourishment. Where do they get all these ingredients from? They get their minerals through water from the earth, which supplies these requirements both to the vegetable and the animal kingdoms. Carbon is absorbed by the vegetation from the air through carbon assimilation. Similarly, nitrogen for our nitrogenous food, which is needed for our body building, is also derived from the atmosphere through the process of "nitrogen-fixation" by the roots of certain plants of the family of *Leguminosae.* Thus we see that there does exist a unity in cyclic order among the mineral, vegetable and the animal kingdoms through the earth, water, air, etc.

We can therefore clearly see that all these are working in close cooperation for the good of one and all. There pervades a continuity of unity among all the elements of nature, helping each other for the common good of the whole.

It is only in the presence of the sunlight that the plants can absorb carbon from the carbon dioxide, assimilate it for their growth and give off oxygen through a chemical process called photosynthesis. There can be no vegetable life without the sun and no animal life, either direct or indirect, without the vegetable life. They are all interconnected through the sun. The sun not only gives us light but is also a cure for a number of our diseases and ailments. Besides, it provides energy to all of us directly and also indirectly.

The sun, being immensely useful in the daily life was worshipped by the ancient Egyptians. Also, some of the cults of the Indians even today worship the sun as the symbol of God because it is the visible source of energy which supports life on this earth. A time may come when the scientists may succeed in harnessing the sun's energy for our daily use. Not only the sun but also the sea may be utilized to provide energy for mankind.

Similarly, as with the sun, our unity with the moon, Mars and other planets can also be traced and proved. There cannot be the slightest doubt that the entire universe is interconnected with the thread of continued unity for the common good of the whole. Why? Because there is one and only one without a second, who is all in all.

We see in this material world that everything is useful to us in some way or the other, directly or indirectly. We may know it or not, but it is so. Nothing is useless. Even discarded bones and our dirty excreta can be utilized as manure for vegetation and also for manufacturing useful chemicals for the benefit of human beings. All are working constantly, offering their usefulness in their own spheres for the common good of all. For example, even the roots, the herbs, the shrubs, the bark, latex, sap, the leaves, flowers, fruits, minerals, etc. are all useful and are being utilized in different ways for our common good. The vegetation not only offers fresh air, sweet fragrance and pleasant sight but is also useful to provide food and medicines, manufactured in the laboratory of nature for our various physical or mental ailments.

The earth, besides producing minerals including precious and beautiful diamonds, medicinal salts, metals, etc., also grows vegetation, provides well water (cold water during summer and warm water during winter) and hot springs even in the lap of the snow capped mountains. The sea provides us with minerals, salts, pearls, energy, a variety of edibles, rain water for the clouds with the help of the sun and also hot streams, (Gulf stream, etc.) to keep our shores warm and convenient. The air, as has already been stated above, is very vital for all of us, the vegetables or the animals. We cannot live without it.

Then we see that the snow of the mountains melts into the rivers which deposit alluvium to make our soil fertile. The water evaporates with the help of the sun to form clouds. The clouds pour water in the form of rain to water our fields and forests. The fields yield agricultural and other products to provide nourishment to the animal kingdom. Even the smallest bacterial objects are constantly at work for the common good of all. Even the seeming calamities, war, destructions, pestilence, fire, etc., are the pruning and leveling instruments to maintain a healthy equilibrium in this universe.

There is thus a continuity of inner unity. That is how all the various factors in nature are working continuously in consonance to help each other, like different organs of our own body, being guided by the same universal force, or soul.

The universal power is latent in all the so-called different objects, which arranges the entire show according to the universal laws of nature. It is on account of this arrangement that men and women are always born where they are needed to maintain their balanced proportion. The negative electricity is by itself created in relation to the production of the positive electricity. If one side of the river has female flowers having pistils then on the other side there must be male flowers having pollen grains in anthers. The botanists tell us that the dispersal of seeds of certain plants is done through special mechanism by air, water, birds, and even by higher animals. This sort of arrangement is very necessary in the interest of the propagation of species. All these faultless and beautiful arrangements go to show that the working of the entire universe has intelligently been planned by the super brain of nature with an exquisite genius and that the seemingly different objects are all interconnected with the same unitary and all-pervading force which designs and organizes the various phenomena to maintain order and regularity.

You must have marked that when there is an itching sensation in some part of your body, your hand automatically reaches exactly the same spot to relieve you of your irritation. If some other person tries to do the same, he cannot do it so well. Why? It is so because your real self is pervading throughout your own body. It is here, there and everywhere in your body. It is on the itching spot and also in your hand which relieves you of your itching sensation. It proves the unity and the all-pervasiveness of "I" in your body. So too is the case with this universe, wherein the all-pervading force (power, energy, God or *Atma*) is present and interpenetrating throughout. When you are in some trouble, the same power in the form of your friends, associates or someone else appears to help you solve your difficulties. This is no uncommon experience in one's life.

It is on the authority of this law that Lord Krishna, the greatest practical teacher of all times, has declared in unambiguous terms in the *Bhagavad Gita* that "when there is decay of righteousness and exaltation of unrighteousness, I manifest myself in some form or other to protect the virtuous and to destroy the evil doers," in order to prevent tyranny, to maintain equanimity and to ensure law and order, so as to give relief to the poor, helpless and the innocent sufferers and to remove the ignorance of the masses. This law is infallible. You can verify its correctness from the very facts in your own history. The whole universe is united into one by the all-pervading universal force, and all its different elements have to work with the common object to safeguard the security and welfare of the whole. It is to implement this law that the *Avtars* (incarnations), the prophets and the saints come down for the common good of all.

On a smaller scale, we see that when some disease develops in your body, its antidote is also simultaneously developed to cure the ailment. This is so not only in your case, but also in that of others, may they be human beings, horses, monkeys or rabbits. It is so because of the underlying unity of the all-pervasive universal law. Here it is under the law of affinity that the necessities and relief for all are provided automatically. When fire burns, oxygen is automatically drawn from the atmosphere to help it.

The sea close to Bengal is called the "Bay of Bengal," the one close to Arabia is called the "Arabian Sea," the one close to China is called the "China Sea," and the one close to India is called the "Indian Ocean," and so on and so forth. Truly speaking, the sea is only one, though it has adopted different names due to its proximity with different countries. Similarly, God is one and is all-pervading and omnipresent. When His power works wonders in the battlefield through a man, He is called by the name of courage or valor. When He works through trees, He is called growth, so on and so forth. In a nutshell, He is recognized in a hero through extraordinary courage and resoluteness and in vegetation through growth, in the massive mountains through sky-kissing, snow-capped heights, in the ocean through extensive vastness, in space through limitlessness, in the sun through dazzling brilliance, though His power working in all is the same. It is God and God alone. As a matter of fact, there is one and the only one force that works in all and controls all the laws, although it may be termed differently, such as force of cohesion, force of gravitation, love, affinity, devotion, attraction, repulsion, intelligence, oratory, valor, courage, greatness, growth, strength, power, energy or vastness.

The great poet and dramatist of England, William Shakespeare, has also said the same thing in his play "The Merchant of Venice," though in a different context, in respect of the Jews and the Christians.

> "Hath not a Jew eyes? Hath not a Jew hands, organs, dimensions, senses, affection, passion? Are not the Jews fed with the same food, hurt with the same weapons, subject to the same disease, healed by the same means, warmed and cooled by the same summer and winter as a Christian is? If you prick us, shall we not bleed? If you tickle us, shall we not laugh? If you poison us, do we not die? We are like you in every respect . . . "

The above quotation is concerning the Jews and the Christians. But it equally holds good in respect of all human beings, irrespective of caste, creed or nationality. We are all alike. Our anatomy, physiology, psychology, habits, thinking, etc. are also fundamentally the same on account of the underlying unity with all.

Then again we find that in our bodies, there are different organs like spleen, liver, stomach, heart, lungs, kidneys, brain, eyes, ears, nose, arteries, veins, nerves, glands, hands, feet, etc. These have different names, different forms and different functions to perform. It may be observed that in spite of their seeming differences, they are united into one because they all perform their different functions in their respective spheres with the common object to maintain normalcy in the same body.

On the contrary, if hands were to say, "We work hard. We earn by our toil and sweat. Why should we feed the mouth?"; if the mouth were to say, "I masticate food and make it soft and palatable; why should I transfer this delicious food to the stomach?"; if the stomach were to say, "I secrete gastric juices, I digest food, why should I allow the digested food to be absorbed by the blood vessels?" and so on and so forth, then you can imagine the chaotic result of such a sort of selfishness. You need not go far to see the damaging effect of this "pull apart." Not only the particular organ will suffer, but the entire body will wither away. The whole system will crumble down. When the kidney, the liver or heart is somehow damaged, the whole body is bound to be affected by the malady. So too is the case with selfishness of men or nations. A selfish man, for want of foresight, attaches too much importance to the false notion of his own prestige and power, insults others, keeps himself aloof only to find that he has been segregated by all to face his sufferings all alone. Nobody cooperates with a selfish man. On the other hand, all cooperate with him who cooperates with all. So too is the case with the nations which disregard or oppose the law of unity. They all suffer and suffer miserably. Selfishness breeds hatred, spite, malice, jealousy, hypocrisy, unpatriotism, undiscipline, etc. As such, selfishness is the main cause of all the man-made troubles in this world. Selfishness is not only the worst crime but also the root of all the sins. We should therefore learn how to live for others and let others live for the good of all. An

Indian poet says,

> It is better for a man to die
> if he lives only to satisfy his own selfish ends.
> But the man who dies for the good of others
> is really immortal.

We must, therefore, set aside our selfishness and live like the different organs of our own body, in a spirit of mutual cooperation with all.

The different objects and elements in nature with their different names, forms and functions, are continuously working in a coordinated way to help the common cause of the universal body (*Virat Sharir*) of mother nature. We are not separate from nature. We should therefore feel our oneness with the whole. This realization of the universal unity is the real strength and the real life of eternity. Accordingly, our motto in practical life should be "One for All and all for One."

The Hindu scriptures say that we all emanate from God, that nothing can exist without God and that the entire universe is nothing but His own manifestation. It is not without reason.

The scientists say that energy is omnipresent because of its indispensability, even though it may vary in magnitude and form. Energy, as you know, means power for working. The force of cohesion which keeps the particles of matter stuck together, affinity, force of gravitation, movements of stars and planets, retention of chemical or physical properties, physical or chemical action or reaction, attraction, repulsion, reproduction, procreation, growth, development, evolution, life, etc. are all dependent on energy because all these phenomena involve work or action which can be accomplished only through energy or power to work. It is therefore this energy which is manifested in the form of matter or life.

You will see that no matter can exist without the force of cohesion, or without the capability to retain the physical or chemical properties and to react to the physical or chemical stimuli. All this requires energy in respect of matter. Then again, no life worth the name can exist without energy, as is quite obvious. As such, no energy, no matter, and no energy, no life.

Upanishads say that the entire creation is simply the thought force *(Sankalp-Shakti)* of God or Brahman. Thought force, or will force, is also power *(shakti)* or energy. The turning of water into wine by Jesus Christ, the making the sea dry to let the Jews pass through it by Moses, the halting the course of the sun by Mohammad, the performance of innumerable miracles by Rama or Krishna, the drinking of deadly poison by queen Mira and continuing to remain alive, etc. are only a few examples of the will force. Mesmerism, hypnotism, auto and hetero suggestions, telepathy, mind reading, etc. are the well known examples of thought force or will force as seen today. Rama has himself seen American patients being cured through will force. By hypnotising a man through thought force, you can make him see a table to be a horse and a horse to be a beautiful lady. After all, thought force is also a force, power or energy. Accordingly, the will force or the *Sankalp Shakti* of God is also power or energy which is capable of accomplishing anything. Even according to this theory, the creation is nothing but the *shakti* or power of God. Be that as it may, the fact remains that the entire universe as we see it is simply the display of energy which is manifested in its diversity. Energy is, so to say, the symbol of God, who, being omnipotent and omnipresent, controls the entire universe. In the Vedantic terminology, you can call it *Chaitanya*, which is all-pervading and the same everywhere. Vedanta requires you to learn the technique of developing your will force, to shake off your feeling of limitedness and to realize your oneness with the Universal Self which you really are. You have to be in complete harmony with nature in an effortless way, with no feeling of duality.

The scientists may or may not agree today with Rama, but he is fully convinced that even the smallest particle of the dust of this universe is a storehouse of energy which may be possible to be released, under suitable conditions, more or less like fire from fuelwood or like heat from coal. In other words, energy is condensed into matter which can be reconverted into energy which is stored in it.

A true scientist may not believe in God as you do, but he cannot deny the universal force which controls the laws of nature and regulates the working of the universe. Science, howsoever material it may be, cannot dare overlook the underlying unity of the moving spirit *Chaitanya*, pervading all that exists.

Now the question is, where does this energy come from? It does not come out of nothing. It must come out of something. What is it? Though the heat or light appears to come directly from its visible source, the sun, the entire energy in reality originates from its ultimate source which bestows effulgence upon all the galaxies and all the suns of various solar systems, moves the planets and runs the grand show of this entire limitless universe. This ultimate source of unlimited energy is *Atma, Brahman*, or God *(Chaitanya)*. That is why He is called all powerful and almighty. He is energy personified. If, however, you are allergic to the use of the word "God" or "Brahman," it makes no difference. Surely you cannot deny the omnipresence and indispensability of energy.

Some yogic schools advise you in the beginning to concentrate with closed eyes on light which is a form of energy. It has the power to travel. Though light itself is invisible, yet it has the power to cause visibility. It also acts on certain salts to bring about chemical changes. It has the power to help carbon assimilation in the plants. So you see that light is energy. The *Gayatri Mantra* of the Hindus therefore directs you to meditate upon the effulgence of light. The prophet Moses saw God in the form of light. Lord Buddha was called the Enlightened One because of his experience of the universal light. So too is the case with the prophet Mohammed, who was blessed to see the *tajalli* (light) of God. Lord Jesus Christ also speaks of the same divine light. Why is there so much emphasis on light? As you know, light is energy. Light also manifests as knowledge because knowledge dispels the darkness of ignorance. As stated earlier, energy is needed at every step. It is God's power, *Chit Shakti*, without which not a blade of grass can grow. Being a symbol of God, it represents God Himself.

It is not possible for the common man, who considers himself to be a limited self, or *jiva*, to concentrate upon the limitlessness of God. Therefore light, being energy and a manifestation of the unmanifested universal Soul, has been prescribed in yogic practices; more so because it is one of the most convenient media to be concentrated upon in order to realize, through it, its ultimate source. You may call this ultimate source the nameless

One, any name you like, but Rama will prefer to call it here God.

Thus you can clearly realize from the above exposition that energy is all pervading. Without it neither anything can exist nor any phenomenon can happen in this universe. Since energy originates from God, it is God and God alone who is manifesting Himself as a continued unity through the process of evolution in the seeming diversity of the universe.

It may however be remembered that there is no evolution in Atma, the universal Self, which is the same yesterday, today and forever. The apparent evolution is only in the so-called matter, mind, intellect, etc., which is nothing but energy, the manifestation of God or *Atma*. The ornaments may change their names and forms, but there is no change in gold itself.

It may also be made clear here that energy, howsoever important it may be, is only secondary to its source, Brahman. He alone is the reality, being the original and the primordial cause of everything including energy. It is the cause which manifests as effect and if you segretate cause from the so-called effect, nothing like effect remains because all the existence is attributed to the cause and none to the effect. So too is the case with Brahman. He is All in all.

The scientists have discovered a number of elements like gold, silver, copper, oxygen, hydrogen, carbon, sulphur, etc. Each element is basically the same throughout the universe, either on this earth or on any other planet. Gold is gold, and silver is silver, everywhere. They, in their present forms, wonderfully retain their basic physical and chemical properties. Not only the individual elements, but also their different combinations called chemical compounds (like copper-sulphate, carbon dioxide) are individually the same throughout in every respect. How or why is there such a continued unity and absolute similarity in the individual elements or in their respective compounds? The reason is the same. It is because of the same universal force (energy), which is here, there and everywhere on this earth, the moon, mars, etc. It is all-pervading, unitary and uniting.

You may however object that if these individual elements or their respective compounds are the same, why do they differ among themselves in their forms and physical or chemical properties? Why silver cannot be gold, and iron not be copper? Why are they different? In reply to this objection Rama will only say that he does not see any difference. How can there be any difference when according to the unfailing philosophy of the Vedanta, the so-called all is one, and the one is the so-called all? There exists One and the only One. The seeming difference is only of name, form, etc. The underlying reality is the same. Let the scientists say that these different elements are quite different from one another in every way. Let them say whatever they like. Their science is still in infancy. It is still in an experimental and developing stage. Rama asserts that, though so far they could not establish the underlying unity, yet a day will surely come when the scientists of the world would be convinced that all these different elements with different names, forms, properties, etc. are fundamentally the same and that they would accept that it is possible to convert one element into any other element under suitable conditions, more or less like heat, light, electricity, etc., which are inter-convertible.

Why? Because, as stated earlier, they all owe their existence to the One, who is the common base or the underlying reality in all. All the phenomena, whatever their names or forms may be, cannot stand alone without the underlying noumenon or common reality. How can they be different when their intrinsic substratum is the same (like gold in the form of different ornaments or like sugar in the form of different sugar toys)? If you dive deep, you will see the unifying reality as one unchangeable, everlasting, immutable principle behind all the names and forms. It is this reality which establishes the unity with all.

Psychologically, too, on the plane of feeling, we are all one. When the lyre is played upon, it brings out a similar note from another lyre placed opposite to it. When you strike a chord on one instrument, a similar chord on the opposite instrument begins to vibrate. Similarly, on a theatrical stage, when an actor weeps, the eyes of the receptive persons in the audience also get moist. Rama has noticed while lecturing that when he laughs the audience also starts laughing. Why so? It is so because of the "law of continuity." Our minds, our feelings, and our psychology are related to each other as one. If our minds were not related to each other the same way as the different waves are related to each other in the same ocean, this fellow feeling would not have been possible. Science has proved that if a body is to act upon another body, there must be continuity between the two. It is because of this "law of continuity" that we are all united to one another psychologically. If you smile at a baby, he smiles, and if you put up an angry face, he weeps. If you sing, others also start singing. A teacher could not have taught anything if the teacher and the taught had not their minds connected directly. If you love a man he will also love you. If you hate him he will also start hating you. Telepathy, hypnotism and mesmerism are all based on this law of continuity. Even the flowers smile, the plants grow and the animals react to this law because we are all one through the universal unity. Now Rama will narrate a few examples of mental or psychological unity.

Professor James, a psychologist, writes that all our actions are performed through suggestions. Actually, we are not aware of the root cause of our own actions. Most of our actions are performed not through our own will but through direct or indirect suggestions, just as a monkey acts by copying others. Similar is the case with other animals. Rama will narrate an incident which he himself had seen.

In the high hills, business commodities are transported on sheep or goats. There was a bridge near the halt at Bhairon valley on way to Gangotri on the high Himalayas. Once a business man was transporting common salt as usual on the sheep and goats. While he was crossing the bridge, one of the goats fell into the river. Seeing this, the other goats and sheep followed suit. All of them fell into the river, one by one, in spite of every possible effort by the owner to prevent them from falling. They all were drowned and destroyed. Why did it so happen? It was so because the thought force of one has got its natural unity with others. If we reflect deeply, we shall know that the invisible currents of the subtle body, called thoughts, are the same in different bodies. As such, there is a continued unity between the different subtle bodies. This subtle unity is possible due to the unitary character of psyche through the law of continuity.

According to science energy is indestructible. It can, however, change its form. During the "reign of terror" in France it was the common desire of all that the government should be replaced by some good administration. Although every man wanted this change, there was none to give shape to this thought in an organized way. Ultimately a man, Napoleon, came forward from amongst the plebeian rank to guide the affairs. Once about a thousand persons came to arrest him. He stood all alone facing them and said in a loud voice, "*avount*" meaning "halt." His voice produced such an awe into the hearts of those men that they at once halted and stopped their advance. This was not the power of Napoleon alone but the cumulative effect of the thought force of thousands of persons which was expressed through his command, "halt."

There is a well known saying, "As a man thinks, so he becomes." We should therefore expand our circle of oneness and unity to the greatest possible extent in order to increase our resulting collective strength. When our unity, or oneness, with the universe is complete in thoughts, words, and deeds, we become one with Him, the Universal Self or nature. Our acts become the acts of nature or God, and we develop unlimited power and authority. It however depends upon the intensity of our conviction of the truth of universal unity.

As a matter of fact, we are already one with nature, which is all-pervading. We are not at all separate or away from nature, but due to our ignorance we are unable to take any advantage of our natural oneness with nature of the Universal Self, because we think ourselves to be limited within the gross physical frame of our mortal body.

So far Rama has dealt with the question of unity in respect of the gross (physical) bodies and the subtle (mental) bodies. Apart from these, there is also a basic unity in respect of the causal bodies and the subjective minds wherein all the fundamental ideas and thoughts rest in store and are expressed from time to time to assert their inherent originality. The very facts that nobody wants to die, that every man considers himself to be wisdom personified or desires to remain independent and that he loves peace and desires permanent happiness go to prove to the hilt that there is an underlying and essential unity in the fundamental psychology of men. It may be explained further.

Since we all emanate and are manifested from the same unmanifested Self, we have inherited its basic nature, just as the seeds of the fruits of a plant or a tree inherit basic qualities of its original seed. The nature of Brahman, call it God, is absolute truth (eternity), absolute consciousness (wisdom personified) and absolute bliss (everlasting happiness). In the Vedantic terminology it is called *Sat, Chit, Anand.* This nature is, therefore, inherent in us. Why should we, then, desire death? Why should we not ignore death, which is associated with our gross body alone? We are not the body after all. We are the *Atma.* Why should we then worry about death? Fundamentally, our real Self is truth, the Eternal Self, which is indestructible and immortal. Death will meet its own death, if it even tries to advance its tentacles towards our real Self. Why should we not then regard ourselves to be wisdom personified when our real Self is absolute consciousness? Why should we not then love our inherent nature of peace and happiness, when we are eternal bliss in reality?

Unfortunately, the pity is that you, through your own ignorance, have forgotten your limitless real Self and have wrongly identified yourself with your limited body, mind and intellect, with the result that you have to feel all the sufferings associated with them. It is really sad that you do not realize that you yourself are the happiness incarnate. Happiness is not to be found in the sense objects. It is you who bestow happiness on the worldly objects. In spite of your identification with your body (Antah Karan), your real Self, which is indestructible and immortal, asserts itself to remind you of your true nature (truth, consciousness and bliss), which is common to all. This explains our fundamental inner unity with All, the all-pervading Universal Self, which we really are.

On a higher plane, a man starts feeling his spiritual unity with all the living beings. Here I may quote the example of Abraham Lincoln, the then president of America. He was once going to address the Senate. On his way he noticed a pig badly entangled in the marshy swamp on the road side. It was practically exhausted. In spite of this it was desperately doing its best to save its life, but unfortunately, the more it struggled, the more it was gripped in the death trap. It was groaning painfully. The president could not bear this pitiable sight. He got off his presidential coach and, with the help of his body guards and others, succeeded in extricating it out of the marshy swamp. His costly clothes were soiled with dirty mud, but without minding it, he went straight to the Senate in the same condition to avoid delay. When the senators came to know about this happening, they started praising their president and remarked that he was very kind, noble and God-fearing. The president felt embarassed and intervened, "No, no, no. Please do not say so. I did not show any kindness to anybody. I was affected, as if by some infectious disease, by the heart-rending groaning of the pig, due to its agonizing pain. I took the pig out of the mire only to relieve myself of the pain in my heart caused at the unbearable sight, due to its death pangs. My heart ached at it, and I only tried to remove my own pain. I did not show any mercy to anyone." Well done!

The man who realizes this underlying spiritual unity and loves all like his own self is really the wise man. He cannot be harmed like Lord Shiva even by carnivorous and dangerous animals, like lions, tigers, snakes, scorpions, etc. One who loves all is loved by all, and the one who hates all is hated by all. This is the law. Why should you then allow yourself to be the target of hatred of anybody? Why not love all by realizing the all-round spiritual unity, and lead a peaceful and blissful divine life?

So, you see, it is very necessary in your own interest to feel and realize your oneness with all. A man has not only to understand this intellectually but also to feel from the very bottom of his heart that this whole universe is one, that he is not separate from it and that he is one with it. The more you realize this truth, your unity with the universe, the nearer you are to God, the Universal Self. This is the law.

A man has to do away with dualism, efface differentiation and feel oneness with all. All the objects have to be realized to be not only one with him, but his own self. All the world has to merge in Him. You have to develop a vision, call it divine, and realize according to *Kathopanishad*, "He who is here is also there and the same He who is there is here as well."

You have to acquire that state in which you realize the entire universe to have become your body. The beasts, the birds, the mountains, the trees are your own self. The flooding rivers are like the circulation of blood in your arteries; the sun and the moon are like your eyes. It is your own heart that is throbbing in the thorax of all. Efface the idea that you are something separate or different from others. Only one conscious power is working throughout the universe. The power, force, energy, nature, or call it God or Brahman, is all-pervading and interpenetrating. You have to realize this universal unity. As a matter of fact, you are really one with it. Rama repeats it again and again so that you may grasp the truth thoroughly and practice it in your daily life. Without this there is no success or realization of Self or God. It is this realization of spiritual unity with all which is the ultimate aim of the true religion. We have to achieve this realization by all possible means.

If you purify your heart by doing away with malice, jealousy, hatred, spite, rivalry, etc., and practice to love all like your own Self, forget and forgive those whom you consider your enemies, opponents, fault-finders and adversaries, you can attain this highest stage of realizing your oneness with all. When this universal unity is realized in this seeming diversity, a man has nothing to worry about. He can really enjoy the resulting eternal peace, everlasting bliss, and unlimited power. The elements of nature are then bound to obey his orders, as if they are his own hands and feet which can be moved at his will.

Realize this underlying spiritual unity with all. In fact we all are one with Him. Feel, feel this unity and oneness, and enjoy the eternal life of Godhood. There is none else besides That and That you are.

Om. Anand! Anand! Anand!

IDEALISM AND REALISM RECONCILED IN THE LIGHT OF VEDANTA

January 13, 1903
Golden Gate Hall, San Francisco

The only Real and Ideal One in the form of ladies and gentlemen,

The subject of tonight's discourse is very abstruse, very difficult. Only those will be able to follow it thoroughly who are already somewhat acquainted with philosophy. To Rama it makes no difference whether all of you go away fatigued and disgusted or the whole world comes to listen. Truth stands above all desire for popularity. Scientific laws were governing the world and are governing the world and will continue governing the whole universe, whether people know them or not, whether they become popular or not. The law of gravitation was the same law of gravitation even before it was discovered by Sir Isaac Newton. There are laws which people may not have discovered, and yet they are governing the world. A magnificent diamond may be lying in a mine, and nobody may go and take it up; the diamond shines in its own glory all the same. Let people pick it up and place it on their foreheads, or let people ignore it entirely; to the diamond it makes no difference.

The subject is difficult, but if you follow it very closely, attentively, you will understand it. You need not say what is the use of speaking upon such abstruse, speculative, philosophical subjects. We require them not; we want hard cash; we want something practical. Rama has been speaking on practical subjects, but theoretical and speculative subjects are also necessary. No fact can be explained without a sound theory to back it; and you know, all your practice is simply your energy transformed into activity, nothing else. When you have to write anything, before your pen begins to move, the whole subject must come into your mind in theory. Theory always precedes activity.

So Rama is trying to drum into your ears and instill into the hearts of all the audience the divinity of the real Self. Let it sink deep into your hearts day by day; let it penetrate your minds hour after hour, and you will see, according to the laws of science, this mental energy which appears to be a vain speculation; this you will see transforming itself into the most noble activity on your part, and this knowledge you will see transforming itself into happiness and bliss for you.

The subject is "Idealism and Realism Reconciled in the Light of Vedanta." In other words, the subject is "The Vedantic Theory of Perception," a most important subject for philosophers.

You ought to be told a little about what Idealism and Realism are. We have no time to enter into details upon these topics. In brief, Realism means a belief or theory which looks upon this world, as it seems to us, to be a real phenomenon. According to Idealism, the world is not as it appears to us; the world is, but it is not what it appears to us. Idealism has several branches. We have Subjective Idealism, the Idealism of Berkeley and Fichte; we have Objective Idealism, the Idealism of Plato and Kant; we have Absolute Idealism, the Idealism of Hegel and Shelley, and many others of the same sort. Realism has many philosophers like Bain and Mill to support it. We shall not describe these several branches of Idealism or Realism. We shall not criticize in tonight's discourse the Subjective Idealism of Berkeley or the Objective Idealism of Plato and Kant or the Absolute Idealism of Hegel or Shelley. We shall just allude to these to such an extent that the Vedantic theory about this matter may be easily comprehended by each and all.

Before beginning with the subject, two words ought to be explained—the words "subject" and "object." You know these words, subject and object, are taken in different senses. In grammar they are used in one sense, in ordinary language they are used in a different sense, and in philosophical language they have a meaning of their own. The word "subject" in the language of philosophy means the knowing one, and the "object" means the thing known. When you see this pencil, the pencil is the object, and you that perceive the pencil are the subject. The perceiving one is called the subject, and the thing perceived, the object. Thus, in ordinary language, the word subject means the understanding or the intellect but according to Vedanta, this subject, this understanding intellect or reason, also should not be called subject; this also is an object. You know, anything that can be perceived becomes an object; you can perceive the intellect; you can think and reason about the intellect and lay down the laws of the intellect. In so far as you can reason about the intellect and conceive the intellect, the intellect is an object and not a subject. The real subject cannot be conceived; the real subject cannot be perceived. How can the knower be known? In ordinary language the word subject implies the understanding intellect or reason. The real subject, or the real knower, is, according to Vedanta, the true *Atman*, the only infinity and is one and the same in all the bodies. It would be very kind of you to remember a Sanskrit word also in connection with this. The word "subject" is called in Sanskrit *drashta*; the word "object" is called in Sanskrit *drishya*; and the real subject in Sanskrit is the Brahman or *Atman*. The word *Atman* might be translated in English either to be the "will" of Schopenhauer or to be the "hard" or "absolute intellect" of Hegel. You know Hegel and Schopenhauer are antagonistic to each other; they are always at daggers drawn with each other, but Vedanta reconciles them. Vedanta tells them that the absolute will of Schopenhauer is in reality the same which Hegel calls the absolute intellect; and so for this Absolute Self we have the word "Brahman" which means absolute will, absolute intellect, absolute existence and absolute bliss.

So the real subject is the true *Atman*, but the practical subject is the *Atman* as shining in the intellect or in the understanding. So the real *Atman* with the intellect as an agent is called the subject.

What are the arguments which the Realists advance on their side and what are the chief arguments advanced by the Idealists? That is a long subject, but we shall go over it very briefly. We have no time to criticize your Berkeley. Berkeley is one of the principal Idealists. How briskly he starts in his philosophy, and how he soars high so long as he is exactly hand in hand with the Vedanta philosophy, and how he loses his way and falls into a meandering, zigzag path, the very moment he departs from the Vedanta philosophy. What a contrast the latter part of his philosophy forms with its original part, and how he is obliged to believe in so many spirits, and how he is obliged to bring in a personal God to control this universe, and how according to his philosophy, no object may be present in this world without a spirit present beside it, and what absurdities he brings in. Well, that is a subject which we shall not take up tonight. Amongst the many arguments advanced by the Idealists, the following two or three are important. The first is that you cannot see or perceive anything without your own activity. It is the subject's activity alone which makes you perceive anything or sense any object in this world. You are writing something, your mind is with the pen, and there passes before you a snake. You perceive not the snake, for you the snake is not a snake, the snake is not there. Now the Idealists say if your activity, if the activity of your mind or the subject's activity is wanting, there is no object there. When you are asleep, the subject is not active, and all the sounds that may be made around are not heard. Sometimes people do not close their eyes when they are asleep. Now before their eyes all the objects are present, all the objects are being reflected on their retina, but they see not the objects. The Idealists say that your mind is inactive, the subject is not asserting its activity, and you do not see the objects. Can you see anything in this world without mental activity? No. Just try to see this table or that wall, try to hear Rama's words, try to perceive anything without the mind's being active. Can you do that? Can you see anything without thinking, without your mind's thought? You cannot. Thus the Idealists say that all this world is nothing else but thought, all this world is simply a projection of your thought. How do you know that the world exists? Through your senses; but the senses by themselves cannot perceive. It is only when the mind is connected with the senses that the senses perceive. In other words, the senses do not perceive; the mind perceives through the senses. So the idealists say, "O people of this world who call this world real and look upon these objects as true by themselves! O forget not yourselves; be not mistaken. All these objects are created by you or projected by your thought; you make these objects." This is what the Idealists say, and it appears that Idealists are something like Vedantins. Rama tells you that all these Idealists—Berkeley, Plato, Hegel, Kant, Fichte, Shelley, Schopenhaeur—have the principles of Vedanta, but the Vedantic theory of perception far transcends all these. These people have conflicts with each other, they have quibbles and quarrels, but the Vedanta philosophy reconciles each and all of them. These people glorify and aggrandize and make much of the self, but Vedanta does not deify and lionize the subjective self as most of these philosophers do. We have to take the truth for its own sake.

Another argument advanced by these Idealists is that this world which people ordinarily take to be real, should not be regarded as such because the world appears to be as it is through the senses only, and we depend upon the senses in calling the world true, real, as it seems to us. Now the senses are not reliable evidence; the senses are not trustworthy witnesses. Take the case of the eye, for instance. The eyes of the ant see differently from the eyes of man. To the eyes of the elephant things appear to be much bigger than they appear to the eyes of man. To the eyes of a frog things are clear when seen in water, and things in air are all hazy, dim, covered with a kind of mist. Now whose eyes are to be relied upon, the eyes of man or the eyes of ants? If your eyes be formed upon the microscopic principle, if the lens in the eyes be fixed in a different way to the retina, to you the world will be entirely different. If the retina of the eyes be adjusted on the telescopic principle, all the world is entirely altered. If the nerves and muscles be differently adjusted, the whole world is changed. You will say that if the nerves and muscles and sense-organs are adjusted in this way, they must remain in this way. It is not so. The law of evolution tells you that they are undergoing a change. Thus the Idealists say that the world is not what it seems. The world as it appears to us is false; the world as it seems to us is unreal, is illusory, a mere delusion. They have many other arguments on their side, but if we enter into details many nights would be taken up by Idealism alone.

We shall now pass on to Realism. The Realists say, "You are wrong, O Idealists! You are altogether wrong. If your statement be true that everything we see is the creation of our own imagination, if that be true, then, O Idealists, please create there a horse where the wall is. Let that wall appear to be a horse. O Idealists, if the whole world is simply the result of this small subject's understanding or mind's creation, then turn this handkerchief into a lion, or make this pencil a big house." The Realists say, "O Idealists, you cannot be right; the world is real. The wall is a wall, and for that reason it always impresses upon your senses as a wall; it does not appear to you a horse tomorrow."

These objections of the Realists are met by the Idealists. They have answers to these objections, but we shall not take up all the questions on both sides. The Idealists say that it is a question of time. You can create anything you like by your imagination. When we begin to think of spirits, spirits appear to us; when we begin to imagine anything, that imagination comes to us. They say that in dreams do we not create things. Our imagination realizes these things. They have answers, and these answers have rejoinders from the Realists. We are not going to enter into detail upon these questions and answers.

Vedanta also looks upon the world as *my* idea, as *my* creation; but even when Vedanta looks upon the world as *my* idea or *my* creation, you cannot call Vedanta Idealism. That seems to be something very strange from the lips of Rama. It will be repeated again. The people in Europe and America think that Vedanta is a kind of Idealism, and almost all the books written by Europeans that have passed through Rama's hand represent Vedanta as Idealism, but Rama tells you that these people have not understood it. Vedanta is not Idealism in the same sense as the Idealism of Berkeley or Plato. It is far higher, far superior.

The Idealists make the world depend upon the little subject, the little understanding, the little mind, but when Vedanta says that the world is *my* idea, that does not mean that the world is the idea of the little subject, of the little understanding, of the little mind. This is something variable, this is something in itself a creation, and Berkeley made a terrible blunder when he said that dreams are the creation of the subject. There the mistake made by him was that he looked upon the subject of the dream land to be identical with the subject of the wakeful state, and you know that the subject in the dream land is different from the subject in the wakeful state. When you wake up, the subject of the wakeful state is of the same sort as the objects of that state. Berkeley took the subject of the wakeful state to be the same as the subject of dreamland. The world is not a creation of the subject of the wakeful state or the subject of the dream land; the world is a creation of my Self, the real God, the real *Atman*.

We come now to the subject, the Vedantic theory of perception. Vedanta says to the Idealists, "O Idealists! You are right in saying that all the names and forms of this world could not come about without the action of the subject. All the qualities, attributes and properties of things depend upon the activity and action of the understanding or the mind or the subject. You are right thus far, but you are not right in saying that there is nothing outside this small subject of yours, that there is nothing outside this small mind of yours." Vedanta says to the Realists, "You are right in saying that this phenomenal world could not appear without the action of any outside reality. Yes, without some sort of action from outside we could not perceive things." So far is Realism right, but according to Vedanta, Realism is wrong when it says that all our perception is due solely and wholly to outside action and not to the subject's activity. Let us make this clearer. In this world take up anything, take up any object, take up this pencil, for example. To what is the color of this pencil due? It is due only to the action of the subject together with a reaction from outside, you might say.. If your eyes are color blind, you will not see this color in the pencil. The color of the pencil is a quality of attribute. Again take the weight of the pencil; it is changeable, and so is its color. If our eyes are jaundiced, we might see the pencil to be of a different color, and if we do not weigh it here but at a great height, or on the moon, or in a deep mine, its weight will be different, and you know that the weight of every object when weighed in London is different from what it is when weighed in India. The weight is changeable; the color is changeable.

You know that the same water you touch in winter appears to be warm and that when you touch it in summer it appears to be cold. Why? Because the observer, or the perceiver, is at different temperatures when he touches the water though the water retains about the same temperature. The apparent difference in its temperatures is due to the difference in the temperatures of our hands. So according to the difference in the subject, there will be difference in the qualities of the object.

Of what is this pencil made? According to Berkeley and some others, it is nothing else but a bundle of attributes and qualities. Take away these qualities and there is nothing left, but according to Kant and according to Plato there is "the thing in itself" behind it, the idea. So here there are qualities. Vedanta says that all these qualities in the pencil are due to the action of the subject. It is true, but why was the action of the subject excited? This is the question. There must be something outside which acted upon the subject and excited a reaction or action of the subject; and when the reaction of the subject was excited, there were these qualities posited, put forth or projected there. We cannot say that before this subject acted these qualities themselves acted upon the mind and excited an action or reaction of the mind, because these qualities make their appearance after the action or reaction of mind; so there must be something outside. There must be some reality in the pencil which acted upon your eyes, which acted upon your ears when the sound was heard, which acted upon your taste when you touched it with the tongue, which acted upon your sense of touch when you touched it. Eat this pencil, and it will tell upon your health. How can you say that there is no reality outside? There is some reality outside too, and when this reality acts upon the senses of a man, they report it to his mind and the mind reacts. Then are the attributes or qualities of the object projected on the scene. In the same way, one wave came from this side and another from that side; the two waves collided, and foam was produced. Action and reaction from both sides produced foam. Here is a match and here is a piece of sandpaper. Strike the match on the sandpaper, and then the flame comes out—action and reaction from both sides. Here is one positive pole of electricity, and there is a negative pole. If they approach each other, we see the electric sparks or hear the report. Thus action and reaction from both sides bring about the phenomenon.

So, according to Vedanta, in your intellect the "thing in itself" is present, what we call the *Atman*. The real Self is living in your intellect, and there is the "thing in itself," or the reality, in every object in this world. The reality outside, the divinity or the absolute in the pencil, and the absolute in the intellect, are like the two waves, as it were. The moment they collide, the attributes of the pencil are posited; they make their appearance like foam. In the language of Vedanta, the very moment the *drishya* and the *drashta* unite, we see the objects. There is *drishya* and *drashta*; there is the true Self or *Atman* in the pencil and the true Self or *Atman* in the intellect. Action and reaction between the two produces the phenomena.

Thus the Idealists are right in asserting that nothing can be seen without the action of the subject, but they are wrong in saying that this action of the subject by itself produces this phenomenon; in so saying they violate one of the most inexorable laws of science which runs thus; "There can be no action without an equal and opposite reaction." So the Realists are right when they say that this world has a reality in itself; we should not say that this world simply hinges upon the subject. However, when they say that the phenomena of this world stand by themselves, they are wrong because the phenomena of this world, the differences of this world, the qualities of the objects of this world, all these qualities and phenomena depend just as much upon the action of the subject as upon the reaction of the reality in the object.

Here comes a great objection. You talk of action and reaction. How can there be action and reaction in infinity? Well, we spoke of action and reaction only to be understood in the same language as other people use. We talk of action and reaction when we refer to the absolute will or the absolute energy as conjoined to the intellect or as conjoined to the object. The absolute entity as conjoined to this object acts or reacts against the absolute entity as conjoined to this adjunct the head, brain, or intellect. Take this illustration. There is space in this vessel and space in that vessel. You might refer to the space as appearing in that vessel and the space as appearing in this vessel; but as a matter of fact, space cannot be divided or torn into pieces. Space is indivisible. According to Kant, space is subjective, not objective, and cannot be divided or cut. Similarly, the true Self or reality, the absolute infinity, cannot be divided or cut, but when we are referring it to the objects of this world, we are justified in talking of it as conjoined to the intellect or to any object. The same reality is conjoined to this or that object as action and reaction.

Thus Vedanta says that when the absolute reality underlying the subject becomes identical with the absolute reality underlying the object, the subject and the object unite. Action and reaction take place, not in reality in the *Atman*, but they take place in the *Atman* as defined by the "limited." Look here. Here is one wave of water coming from one side; another, from the other side. One wave is water just as much as the other, and even when the waves collide both will remain water; they do not undergo a change and yet the action and reaction take place between the waves. This collision brings about the phenomenon of foam. Now this fact is not made quite clear that all the objects in this world have the same reality behind them. Here is a pen. This pen consists of some qualities or attributes and also the underlying reality. It consists of some qualities, which we will call Q, and of the underlying reality, which we will call X. The pen is equal to the qualities which make it a pen. There we have a table. The table has also some qualities which make it a table, QT plus X, the absolute reality. Here you may ask why we assume this X to be the same as the previous. The question arises that this pen may have some other reality underlying its qualities than the reality which underlies the qualities of the table. Thus it may be suggested that before the qualities of the pen were projected, some reality may have acted upon our senses, and the qualities which make this a table were projected by some other reality, which we might call X, which has acted upon our senses. You might question that we have no right to look upon this X to be the same as the other X.

Here mark the mistake made by Plato. He looks upon these underlying realities as different, which apparently they are, and you have also taken them to be different. There is a fallacy in this argument by the method of *reductio ad absurdum*. We can show that this assumption is wrong. The qualities and attributes of the pen, its color, weight, softness and other qualities, were the result of the reaction of your intellect or mind. We have assumed that the absolute reality in this pencil precedes the projection of these attributes or qualities. Thus the absolute reality transcends all qualities, all properties or all attributes. This X also transcends all qualities or attributes. X' also transcends all qualities and attributes.

To what then are differences due? Reflect a little please. All differences in this world are due only to qualities. Could you distinguish between this piece of chalk and that pencil without referring to their qualities? How do you know that this piece of chalk is different from that pencil? Through qualities alone.. If you make this X different from that X', you make this absolute reality subject to qualities again. You began by taking them to be beyond qualities, and you end by taking them to be with qualities.

Thus you have no right to say that the underlying reality in this pencil is different from the reality that underlies this piece of chalk. You have no right to say that the reality which underlies the mind, subject or intellect is different from the reality which underlies a cow or bull. You have no right to say that the *Atman* which underlies this table is different from that *Atman* which underlies this pen. No, you have no right. It is one and the same infinity, the same absolute, unchangeable reality.

It might be made more clear by an illustration. Here is a beautiful white wall. All of you are sitting here. One of you is tracing upon that wall beautiful geometrical diagrams, triangles, circles, ellipses, etc. Another is tracing upon the same wall, suppose, a picture concerning a great war. Another one of you is tracing upon the same wall a picture of his wife, friends and relatives. Yet another is tracing something else. All of these pictures have the same reality behind them. Similarly all the things that you see in this world have the same reality behind them. Here, suppose that you see a horse; you observe a cow; here, a dog; there, an elephant, and there, a man. All of these pictures are traced upon one and the same absolute X, the same white wall. Thus the same *Atman*, the one infinite Rama, underlies each and all, the same, the same, the same. In your dreams you see an ox; then you see a dog; then, a man; then, a woman, but you know that in your dreams the ox, the dog, the man and everything, all those are pictures upon one and the same absolute reality, the true *Atman*. When you wake up, you know the horse, the mountain or the river that you saw in your dream are nowhere.

What about these qualities which make up the world? The phenomenal world consists of these qualities, and they depend upon the absolute reality. Here is a very subtle point which you will not be able to understand just now, but still you had better hear it; you will understand it thoroughly in some of the succeeding lectures.

According to these qualities, the absolute reality has a quality too; namely, the quality of supporting them, the quality of keeping them up. If so, the absolute reality is not absolute, because the absolute reality has at least one quality of supporting all these qualities. How then can we say that such a reality is absolute? We say this from direct experience. Just as you say that this world is real on the authority of your personal experience, so on the authority of the higher spiritual experience, on the authority of the supreme spiritual experience, we say that when the absolute reality is realized, all these qualities, all this time and space, vanish. Thus from the standpoint of the absolute reality, these qualities never existed, but from the standpoint of the qualities, these depend upon the *Adhishthan*, the absolute. Here is an antinomy to be solved; here is a great problem. It is called the problem of *maya*. In fact the absolute reality is absolute, is beyond all qualities, but these qualities depend upon the absolute reality from their own standpoint. Here is the one chief problem, the solution of which solves all the difficulties in this world.

European philosophers make these subjects simply matters of speculation, but it is not so with Indian philosophers. With them any subject which is proved theoretically is half proved only if it is not verified through experience, if it is not realized and experimented upon. This is a subject which is so sweet when we hear it intellectually; Oh! but it is the quintessence of sweetness and all joy when we once realize it. It is worth while to realize it. If you live this idea, that you are that One Infinite X which underlies all the bodies in this universe, that you are that absolute reality, then you are above the body, above the mind. This body is not the subject; it is a mere object brought into existence by one wave coming into collision with another from another side. This foam of a body you are not. You are the absolute reality in which all this world, all the phenomena of the universe are mere waves or eddies. Realize that, and become free, absolutely free. Is it not the wonder of wonders that you, the true reality, the real absolute, do not realize it? Oh, be that. What good tidings. What a blessed Gospel. You are that absolute reality, the real X you are. Realize it and become free.

Let that be your state—
The body dissolved is cast to the winds,
While Death, Infinity me enshrine;
All ears my ears, all eyes my eyes,
All hands my hands, all minds my minds.
I swallowed up death, all difference I drank up,
How sweet and strong and good I find.

Om! Om! Om!

MAYA OR THE WHEN AND THE WHY OF THE WORLD

January 15, 1903
Golden Gate Hall, San Francisco

The Ruler, Governor, Controller of Maya in the form of ladies and gentlemen,

The subject of tonight's discourse is *Maya.* This is a subject which superficial critics look upon as the weakest point in the philosophy of Vedanta. Today we shall take up that weakest point. All those philosophers and thinkers who have studied the philosophy of Vedanta say unanimously that if this *maya* could be elucidated, then everything else in it would be so natural, so plain, so clear, so beneficial and useful. This is a vast subject. In order that we may exhaust it thoroughly, about ten lectures ought to be devoted to this subject alone, and then can the subject be placed on such a clear, lucid basis that no doubt or question under the sun or on the face of the earth would be left unanswered and unmet. Everything can be made plain, but it requires time. Hurrying readers and hurrying listeners are not expected to understand that thoroughly.

The question is "Why this world?" "Whence this world?" or to put it in Vedantic language, "Why this ignorance in the universe?" You know, Vedanta preaches that this universe is unreal, is merely phenomenal. Ignorance is not eternal. All these phenomena are not real or eternal. The question comes, "Why should this ignorance which is the cause of these phenomena, or this *maya*, which is at the root of all this *meum* and *tuum*, differences and differentiation, overpower the true Self or *Atman*? Why should this *maya*, or ignorance, be more powerful than God?" This is the question.

In common language, in the language of other philosophers and theologians, the question is, "Why should this world exist at all?" Why should God have created this world? Vedanta says, "No, brother, you have no right to ask that question. There is no answer to this question." Vedanta plainly says that there is no answer to this question. Vedanta says that we can prove it to you experimentally and directly that this world which you see is in reality nothing else but God, and we can show to you conclusively through experiment that when you advance high enough in the realization of the truth this world will disappear for you. However, why does this world exist at all? We desist from answering that question. Vedanta plainly confesses its inability to answer that question. Herein all the other theologians and dogmatizers and all superficial philosophers come forward and say, "Oh, Vedanta philosophy is imperfect; it cannot explain "the why and the wherefore of the world." Vedanta says, "Brother, examine the answers that you yourself give to the question of 'the why and wherefore of the world' and you will see that your answers are no answers at all." It is mere waste of time to dwell upon that question, a sheer waste of time and labor. It is letting go a bird in the hand in search of two in the bush. They will fly away before you reach them, and you will lose the bird in your hand. Vedanta says that all philosophy and all science must proceed from the known to the unknown. Do not put the cart before the horse. Do not begin from the unknown and then come to the known.

There was a river on the banks of which some people were standing and philosophizing as to its origin.

One of them said, "This river comes from rocks, from stones, from hills. Out of hills water gushes in spring, and that is the cause of this river." Another man said, "Oh, no, impossible. Stones are so hard, so tough and so rigid, and water is so liquid and soft. How can soft water come out of hard stones? Impossible, impossible. Reason cannot believe that hard stones are giving out soft water. If stones could give out water, then let me take up this piece of stone and squeeze it. Out of this no water flows. Thus the statement that this river flows from those mountains is absurd. I have a very good theory. This river flows from the perspiration of a big giant somewhere. We see everyday that when a person perspires, water flows from his body. Another man said, "No, no, it is somebody standing somewhere who is spitting, and this is the spit." Another man said, "No, no. There is somebody who is vacating his water, making water, and this is the cause of the river."

Now these people said, "Look here, look here. All these theories of ours are feasible; all these theories of the origin of water are practical. Every day we see such things, but the ordinary intellect of a man who has never seen water gushing out from stones, who has never been on the mountains, will not accept the theory that water flows from stones and yet it is true." On what does the truth of this theory rest? On experience, on experiment, on direct observation.

Similarly, the origin of the stream of this world, the origin of the stream of the universe, the river of life is described differently by different people. The origin of the world, according to the people of that kind of intellect which ascribed the origin of the river to spittle and to perspiration, is taken to be something of the same sort as they observe every day around them. They say, "Here is a man who makes boots. The boots could not be made without somebody with some intention or design of making. Here is a man who makes a watch. Now the watch could not be made without somebody with some intention or plan or design of making it. Here is a house. The house could not be made without somebody having the plan and design." They see this every day, and then they say, "Here is the world. The world could not have been made without some kind of a person of the same sort as the shoemaker, the watchmaker, the housemaker; there must be a world maker, who makes this world." Thus they say that there is a personal God, standing upon the clouds, not taking pity upon the poor fellow that he might catch cold. They say some personal God must have made this world. Their argument seems to be very plausible, very feasible and very reasonable. It seems to be of the same sort as the arguments of those people who look upon the origin of the river to be of the same sort as the water coming out of the bodies. The world also must have been made by somebody.

Vedanta does not propose any theory of that kind. Vedanta says, "See it; make an experiment; observe it. Through direct realization you see that the world is not what it appears to be." How is that? Vedanta says, "How the water comes out of the stones, I may or may not be able to tell you, but I know the water comes out of stones. Follow me to that place, and you will see the water gushing out of the stones. If I cannot tell why the water comes out of the stones, do not blame me. Blame the water; it is coming out of the stones. I am unable to tell you how the water comes out of the stones, but it remains a fact; you can verify it yourself."

Similarly Vedanta says, "Whether or not I am able to tell you why this *maya* or ignorance is, it remains a fact. Why it came, I may not be able to tell you." The Vedantic attitude is merely experimental and scientific. It establishes no hypothesis; it puts forth no theory. It does not claim to be able to explain the origin of the world; this is beyond the sphere of intellect or comprehension. This is called *maya*. Why does the world appear? Vedanta says, "Because you see it." If you do not see, there is no world. Close your eyes and a fifth of the world is gone; that part of the world which you perceive through your eyes is no longer there. Close your ears, and another fifth is gone; close your nose, and another fifth is gone. Do not put any of your senses into activity, and there is no world. You see the world, and you ought to explain why the world is there. You make it there. You should answer yourself.

There was a child. It saw in a mirror the image of a little boy, and somebody told the child that in the mirror there was a very beautiful, dear little child. When he looked into the mirror, he saw a dear little boy, but the child did not know that it was his own reflection; he took it to be some strange boy in the mirror. Afterwards the mother of the child wanted to persuade him that the boy in the mirror was only his own reflection, not a real boy; but he could not be persuaded, he could not understand that in the mirror there was not really another boy. When the mother said, "Look here; here is a mirror; there is no boy in it," the child came up to it and said, "Oh Mamma, O Mamma, here is the boy! Why! The boy is here." When the boy was saying, "Here is the boy," in the very act of saying he cast his own reflection in the mirror. Again the mother wanted to persuade him that there was not a real boy in the mirror; again the boy wanted to have a proof or demonstration. The boy went up to the mirror and said, "Look, here is the boy," and in the very act of proving that there was a boy in the mirror, the boy put the object in the mirror.

Similarly when you say, "Why the world, whence the world, how the world," the very moment you begin to investigate the origin and the why and wherefore of the world, that very moment you create the world. So how can you know the origin and wherefore of the world? How shall we know beyond it? How shall we transcend it? This ought to be made more clear from both the micro-cosmic and metaphysical standpoints. Some say that a mundane god created the world. Now the question is that this creator, in order to create the world, must have stood somewhere. Where did he stand? If he stood somewhere, if he had a resting place, then the world was already present before it was created, because the resting place must be somewhere in the world. The world was present before it was created. When you begin to examine when the world began, you want to separate two ideas, the idea of when, why and wherefore on one side and the idea of world on the other. The words why, when, and wherefore, the idea of time, space and causation, are they not a part of the world? Mark it. Time, space and causation are also in the world, not beyond the world. The very moment you begin to say, "When the world began," the world is on one side, and the idea of when, on the other side. There you keep the world before the world. This is very subtle and very difficult, and you will kindly attend closely, most carefully.

It will be explained in a different way now. Here is a man asleep, and in his sleep he sees all sorts of objects. He is the subject and the object, the bewildered subject of the dream and the woods, rivers, mountains and other things. There the objects of the dream and the subject make their appearance simultaneously, as was shown the other night. Could the subject in a dream, the traveller in the dream, tell when these rivers, mountains, lakes, and other landscapes came into existence? No, never. When you are dreaming to you the rivers, dales, mountains and landscapes will appear to be eternal. You can never know their origin; you can never know the why, when and wherefore of the dream so long as you are dreaming. Wake up, and the whole is gone; wake up and all disappears.

Similarly in this world you see all sorts of objects; they seem to be real, and there seems to be no end to them, just as in a dream there is no end. You cannot know when the dream began; can you tell when time began? This is an antinomy pointed out by Kant also. When did time begin? When you say time began at that time, you posit time. This question is impossible. Where did space begin? The question is impossible. Beyond where space began, you place a point where it began. The beginning of space is surrounded by the idea of where, and the idea of where includes that of place. Where did the chain of causation begin? The question is impossible. Why did the chain of causation begin? This question is likewise impossible. Oh, if you point out any beginning of the chain of causation, there you see that the idea of why is itself causation. This is a question which is unanswerable. There is no end to time, space or causation whether on this side or the other. Schopenhauer proves it; Herbert Spencer proves it. Every thinker will show to you that there is no end to it, no end, no end.

When the (dreaming) subject wakes up, the whole problem is solved. Waking up, the (dreaming) subject says, "Oh, that was a dream; there was no reality all along." Similarly on waking up to a realization of the truth, on achieving that perfect state of liberation which Vedanta holds up before everybody, you can see that all this world was a mere joke, mere plaything, mere illusion, nothing else.

The same question of *maya* is put in this way also, "If man is God, why should he forget his real nature?" Vedanta answers, "The real God in you never forgot its real nature. If the real God in you had forgotten its real nature, it would not have been all the time controlling, governing and ruling this universe. The real God has not forgotten at all. It is still controlling, governing and ruling this universe." Then who has forgotten? Nobody, nobody has forgotten. It is just like a dream. In the dream, when you see different kinds of objects, in reality it is not you that see these things; it is the subject in the dream, created along with the other objects in the dream which sees all those scenes and dwells in those dales, mountains and rivers. The real Self, the *Atman*, the true God, has never forgotten anything. This idea of a false ego is itself the creation of *maya* or an illusion of the same sort as the other objects. When you ask, "Why did God forget himself into a man, into a little egotistical self?" Vedanta says that in this question of yours there is the fallacy which logicians call *circulus in probando*, the fallacy of a circle in the proof. To whom are you putting this question? Are you putting this question to the dreaming subject or to the wakeful subject? To the dreaming subject you should not put the question because the dreaming subject has not forgotten anything, being a creation like the other objects it sees, and to the real subject in the wakeful state you cannot put the question. Who will put the question? The questioner must be in the dream itself, and when the dreaming subject is removed, then who will put the question? All duality of questioning and answering is possible only so long as the dream of *maya* continues or lasts. You can put the question only to the dreaming subject, and the dreaming subject is not responsible for it. Let the dreaming subject be removed; and the whole panorama, the whole dream, vanishes; and nobody is left to put the question.

Now the question remains, "Is the world real?" Vedanta says, "*Neti, Maya*, not that, nit. You cannot call it real." Why not? Because reality means something which lasts forever, which remains the same yesterday, today and forever. Now does the world last forever? It does not last forever; therefore it does not satisfy the definition of reality. In your deep sleep it disappears; in your state of realization, perfection or liberation it disappears. Consequently you have no right to call it real. Is the world unreal? Vedanta says, "*Neti*, not that, *maya*, nit." This is very strange. The world is not unreal. Vedanta says, "No, it is not unreal, because unreal means something which never is, like the horns of a man." Did a man ever possess horns like a cow? Never. That is unreal, and the world is not unreal because it appears to you to be present just now. Is the world real? "*Neti*, nit." Is the world unreal? "*Neti*, nit." Then is the world partly real and partly unreal? Vedanta says, "*Maya, neti,* nit." Not that even. Unreality and reality cannot subsist together. The answers to these questions are called the *maya* theory of Vedanta. Such answers to these questions have another name, *mithya*. It is a word which is cognate with your word mythology. It means something which we cannot call real and which we cannot call unreal, and which we cannot call both real and unreal. Such is your world.

Atheists say that there is no God. Vedanta says, "*Neti*, nit, *maya*." They are wrong; they have no argument for saying that there is no God. Some people say that there is a personal God. Vedanta says, "*Neti*, nit, not that." You have no right to make a statement of that kind. Vedanta says that here is a realm where you ought not to tread; here is a realm upon which you cannot bring your intellect to bear. Your intellect has work enough to do in this world; let it work there. "Render unto Caesar the things that are Caesar's, and render unto God what is God's." Your intellect has work enough in the material plane, in the empirical realms, but in the realms of metaphysics you have to come only by one way and one way only; and that one way is of realization, that way is the way of love, feeling, faith, rather knowledge—strange kind of knowledge, strange kind of God-consciousness. When you come to this region through the proper channel, all questions cease; all problems are solved. In the *Kena Upanishad* of Sama Veda, we have a passage which translated into English is something like this:

> I cannot say I know it:
> Nor can I say I do not know it;
> Beyond knowing and not knowing It is.

This is exactly what the thinkers of today say Herbert Spencer in the first part of his *First Principles,*

"The Unknowable," comes to the very same conclusion as that at which Vedanta arrives. Rama need not read to you all that he says, but a small passage might be read. "There must exist some principle which, being the basis of science, cannot be established by science. All reasoned-out conclusions whatever must rest on some postulate. There must be a place where we meet the region of the unknowable, where intellect ought not to venture, cannot venture to go."

All the philosophers have something to say to the same effect on this point. Just mark what a fallacy is committed by the people when they ascribe motives to God, when they say God must have done this, God must have mercy, God must have love, God must have goodness, God must have this attribute or that. What a fallacy is committed by such people, for all classification is limitation. You call God infinite and finite in one breath; you say on the one hand that He is infinite and on the other hand you say, "Oh, He possesses this quality, and he possesses that quality." When you say that He is good, that He is not bad, then He is limited. Wherever there is bad, good is not. When you say that He is the Creator, that He is not the creature, then you limit Him; there you point out a place where He is not. He is the All. Similarly when you hold God responsible for anything or attribute to Him any motives, designs or plans, you practically make yourself a magistrate or judge and God a person who has done certain deeds, who has come before you to give an account of His work. There you limit Him. Vedanta says that you have no right to bring God before your tribunal. Give up this question; it is illegitimate.

Now Rama will explain to you this problem of

maya in the way of the Hindus and how they have described and explained it in their old scriptures. They explain it practically, experimentally. They call this *maya anirvachaniya*, the limited meaning of which is illusion and the explanation of which is something that is indescribable, that cannot be called real, that cannot be called unreal, and that is not a combination of reality and unreality. This whole world is *maya* or illusion, and this illusion is of two kinds. We might call them extrinsic and intrinsic illusion.

Suppose you see a snake in the dark. It frightens you to death; you fall down and are hurt. What was the snake? Was the snake real? Vedanta says the snake is not real, because afterwards when you approach the spot where the snake was, it is not there, and in its place you find a coiled rope. But is the snake unreal? Vedanta says, "No, no." You have no right to say that the snake is unreal. Had the snake been unreal, you would not have received the injury. The snake is an illusion; and an illusion is not a reality; it is not a non-reality either because unreal means something which never appears to exist. You see a rainbow. Is the rainbow real? The rainbow is not real because when we approach the spot, we do not find it and if we change our position, we will find the position of the rainbow changed. Is it unreal? No, no, because it appears to exist there; it produces some effect on us. It is not unreal either. It is an illusion.

You see in the mirror your image. Is your image unreal? Vedanta says, "No, it is not unreal, because it produces an effect on you; you see it." Is it real? No, it is not real either. You turn your face this way, and it disappears. This is an illusion. Now this illusion is of two kinds, intrinsic and extrinsic. Intrinsic illusion is as in the case of the snake seen in the rope. A peculiarity of intrinsic illusion is that when the illusory object is there, the real object is not seen; and when the real object is seen, the illusory object is not there. Both cannot co-exist. If the snake is there the rope is not there, and if the rope is there the snake is not there. The one or the other must perish. The one or the other must exist.

However, in the extrinsic illusion both co-exist. The reality as well as the illusion can both co-exist as in a mirror. In the mirror the object, the image, is unreal, or in the terms of scientists it is a visual image, an illusion. The face is the real object; now the face as well as the image co-exist. Another thing about extrinsic illusion is that a medium is seen, a medium like the mirror. The mirror is the medium, the illusory object is the image, and the real object is the face. So in fact, in an extrinsic illusion, three things are present for the time being. In an intrinsic illusion only one thing is present for the time being.

The experiments of Vedantins and their religious development and realization of the truth, prove this world to be made up of both kinds of illusions, extrinsic and intrinsic. When a man begins religious life and realizes the divinity within himself, he overcomes only the extrinsic illusion. All the religions on the face of the earth, Christianity, Mohammedanism, Buddhism, Zoroastrianism, have done a great deal in overcoming the extrinsic illusion. Vedanta says they are all right, but Vedanta goes one step further. It overcomes the intrinsic illusion also at which other religions as a rule stop short. There they say, "Vedanta is opposed to us." No, no, it is not opposed. It simply fulfills what they began; it supplements them.

Now something very subtle is going to be told, so attend most carefully. A rope is mistaken for a snake or a serpent. In the rope there appeared a serpent. To what kind of illusion was the serpent due? The serpent was due to the intrinsic illusion. You know, if the serpent is there, the rope is not there; if the rope is there, the serpent is not there. Only one thing is seen at one time. That is intrinsic illusion. Now you recall the example of the mirror which serves as a medium to you, and that you see in the mirror an illusory object; we say, an image. You have in the case of the mirror an extrinsic illusion. Now it will be shown that while in the case of the rope, the serpent appears on account of intrinsic illusion, this serpent will serve as a medium or as a mirror to the underlying reality of the rope, and we shall have an extrinsic illusion also on the spot.

A boy comes to you and says, "Papa, papa, I am frightened; there is a snake." We ask, "Child, how long was the snake?" and the boy says, "The snake was about two yards long." "Well, how thick was the snake?" and the child says, "It was very thick. It was as thick as the cable I saw the other day in the ship which was leaving San Francisco." We ask, "Well, what was the snake doing?" He said, "The snake had coiled itself around." You know that the snake was not there; the snake was unreal; only the rope was lying there. The rope was about two yards long, and was as thick as the cable which he saw on the day when the ship was leaving San Francisco. The rope was coiled around on the floor, and there the properties of the rope, its thickness, length and position, have mirrored themselves as it were in the illusory serpent. The serpent was not so long; the length only applied to the rope. The serpent was not of that thickness; the thickness only applied to the rope. The serpent was not in that position; the position only applied to the rope. So you mark that originally we had the serpent as the result of intrinsic illusion and subsequently we have another kind of illusion in the serpent which we might call extrinsic illusion, the properties of one being attributed to the other.

This is the second development of the illusion. In order to remove these illusions what process is to be adopted? We shall remove one illusion first and then the other. The extrinsic illusion will be removed first and then the intrinsic illusion.

According to Vedanta all this universe is in reality nothing else but one indivisible, indescribable reality, which we cannot even call reality, which transcends all language, which is beyond time, space and causation, beyond everything. In this rope of the reality, in this underlying substratum, substance or whatever you might call it, appear names, forms and differentiations; or you might call it energy, activity, or vibrations. These are like the serpent. There we see that after this intrinsic illusion is completed the extrinsic illusion comes up, and on account of the extrinsic illusion we look upon these names and forms, these personalities and these individualities, as having a reality of their own, as existing by themselves, as real on their own account. Here is the second, or extrinsic, illusion put forth. You will understand it now when we reverse the process.

What have religions done? Be it said to the credit of beloved Christianity, beloved Mohammedanism; be it said to the credit of these religions that they have done a great deal in removing extrinsic illusion; they have shown to mankind that if a man lives a pure life, a life of universal love, a life of divine ecstasy, if a man lives a life of hope, faith and charity with unbounded love gushing forth from him in all directions, filling the whole universe with divinity, then he finds God in everything. Just mark. The real saint or sage, the true Christian, the beloved Christian, finds God even in the names. He hates not the enemy, but loves the enemy. Oh! "Love your enemy as yourself," that blessed saying of Jesus! He finds the same God in the flowers. Have you ever realized that state? The truly religious people have. Flowers speak to you; and you find sermons in stones, books in the running brooks. The stars speak to you; divinity looks at you through a man's face. Does divinity require any intellectual proof? No, it carries its own proof with itself. It rests on a proof which transcends all worldly logic and worldly philosophy, on a person who feels God everywhere, lives, moves and has his being in God, in divinity. Through this kind of religious life, through practice and through experience, through experiments, he overcomes the extrinsic illusion. How is that? You say that God is in all these forms; God is in all these phases and forms and differentiations. All these are like the serpent; still if you look behind them, you see beyond them the underlying rope beneath the serpent. The length, breadth and thickness you attribute not to the serpent but to the underlying rope. There you dispense with one kind of illusion only. You see God behind everything, and when you realize this state of religious life, you do not impute motives to your friends or foes. You see divinity in them, you say that the one divinity, or the one All, which is God, is doing all these things, and I should not impute motives to my friends. This is one step in your advancement, but Vedanta tells you, "Brother, if you say that God is in all these, that is not the whole truth; go beyond that." All these forms and all these images and differentiations themselves contain God, but at the same time all these different illusions and forms are unreal, and they are like the serpent in the rope. Go beyond that, and you reach the state beyond all ideas, beyond all words. These are unreal even. There you see that Vedanta is the fulfillment of all religions. It does not contradict any religion in this world.

It will be shown that it is unnecessary to say that this world must have been created by this God or that God. It will be proved that these forms and figures, these different figurations and situations, are this world and nothing else.

Here are two triangles and one rectangle—

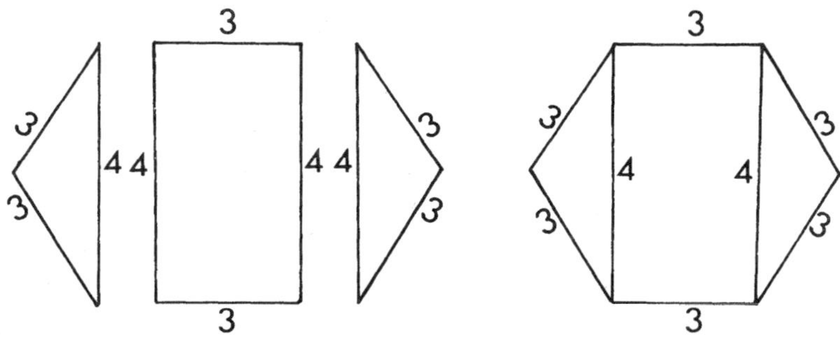

Both these triangles are isosceles—two sides are equal. The two equal sides are marked "3"; and the third side, "4." In the rectangle the shorter sides are marked "3"; and the longer sides "4." Place them in such a way that they may form one figure, so the bases of the triangles may coincide with the longer sides of the rectangle. What will that become then? We shall get a hexagon of which all the sides are 3. You know the sides marked "4" have come within the figure, and they are no longer sides. How do we get this hexagon? We get this from a different position or a different combination of the triangles and the rectangle. What about the properties of the original figures and of the resulting figure? The properties of the resulting figure are entirely different from those of the component figures. The component figures have acute angles; the resulting figure has no acute angle whatsoever. One of the component figures (the rectangle) has right angles, and the resulting figure has no right angle whatsoever. The component figures have sides four units in length; the resulting figure has no side of that length. None of the component figures were equilateral. The resulting figure is equilateral, and it has also all its angles equal. Here we see a creation, all of whose properties were entirely unknown before. Wherefrom have these entirely new properties come? Just mark that these entirely new properties have been created by no creator. These entirely new properties have not come out of the component elements; they are the result of a new form; they are the result of a new position, a new configuration which Vedanta calls *maya. Maya* means name and form; they are the result of names and forms, mark that. Again see. Let each of these two isosceles triangles represent H, Hydrogen, and the rectangle O, Oxygen; this gives you H_2O, water. These original elements, hydrogen and oxygen, have properties of their own, and the resulting compound is an entirely new something. Hydrogen and oxygen give us water. Hydrogen is combustible, and oxygen aids combustion, but water does not. It has a property of its own, entirely new. We see again that hydrogen is very light, but oxygen does not possess the same lightness. Hydrogen fills balloons and takes you up to the skies; but water, the resulting compound, does not. The properties of the component elements are entirely different from those of the resulting compound. Wherefrom does the resulting compound get its properties? Does it get these properties from the creator or from the component parts? No, they come from new form, from new position, new configuration. That is what Vedanta tells us. It tells you that what you see in this world is simply the result of name and form. You need not posit the existence of a Creator for this and that which are the result of name and form.

Here is before you a piece of charcoal, and there is a brilliant diamond, a dazzling bright diamond. The diamond has properties entirely different from those of the piece of charcoal. The diamond is so hard that it can cut iron; the charcoal is so soft that it leaves its mark upon a piece of paper when you scratch it on the paper. The diamond is so priceless, so precious and so brilliant, and the piece of charcoal is so cheap, so ugly and so black. Mark the contrast between the two, and yet in reality they are one and the same thing. Science proves that. Oh! you will say, "My intellect will not grasp it." Whether you accept it or not, it is a fact. Similarly Vedanta tells you, here is something bad and there is something good. The diamond is good, and the charcoal is bad. Here is something which you call friend, and there is something which you call foe. Just as the carbon appears in charcoal as in diamond, so in reality it is only one and the same divinity that appears in both places. In name and form lies the difference, in nothing else.

Similarly the difference between good and bad is due only to *maya*, to name and form, nothing else. These names and forms are not real because they do not last forever. They are unreal because we see them at one time and not at another time. This phenomenon of the universe is nothing but names and forms, nothing but differentiations, variations and combinations. So these different variations and combinations are due to what? They are due to intrinsic illusion. In these names and forms which are due to intrinsic illusion the one divinity manifests itself. God manifests Himself in these names and forms of the world which are called *maya*. Get beyond that, and you are everything. He sees indeed who sees in all alike. He is a man with eyes open who sees the one divinity in all alike.

Om! Om! Om!

KARMA OR ACTION*

January 5, 1902
Social Association, Mathura, U.P., India

Some say that whatever happens happens with the will of God. Some deny it. They say that whatever happens happens with the efforts of man. The former believe that everything is done by the will of God and that we have no hand in His will. The latter are convinced that everything is done by man through his own efforts and that God has nothing to do with it. They argue that "history" supports them. Napoleon Bonaparte had conquered the whole of Europe with his courage, efforts and resolute will. So is the case with Nadir Shah, Mahmood Ghaznavi and others in respect of their attack on India. Had these brave men ignored courage, efforts and the strength of their will and stayed at home only with faith in God, they would never have conquered Europe or India. This goes to prove that man's own courage and efforts are very essential. It is to make ourselves coward and lazy, if we keep faith only in God and sit idly at our homes." This is how they argue.

In this connection Vedanta says that there is no difference between the two points of view. The only difference is between their angles of vision. To tell you the truth, they do not reach the root of the problem.

Vedanta wants to know from those who say that God does everything what their conception of God is. Is He with or without a form? Is He a doer or a non-doer? Is He related or unrelated, attached or unattached? If and

* Translated from the Urdu.

when these questions are properly answered, the problem whether God or man is responsible for all that happens will be automatically solved. Those persons who attach all importance to courage, efforts and resolute will, who ignore the will of God and prove their case by quoting examples from history, have not enough intelligence to probe deeper into the matter. However, taking them as his own dear self, Rama wants to tell them politely that had they read the history with intelligence, they would not have come to this conclusion. Even now if they again read history with understanding, they would certainly change their present opinion. On the other hand, they will now discover much higher causes for the secret of success.

Those who refer to the heroism of Napoleon will certainly discover that when he was actually in the battlefield and winning a war, it never occurred to him that it was he who was acting or doing anything. He could win battles only when he was completely lost in fighting. At that moment he had no idea either of losing or winning the battle. He was all absorbed with one-pointed concentration on the very act of fighting. This was the secret of his success. On the other hand, whenever any man fought with pride and vanity, he was defeated and was made a prisoner. This is the law of nature. "Wherever there is pride, there cannot be any success." This is the experience of all thinking persons. You can however be sure of your success if you make earnest efforts in right direction and are above pride, vanity and egoism. This is the law which applies to all.

Here a doubt may be raised. When at the time of success there was no pride in Napoleon, and when he was above egoism, who will be said to have achieved the success in the work done through him? Vedanta here answers that when a man is wholly absorbed in action, he is above pride or egoism, and the power that works within him is free from selfishness. In Vedanta they call this power, which is above body, mind or egoism, God. Therefore at the time of success only God works. Though Napoleon appeared to be gaining success, and the success may also be attributed to him, yet at that time it was only God and His power that was working through him. In other words, you can say that it was God and God alone, who was working or acting. God is all-pervading and omnipresent. When His power works through a man, He is called by the name of courage or valor, and when He works through trees, etc. it is termed as growth. In a nutshell He can be recognized in Napoleon through courage or resoluteness and in vegetation through growth. There is only one Power working in all; all the work is done by the same Power. It is God. Therefore, it is wrong to say that it was Napoleon who won the battle. It proves that the man who says so does not know the truth about the secret of success.

Now, let us measure the extent to which a man is free and helpless or bound. We have now to examine how far a man is free to act independently and how far he is bound to reap the harvest of his past actions. Both *karma* (actions) and *prarabdha* (the result of previous actions) will be explained in two ways—in the case of an individual and in respect of the whole.

There are two elements in a man. One is independent, or free, called *karma*; and the other is dependent and binding, called *prarabdha* (or destiny), which we are bound to suffer. A silkworm is free so long as it has not produced silk. But once it has produced silk, it is bound to be imprisoned in its own cocoon. So is the case with a man. He is free and independent so long as he has not done any action. But once he has done action, he is bound to face its results. There is no escape then. However, if he has not done anything, the question of facing its result does not arise. He is completely free to act or not to act.

A spider is free to create its thread or not, but once it has woven its thread, it is bound to limit itself within the cobweb. A railway bogie is free to go any way, but when the rails have been laid down, it is bound to run only on those rails. Similarly a man is quite free before doing any deed. He is also free to act or not to act, but once he has acted, he is bound to suffer the result of his actions, good or bad. Therefore, in accordance with these two elements, *karma* and *prarabdha*, he is free or independent and also bound or dependent. These elements are *prursh-artha* (efforts) and *prarabdha* (destiny).

Some people keep *karma* (efforts) and *prarabdha* (destiny) in the same continuity. They say that they mean the same thing because the result of the actions is ultimately the destiny. But in Vedanta, the term "destiny" means the result of our past actions which we must suffer and for which we have no freedom to avoid. We are dependent on or bound to suffer the result of our deeds, good or bad. Concerning *karma*, the actions, we mean that man is quite free to act or not to act. If he acts, he is again free to act in any way he likes. It is his own option.

In English there is a saying that man is free to make his own destiny. In other words man is the architect of his own fortune. This is also the principle of the scripture, "as you sow, so shall you reap." This means that you will have to face the result of your past or present actions, either in this life or in other lives, in the form of your destiny. People complain incessantly that their desires are not fulfilled. Vedanta says that if you at all feel sorry that your desires are not fulfilled, you must weep bitterly because your desires cannot remain dormant, without fructifying. They must materialize one day. Vedanta says that at the root of the source of the desires is your own *Atma*, which is truth personified. As such, all the desires, good or bad, must be materialized. They must be true because they emanate from *Atma*, the truth incarnate. This very *Atma*, which is the source of all power, is called God, or *Ishwara*. Therefore, all his desires must indubitably be fulfilled.

Now here another doubt may be raised. If all our desires are fulfilled sooner or later, then what is the significance of destiny, which is usually mentioned in our scriptures? In answer to this question, Vedanta says that the desires, being innumerable, are often left unfulfilled at the time of the death of a man. To desire is also a sort of action. A man therefore takes other birth or births to see his desires fulfilled. The materialization of these unfulfilled desires may be called destiny. That is why our scriptures have mentioned that it is because of our own desires, hopes and aspirations that we take other birth or births after death.

It is said that a man is reborn according to his thoughts at the time of his death. How then can this belief be reconciled to the theory that the rebirth is caused by the unfulfilled desires to be fulfilled in the next life? In this connection it may be mentioned that Vedanta does not disagree with this common belief. As a matter of fact, it supports it. The ideas and the thoughts which come at the time of the death of a man are responsible for his next life. At the same time Vedanta asserts that at the time of death only those thoughts and desires come to the mind which were uppermost during the life of the man. In the examination hall the correct answers will come to the mind of only that student who has previously studied the subject, but it is impossible for the student who has never cared to study throughout the year to answer the question paper correctly or to pass the examination. In fact that student alone can be successful in his examination who has been regularly studying his subjects. Similarly for the man who has throughout his life been thinking of evils and entertaining all sorts of mean desires, it is impossible to have good thoughts at the time of his death. So too it is impossible for man who has been good throughout to have evil thoughts at his last moments. Only those thoughts, good or bad, which were entertained and practiced by a man in his life come to his mind at the time of his death. Also, all the desires which could not be fulfilled till his death remain uppermost in his mind. Such desires are also recalled by him at his last moments. It is, therefore, according to such thoughts and unfulfilled desires that a man takes his next birth.

It is then proved that the unfulfilled desires of a man are responsible for his rebirth. The man who has already stopped entertaining any desires during his lifetime cannot think of any good or bad desires at the time of his death. As such, he will have no rebirth. Usually such a state of mind is developed only in the men of divine knowledge or in those who have freed themselves from all the desires during their very lifetime.

When it is proved that the man has positively to suffer the result of his past desires and actions and that the destiny is nothing but the result of his past desires or actions, then it should be quite clear that in respect of destiny or *prarabdha*, the man is helpless and is bound to face it. He is not free. However, the other element in man is free. It is in respect of his actions. Here he is free to act in any way he likes. He is free to choose his own line of action and to act or not to act accordingly. It is his actual acts which determine his destiny or lot. That is why wise men have said that man is the architect of his own fortune. He can make, or mar, his future by his own actions.

As has already been said, a spider is free to take the thread out of its mouth, but once it has done so and spread the net, it is bound to be imprisoned in its own cobweb. So too, man is free before doing any action. When once he has done something, he is bound to face its result.

This in short has been narrated in respect of an individual. But when we examine the whole thing from the collective point of view, we see something more interesting. Mr. Herbert Spencer says that a man can create the conditions in the country according to his own liking. This is correct. When we consider it from the collective point of view, we find that Napoleon, who appeared to be working independently, according to his own free will, was certainly forced to come in this world at the right time in the right period. Therefore, when we examine the whole affair in a collective way, we find that divine power, which is latent in us, arranges the whole show. It is on account of that divine force, or will, that men are always born when and where they are needed. Also, due to the same force or will, the number of men and women in the world remains equal. Just as both the forms of positive and negative electricity are present in every object, so too when a man with unfulfilled desires is born, the other man to fulfill his desires is also born simultaneously. Thus both the scales are properly balanced. According to this law, Napoleon, whom we call free and independent to act, was also not free. He was born in accordance with this very law. In other words, even those men who are said to have freedom to act are not free. They are also governed by the universal force in respect of their birth, etc. In this way, you will see that though individually a man appears to be free to act, yet if we take an overall position, we find that man is dependent and bound both collectively and individually in regard to destiny.

Now another doubt is created here. When it is proved that collectively all the work is done by the one and the same universal force, how then can a man think that he is free and independent? How then can it be said that man is both free and not free?

A poet says, "You have tied me to a plank and thrown me in the river. How then do you expect me not to be wet with water? How is it possible?" This is an interesting question. When you are bound, how can you have the feeling to be free? The dualists have not yet been able correctly to explain your freedom to act. Vedanta answers this question forcefully but lovingly. This mysterious secret could not be unveiled by the dualists and other religions. They have failed miserably to solve this mystery, but Vedanta says that your freedom to act in any way you like is due to your real Self or *Atma*, which is absolute freedom. It is due to *Atma* or God, who is declaring from within every man, "I am free," whose mere wish is responsible for the creation of this universe and who is present within every being. It is He who is the real Self of all. He is within; He is outside and He is everywhere. The Vedas say, "He is here, and verily He is there. He, who is there, is certainly here as well. He, who sees differentiation or diversity, will certainly go from one death to another."

This secret is clearly being revealed by all the other Vedas as well. He who is outside is also within you. "I am both animate and inanimate. I am far and near both. I am within and outside every one. I am All, Light."

This secret has been clearly revealed and explained at many place in the Vedas. If we start writing about this, it will cover book after book. Therefore only this much would suffice to say for the present.

As has already been mentioned, according to Vedanta there is an element of freedom and an element of dependence in man. It only means that in view of your real Self, *Atma*, which is within you and which you really are, you are free. However, from the point of view of your body, you are dependent, limited and under bondage. It is not correct to say that the body is free. From the body's point of view there is always something to subjugate it and to have control over it. The body is vulnerable to all sorts of diseases and is also bound to suffer the results of previous actions. It is also subject to change. It cannot therefore be called free. If at all you can be called free, it is because of your real Self which makes you say, "I am free, I am free." This real Self, which is within you, is within all. It is all-pervading and interpenetrating.

This is God which you really are.

At this moment, although the subject under discussion seemingly concerns dualism, yet it is meant to take you up towards monism. In order to explain the mystery to the dualists, we have to use their own language. You might have observed that the tutor while teaching a child often mispronounces a letter or even a word to suit the intelligence of his ward in the beginning. He does so only to make the child ultimately pronounce the letter or the word correctly. So too here, we have talked of *Atma* (real Self) and body as separate, or the inner and outer as different in the language of dualism. It does not mean that we want to inculcate in you the theory of dualism. On the other hand our aim is to take you through dualism towards monism. Through this process the mystery can be explained and solved more easily. Here you have first to understand that your real Self which is proclaiming from within you, "I am free; I am free," is the same Self which is interpenetrating in the outside objects as well.

You might have marked that when some part of your body is itching, your hand goes exactly on the same spot to relieve you of that sensation. But another person cannot do so. Why? It is because your own real Self is pervading throughout your body. Your own power is here, there and everywhere in your body. You are on the itching spot and also in your hand which relieved you of your itching sensation. Although we say, "I felt itching, and my hand relieved me of that sensation," yet the purpose of all this is to show the unity of "I" with the itching spot and also with the hand which removed that sensation. It also proves that the same real Self is pervading throughout an individual body.

A poet says, "You must lose yourself to such an extent as to do away with any trace of dualism." Seeking Him is also an evil, though beautiful. I am searching for the means to end all seeking, i.e., I want to be one with Him. My desire to meet Him is also like a curtain which prevents my union with Him. I therefore desire to be desireless, i.e., when I shall be one with the object of my desire, I shall cease to have any desire. I shall be then one with Him."

This means that our prayers are accepted only when we are lost in our real Self, when there is no idea of "I" or "Thou." In other words, when we are above narrow considerations of dualisms, "I" and "Thou" and when we have reached a stage where even intellect cannot reach, our prayers are accepted.

A poet says, " If I advance even to a hair's breadth, my (intellect's) wings will be scorched and burnt." It is only under such circumstances that our prayers are accepted, because at that moment the person praying is established in his real Self which is truth personified. As such, his prayers are bound to come true. Here at this stage, every desire is bound to be materialized, and every prayer granted. At that stage, this little "I" is free from egoism or selfishness. Vedanta does not recognize any God separate from you to listen to your prayers. There is no personal God to appear before you to accept and grant your prayers. At that stage you alone are all in all to listen to, to accept and to grant you your object of prayer.

From the above discussions it is clear that your own Self, which is one without a second, grants all the requests and prayers in this world. Your own real Self is also the Self of all. You are truth incarnate and whatever you think or resolve must come true. The wonder of all the wonders is that we do not even try to know or to realize that Self which is at the root of all the success in this world.

There is a story that a certain king had innumerable queens who were all devoted to please him. One day the king called all of them and said, "I am very much pleased with you. Express your desires. I will grant all your requests." At this someone made a request for a priceless pearl necklace; someone for ornaments studded with precious stones; some for a portion of the king's kingdom. There was only one queen who demanded the king himself. By so doing she made the king her own, and as such she became the owner of all the treasures and his entire kingdom. Similarly it is a pity that usually men only pray for the objects of worldly pleasure, which are valueless and transitory, instead of praying for God Himself, who controls this universe, who has the power to grant any request and who is almighty. Do not such persons deserve sympathy and compassion?

It is not only surprising but also sad that instead of rising above body and egoism we care more for our bodily connections than for trying to realize the eternal bliss through our real Self. We should have left the bodily enjoyments to our destiny and worked hard to achieve the stage of realization of Self. Alas, we act in a way which causes our degradation instead of spiritual sublimation.

A patient was suffering from two ailments, one concerning eyes and the other with regard to stomach. He went to the hospital and mentioned to the physician about his two ailments. The doctor gave him *surma* (eye powder) for the eyes and a digestive powder for his stomach ache. Unfortunately, the patient confused the packets of the two powders. He ate the eye powder and put the digestive powder into his eyes, with the result that both of his troubles were very much aggravated. Similarly, there is a great confusion with regard to the conduct in our daily life. We should have left the body and the body connection to destiny, but instead we make efforts for it. In other words, we are eating the eye powder. We should have made earnest efforts for realization of the Self, but instead we have left it to destiny. It means that we are applying the digestive powder to our eyes. That is why we are going down instead of rising up. Under such circumstances it is impossible for anyone to enjoy the true happiness without God realization.

Dear friends, if you are really keen to enjoy the real happiness due to realization of the Self or God, you have to work hard very sincerely to achieve that end. You have to give up all desires, and leave the bodily enjoyments to destiny, which will automatically look after them. Your real efforts should be to lose yourself in *Atma* and establish yourself in Godhood. In this way you will be in a position to enjoy the eternal bliss in the kingdom of heaven. This is the real *purushartha*. If you only sit on the royal throne of your Godhood, you will see that all your desires will be automatically fulfilled even without your wishing.

When the judge sits in his chair in the court, his only work is to listen to the cases and deliver his judgement. The remaining jobs in the court are automatically done. So too, when a saint is merged in Godhood, all his worldly jobs are automatically performed by nature, even without his gesture. Dear friends, you will reach this stage only when you make the right use of your efforts, i.e., when you leave the body enjoyments to destiny and make earnest efforts to achieve spiritual development.

Once the Romans asked Lord Jesus if they should pay tax to the king. This question was put to him with an ulterior motive. If Christ was to reply in negative, they would immediately inform the king that Jesus was preaching sedition. If he replied in affirmative, it would mean that he was not the "king of kings" as he called himself to be. They would then get an excuse to call him a liar. In reply to their question Lord Jesus put a coin in his palm and put a counter question to them asking the name of the king whose seal was on it. They all said that it bore the seal of Caesar. Then Jesus said, "Render unto Caesar that which belongs to Caesar, and render unto God that which belongs to God."

Similarly, put all your efforts to achieve God-realization, which has the seal of God, and leave your body enjoyments to destiny, which controls them. When a man works for a higher position, all the lower jobs are automatically achieved. Similarly, as a man makes efforts to advance towards his goal of God-realization, all his worldly necessities connected with his body are automatically fulfilled. This is the law of nature.

Om! Om! Om!

THE SACRED SYLLABLE OM

December 22, 1902

Hermetic Brotherhood Hall, San Francisco

My own Self in the form of ladies and gentlemen,

The other day a few words were spoken on the sacred *mantram* OM, and it was also explained that the subject could not be exhausted in seven or eight lessons. Volumes have been written in the Sanskrit language and are still being written today on this sacred syllable. In fact, all the Vedas, all Vedanta, all the sacred scriptures of the Hindus are contained in this syllable Om.

There are many different sects in India, but all the sects pay their heartfelt homage to Om. The Hebrews, the Mohammedans and the Christians, all end their prayers with "Amen." Mohammedans also do that, although they do not pronounce the word as "Amen" but as "Ameen."

In your ordinary prayer what part does "Amen" play? It comes in at a place where all speech stops, where all talk terminates, at a point where the soul melts into divinity. You go on pouring the language of the heart until that point is reached where the whole being is about to be melted into divinity.Where the ineffable, the unspeakable, the inexpressible is reached, there is Amen. Then what is Amen? It is Om, nothing else. In all your sacred prayers Amen or Ameen occupies a palce that exactly satisfies the meaning of the word "Vedanta" or "the end of speech" and very nearly represents the essence of Vedanta; that is Om.

The literal meaning of Vedanta is the end of knowledge, the end of speech, a point where all speech, all thought stops, and among the Hindus the whole of Vedanta is represented by Om. The meaning in which that word is used in the Vedas will now be brought to your notice—Om. A-U-M.

The Tantriks explain Om in their own way. The Shaivas have their own way. The Vaishnavas have their own interpretation, and all other Hindu sects have their peculiar explanation, but the interpretation that is about to be given is universal; it is to be given as the very fountainhead of Vedanta.

Om consists of A-U-M. The sound A, in accordance with the teachings of Vedanta, represents the so-called material universe, the solid-seeming world, the world of gross senses, all that is observed in your wakeful state. All the experiences of the dreamland are represented by U (oo). The observer as well as the things observed, both the subject and the objects of the dreaming state, are denoted by the sound U. The psychic or astral plane, the world of spirits and all the heavens and hells, are signified by U. M represents all the unknown in the deep sleep state and even in your wakeful state all that is unknown, all that is beyond comprehension of the intellect.

Thus Om, or A-U-M covers all the three-fold experience of man and stands for all the phenomenal worlds. There is in A-U-M the common principle called *Amatra*, that which signifies the imperishable, immutable *noumenon*, or "the thing in itself" running through and pervading the threefold phenomena. This *Amatra* will be treated fully in another lecture. Suffice it to say that Om represents the All.

All the philosophy of Europe and America is based on the experience in the wakeful state and takes little or no notice of the experience of the dreaming or deep sleep state. The Hindu says, "You start with imperfect data. How can your solution of the problem of the universe be correct?"

Philosophers limit themselves to the wakeful state. Mill, Hamilton, Berkeley, even Spencer—all of them—base all their discoveries and investigations on the experience gained in the wakeful state alone. There they want to discover the fountainhead of all force, energy or any name they may please to give it. Now see here; if you are given a mathematical problem and are asked to draw a conclusion, all the premises, the whole hypothesis, you will have to consider. How can you solve a problem correctly when you take up only a part of the data? Vedanta takes the whole data. Your data are threefold; your worldly experiences are threefold, and all these should be considered. The world of wakeful state disappears entirely in the other two states and yet you, that is to say, the Self, lives in the dream state and in the deep sleep state. You are not dead, are you? The intellect and personal consciousness vanish entirely in the deep sleep state, and yet the real Self, the real "you," remains the same. The unchangeable and immutable principle, this reality, runs through the threefold worlds as your true *Atman*, or Self. This is Om. You have no right to take mind, intellect or brain as yourself. How do you know that the world exists; how do you know that the universe is here? Because you touch things, you see things, you hear things, you taste and smell things; that is the only proof. You could say that here is Victor Hugo, Robert Ingersol, Emerson; all these great thinkers are writing so much about this world, and so the world must exist. We ask how do you know that religious books are there? You know they are there through the senses.

Your senses are the only direct or indirect proof of the existence of this world.

Sensation is the primary cause of all perception, intellection, etc. Sensation is not limited to your wakeful state. In your wakeful state your senses are in the gross form, but do you not sense and perceive in your dreams; have you not sense organs peculiar to that state? The outer eyes and the outer ears are not working there. In the dreamland you create objects of senses and the corresponding sense organs or senses simultaneously. Thus we see that in the dreamland the senses and the objects sensed are like the positive and negative poles of the same power or like the obverse and reverse of the same coin. In dreams the subject and the objects spring up together. Both the subject and the objects of dreams are comprised by the sound U in A-U-M, and the underlying reality in which both the subject and the objects appear as waves is the real *Atman*, or Om. According to Vedanta in your wakeful state your senses and the objects are co-related to each other just as the positive and negative poles of the same power. In dreams even though the objects are produced instantaneously, they appear to have a long past of their own. Similarly in the wakeful state the objects of the world together with their past history make their appearance simultaneously with the percipient subject. When you say that this world is real, that this is the solid, rigid world, the statement is entirely founded on the evidence of the perceiving senses or subject, which is equivalent to the dreaming ego calling the objects of the dream real or to the man calling his dog in the picture on canvas real, whereas in reality both are unreal.

What brought the senses into existence? The

elements. How do you know of these elements? Through the senses. Is not that reasoning in a circle? This establishes the illusory nature of the world in the wakeful state. As in dreamland so long as you are dreaming, the objects are real. Those objects are no more when we rise in the wakeful state. In the wakeful state all things are solid, but when we are in the deep sleep state, where is the world? Nowhere—gone, gone. Here we see that the definition of reality does not apply to the phenomena of the waking or dreaming state.

The Hindus define reality as that which persists in all circumstances. That which appears to exist at one time and like a shadow disappears after a while must be a delusive phenomenon. The same definition of reality is given by Herbert Spencer. Why do you say that the dreamland is unreal? Because when you are awake it is not there. Then so does not this very definition of unreality apply to the wakeful state? When in the dreamland or deep sleep state the wakeful world exists no longer.

The sound A in A-U-M indicates the apparent subject and objects of the wakeful state as mere manifestations of the underlying reality, "me." The first letter A stands for this stern reality, your Self as underlying and manifesting the illusory material world of the wakeful state; U represents the psychic world, and the last letter M denotes the absolute Self as underlying the chaotic state and manifesting itself as all the unknown. When chanting Om, the wise have to concentrate their attention and put forth feelings in realizing their Self to be the stern reality which manifests the three worlds and also destroys the three worlds, just as the sun reveals the colors at sunrise or dawn and also absorbs them back into himself before noon.

These worlds are phenomenal. In your dreaming state you see a wolf and fear that the wolf will devour you; you are frightened, but it is not a wolf that you see, it is yourself. So Vedanta tells you that even in the wakeful state it is "Ye that are the enemy or the friend. Ye are the sun and the pond in which the sun is reflected. Ye are the lamp and the moth. The bitterest enemy that ye have, ye are that enemy, nobody else." While chanting Om, you have to work your mind up to such a pitch of realization of this fact that all jealousy and ill will may be rooted out of the mind, may be voted out. Weed out this idea of separateness. The figure and form of the friend or foe is a mere dream. You are the friend and you are the foe. Are the things you did yesterday with you today? Are they not a dream? They are gone. The things of yesterday—where are they, are they not gone? In this sense also the experience of the wakeful state is a dream; the experience of the dream state is a dream. The hard cash, the stern reality, the real Self, is behind them. Realize that.

Some people want to materialize thought rather than to realize all matter is mere thought. They regard the material plane to be real as compared with the astral world or the world of thought. According to Vedanta the material as well as the astral worlds are unreal. You must rise above both because rest, true peace, happiness can be had only when the reality, the hard cash behind the scenes, is realized.

In AUM, A (ah) is sometimes called a *matra* or form; U is often called a *matra* or form; M is called a *matra* or form. However, Om does not stop at *matra* or form; it stands for the reality, the hard cash, which runs through, which underlies all these *matras*. People say, "We want life; we don't want mere ideas." O, what is life? Is it the life of the dream state or the deep sleep state, or is it the life of the wakeful state that you want? All this is only apparent. The reality, the true life, is your Self. There are stern laws which will not allow you enjoyments of pleasure forever through the senses. Is it possible for you to sell yourself to the senses, to the sense plane, and be happy? No, it is impossible. There are most unrelenting, unrestrainable laws which cannot allow you to be happy in sensual pleasures.

The *Atman* is the real life, the hard cash. Realize that, and these material pleasures will begin to seek you. Just as the moth comes to the burning flame, just as the river flows to the ocean, just as the small official pays his respects to a great emperor, just so will pleasures come to you, when you have perfectly known and felt your true Self, your divine majesty, the real glorious *Atman*. This *Atman* is represented by Om.

It has been shown how out of A-U-M, these three *matras*, the Hindus, especially the Vedas, give you a clue to the underlying reality that you are. Om means the underlying reality behind the scenes, the eternal truth, the indestructible Self that you are. Thus when you sing this sacred *mantram* Om, you will have to throw your intellect and your body into your true Self, to make these melt into the real *Atman*. Realize and sing it in the language of feeling; sing it with your acts; sing it through every pore of your body. Let it course through your veins; let it pulsate in your bosom; let every hair on your body and every drop of your blood tingle with the truth that you are the

Light of lights, the Sun of suns, the ruler of the universe, the Lord of lords, the true Self. The sun and stars are your handiwork and the heavens and earth your workmanship. Everything declares your glory, and all nature pays you homage.

Om! Om! Om!

THE SUN OF SELF ON THE WALL OF MIND

January 12, 1903
Golden Gate Hall, San Francisco

The greatest *sadhu*, the greatest Indian monk, the greatest swami in this world is the sun, the rising sun. The rising sun comes to you every day dressed in the apparel, in the costume, of a Vedantic monk. In tonight's discourse this sun will represent to you the Immutable with reference to the changeable bodies. We shall take the sun, the swami, the *sadhu*, the red-appareled sun, symbol of the true *Atma*, the real Self, which is unchangeable, which is immutable, the same today, yesterday and forever. With reference to the sun we shall point out the changeable, the variable things which stand for the changeable bodies in man. Man has got the changeable things in him, and there is in man the immutable, the unchangeable, the eternal real *Atman.* The real *Atman* is like the sun, and the changeable elements are the three bodies, the gross body, the subtle body and the seed body. These are names that Rama gives to these bodies. In Sanskrit they are *sthula, sukeshma* and *karana sharir*. These are not the self but the non-self. These are variable, fickle; these are not your Self. Your Self is the immutable, the unchangeable. This is to be shown.

In order to give you a clear idea of the three bodies and the true *Atman*, we shall resort to an illustration. You will kindly attend very carefully. Tonight there will be talked to you no logic, no great argumentation. Tonight the proposition of man as proved by the Hindus will be made clear to you. It will be clearly enunciated so that you may at once comprehend it, and afterwards, if time be, we shall enter into philosophy and reason out every side of the question. You know that before bringing logic to bear upon a theme we ought to understand what the proposition is. So tonight the meaning of the proposition will be made clear, and you will see that even in this enunciation, or this clearing away of the clouds, and the understanding of the proposition, there will be, as it were, a proof by themselves. As Pope puts it—

> Virtue is a fairy of such beauteous mien,
> As to be loved needs only to be seen.

So the truth has such a glorious beauty that in order to enter deep into your hearts, it is necessary only to see it clearly. The sun requires no other proof of its existence. To see the sun is to prove the sun. Everything that is, is seen in some outside light, but light itself does not require some other light in order that it may be visible. So tonight the proposition is simply to be laid before you without any arguments and without any logic, so called. Now we come to the illustration.

You will kindly take yourself with Rama to the Himalayan glaciers. There we see all dazzling scenes—diamond mountains, all white, an ocean of white glaciers so dazzling, so sparkling, so beautiful, splendid, inspiring. There we find no vegetation, no animal life, no man, no woman. There is upon these glaciers to be seen one source of life, the sun, the glorious orb that shines upon these fairy scenes. Oh, what a splendid sight! Sometimes the light of the sun sifted through the clouds falls upon the land and makes the whole landscape blaze up in the color of fire, makes the whole scene assume the swami's garb, converts the whole scene into a *sadhu*, an Indian monk. After a while the whole scene becomes yellow, but there is one thing, and one thing only, on the scene, nothing else. That is the sun.

Now you observe that in these glaciers there are the greatest rivers of Hindustan, concealed, latent. All the big rivers of India emanate, flow out, from these glaciers. Here in these glaciers is the source, or the seed body, of the river. You will kindly come down with Rama to the second stage of the river life.

Here we come to another phase; we come now to other kinds of sights and landscapes. We are still in the mountains, but not at the snow-capped summits; lower down we are. Here for miles and miles, for dozens and scores of miles, we have magnificent roses covering every spot, and the whole air fragrant, redolent with the sweet, delicious scent of the roses. Here we have beautiful nightingales and other birds singing, indicting valentines all the year round. Here we have magnificent warblers filling the air with their sweet notes. Also we find amongst the magnificent, beautiful, charming trees the most attractive Ganga, or some other stream, treading its winding course in a zig-zag way, playing, frisking about in the mountains. Oh, beautiful brooks, beautiful rivulets we find here. Here in these beautiful brooklets are the shadows of the trees on the banks reflected; and these brooklets are going about in a most charming, in a most playful way, now taking this trend and now that trend, going around and around, turning this way and that way, and singing all along, flow these rivers, brooklets, rivulets.

What is this? This is the second stage of the river's life. Here the river is in its subtle body. This subtle body emanated from the seed body of the river. You know that upon the seed body of the river the sun was shining, and through the action of the sun's heat and light upon the seed body of the river, the subtle body of the river came out. This is the subtle body. It is very fickle, vague, meandering, zig-zag. It is now jumping down and taking long leaps in hot haste and in great fury, then it subsides into a lake or a calm. It is very vague, fickle, changing.

Let us descend a little to the plains. Now in the plains we have different scenes. The same river which we saw present in the seed form upon the snow-capped glaciers and which adopted a most fantastic and most poetic aspect in its subtle form lower down on the mountains, the same Ganga, becomes a mighty stream. It has undergone a great change. It has put on new clothing, new color. It does not keep its original transparency and its original limpidness; it becomes dirty, turbid, and it becomes changed in color. Muddy it becomes, and at the same time it changes its speed. As it becomes now slow, very slow, it becomes more useful. Upon the surface of this mighty river float boats, float ships; traffic is carried on. People come and bathe, and the water of the great river is utilized in canals and aqueducts for irrigating the lands and for fertilizing the country around. This third stage of the river's life is the gross body of the river. Still what about the life of the river? What about the real motive power of the river? The real motive power of the river is the sun, the glorious orb. Now let us apply this illustration to man.

Where are your three bodies, and how are they related to one another and to the real Self, your true Self, or the *Atma*? What are you in reality in your deep sleep state, where you are unconscious of everything else, where you know nothing about the world, where father is no father, mother is no mother, house is no house, and the world is no world, where there is ignorance, ignorance and nothing but ignorance, where there is a state of chaos, a state of death, a state of annihilation, so to say, a state of nothingness?

Vedanta says that there in that state which you have never examined, we have the seed body of man, lying prostrate and flat beneath the true Self, or *Atma*, of man. There, if we compare man's life to the river's life, we have the true Self like the sun, shining over the glaciers. In your deep sleep state this world is not present, nor is it present in the dreamland; there is only dreamlessness. When you wake up, you say that in that deep sleep state is present nothing, nothing, nothing. Vedanta says that indeed in that deep sleep state nothing is present. However, you know that Hegel has clearly shown (the Hindus have anticipated Hegel, that German philosopher) and has proven that this nothing is something, that this nothing is also the seed body; this is the glacier of your life. The Bible puts it that out of nothing was something created by God; so the Hindus have also shown that out of this seed body, which you describe as nothing after waking up, there springs forth the whole world. If philosophers come out and say that out of nothing something can never come, Vedanta says that this which we have called nothing is in reality not nothing; it is called nothing by you only when you wake up. It is the seed body; it is like the glaciers. Realize the sun within, realize the God within, realize the *Atma*, which creates out of this glacier of the seed body this whole universe. Realize that sun or God or *Atma*. You will ask what this means. Listen please.

When you get up, you say, "I slept so profoundly

that I saw nothing in my dreams." Vedanta says that this statement is just like a statement made by a man who said that at the dead of night, at such and such a place, there was not a single being present. The judge asked him if this statement was true. He said, "Yes." "Is this statement made on hearsay, or is it founded on your own evidence? Are you an eyewitness?" asked the judge. He said, "Yes, I am." "All right. Then, if you were an eyewitness, and if you wish us to understand that your statement is correct, that there was nobody present, then in order that your statement may be right, you, at least, must have been present on the scene. But if you were present on the scene, this statement is not literally true. Since you are a human being, at least one human being was present on the scene. Thus the statement that nobody was present, that there was not a single human being present on the scene, is false; that is a contradictory statement. In order that it may be true as you wish us to understand it to be true, it must be wrong."

Similarly when we make this statement after waking up, "Oh sir, I slept profoundly, and I enjoyed such deep slumbers that nothing was present on the scene," Rama says, "Sir, you were present. If you had been asleep, if your true Self, the real *Atma*, and the real sun, the real orb, the real God, had been asleep, then who would have borne witness to the nothingness of the deep sleep or chaos of the dream? As you bore witness to the nothingness of the deep sleep or chaos of the dream, you must have been present there." Thus in your deep sleep state, Vedanta says that there are two things, at least, to be seen, the nothingness which is like the glaciers or like the seed body and the withness light, the sun, the glorious

Atma, the resplendent Self or God, which is witnessing all that and shining even upon the desolation of the deep sleep state. There that true Self is the sun immutable, and that nothingness of the deep sleep state is the seed body, which is changeable, mutable, alterable and fickle. Why is it changeable and fickle? Because when you come down to the dreamland, that nothingness is gone; that nothingness is no more. If that chaos or nothing of the deep sleep state had been your real Self, it would have lasted forever, but it changes. When you descend into the dreamland, the very capability of changing implies that it is not real. That seed body is not real. You will be astonished; you will ask how this phenomenal world of ours did emanate from that nothing. It is a fact. You have been thinking matters differently in Europe and America; you have been taking matters in a topsy-turvy state. Believe Rama that this is a truth which must permeate every individual, which must enter the heart of each and all in this universe, sooner or later.

Here people are accustomed to take things from the bottom to the top. They want to make rivers flow uphill, the unnatural course. So you will be astonished at this statement just now made by Rama that out of that nothingness of your deep sleep state comes your dreamland experience. Just examine; just reflect. Is not that the plan of nature? Wherefrom did this earth of yours come? This earth of yours was once in the nebular state. All this was once in a state which had no form, which was akin to your deep sleep state. Out of that chaotic state have sprung up by slow degrees your vegetable kingdom, animal kingdom, and man. Vedanta tells you that what you find in the whole of nature, what you find true from the physical standpoint, the same is true from the metaphysical standpoint. If this whole world springs from chaos or nothing, so to say, your dreamland and wakeful state also sprang from that deep sleep or chaotic state, the state of nothingness. Just so it is found in the life of every man. When a baby he is in a state most resembling the state of nothingness as it were. Out of that state by slow degrees he comes into the other state which you call higher, though higher and lower are relative terms.

What is the rule in the whole universe is the rule with the ordinary life of every man. Out of the deep sleep state springs this dreaming state. People want to explain the dreaming state as dependent on the wakeful state. You will be astonished when Vedanta puts matters to you in their true light and shows that all the European philosophers, all your Hegels and Kants, cannot explain thoroughly the phenomena of dreams. We have no time tonight to dwell upon the subject, but this will be proved to you either in a lecture or in a book form.

We come to the dream state. In the dreamland we come, as it were, from the glaciers to the lower mountains. You are still on the mountains, asleep. Here the subtle body, the dreaming self, finds itself in a fantastic land, in a poetic region; the dreaming self of yours is now a bird, is now a king. Immediately it becomes a beggar. It is now a man who has lost his way on the Himalayan mountains and then it becomes the citizen of a big city like London. It is now in this city and then in that city. How changeable! Just as the streams in the mountains are changeable, meandering, fickle, taking different turns every now and then, such is the state of your dreaming self. You live in a land of imagination. There the dead becomes alive, and those people who are living you find sometimes dead—strange land, the land of fantasy and the land of poetry!

After the dreaming experience, passing through the mountains, as it were, in your second stage, you come down to the plains; you wake up. In your wakeful state you make up the gross body, just as the river acquires a gross body when descending upon the plains. You know when the rivers come down from the mountains and enter upon the plains, their subtle body remains just the same, but it puts upon itself a red or muddy mantle. That fresh, pure water remains hidden in mud and in the clay and soil of the plains. There the subtle body of the river as it was seen in the mountains has not changed, but it is simply wearing new clothing, it has put on a new costume. Thus when the subtle body of the river has descended to the plains and put on a new muddy costume, we say that the river is in its gross body. It was not so when the subtle body came from the seed body. Then the seed body had to melt down and produce the subtle body. Now in the wakeful state, the subtle body had not to melt or change; it had simply to put on new garments, new costumes. That is what actually happens.

The sun which was shining upon the seed body, the same sun shines equally upon the subtle body of the river; and the same sun which shines upon the seed body and subtle body of the river shines equally upon the gross body of the river. The true *Atma* or real Self, which was seen shining upon the deep sleep state's body, shines also upon your dreamland and upon your wakeful state, upon the gross body, but where lies the difference? The difference lies in the reflection of the sun. When the sun was shining upon the seed body of the river, upon the glaciers, the image of the sun was not seen there. The action of the sun was intense upon the glaciers, but the reflection or image of the sun was not seen. But when the sun began to shine upon the subtle body of the river, the sun was reflected.

What does this image imply? This image in origin is the real Self, the true *Atma*, the unchangeable, the immutable in you, the true divinity, *Atma* or God. The same God that is present in you when you are in the deep sleep state shines upon your seed body, but examine that in the deep sleep state no egoism is present; you have no idea of "I am asleep," "I grow," "I digest the food." The real Self is there, but no ego is there. This false, apparent ego, which is looked upon as the self by people, is not there. In the dreaming state it becomes apparent, and it becomes apparent also in the wakeful state. However there is a difference in the ego of your dreamland and the ego of your wakeful state. In your dreamland the ego which has been to you as the reflection or shadow of the true *Atma* or God is fickle, changeable, vague, unsettled, hazy, exactly as the reflection of the sun in the stream when it is upon the mountains is vague, meandering, changeable. On the other hand, in your wakeful state this ego is definite, permanent, as in the slow stream, slow river, when it is flowing upon the plains.

Here is something more to be told. People ask what right you have to call the gross body the after-effect, or resultant, of the subtle body. People ask what right you have to place the dream state above the wakeful state. Mark it. Of what elements is your wakeful experience composed? Your wakeful experience rests upon time, space and causality. Can you think of any substance, anything in this world, without the idea of time, space and causality entering into it? Never, never. You cannot conceive of anything without time, space or causality. Now this time, space and causality are like the web and weft of your world. Mark them. They are in your dreamland, and they are in your wakeful state. You know Max Muller, while giving his introduction in his translation of Kant's *Critique of Pure Reason*, says that Kant teaches the same philosophy as Vedanta. He says that Kant has clearly shown that time, space and causality are a priori, and the Hindus have not shown it. Rama is going to tell you that Max Muller did not read enough of the Hindu scriptures. Rama is going to tell you that the Hindus proved time, space and causality to be a priori, to be subjective, and out of that it is shown that the wakeful experience of yours is from one standpoint the after-effect of your dreamland experience. You will patiently listen. In your deep sleep state you have no idea of time, no idea of space, no idea of causality. You come down to the dreamland. There time makes its appearance, space comes into existence, and causality also comes into existence. The Hindus tell you that the time, space and causality of your dreamland come out of your deep sleep state in the same way as the tiny sprout comes forth from the seed in its feeble, weak form. In your wakeful state, time, space and causality ripen into the state of a mighty tree. They become strong and ripen into the state of a mighty river; they assume their gross form. Just as you develop, the ideas of time, space and causation also develop with your understanding. Thus the subject is nothing else but a resultant of time, space and causation as they develop. In your dreams you have time, but compare the time of your dreams with the time of your wakeful state. The time of the dream is fickle, vague, hazy, dim, unsettled, indefinite, and the time of the wakeful state is naturally the ripened form, Rama says, the strong developed form of your time in the dreamland. In your dreams you know that the dead become alive and the living become dead sometimes. It is not so in your wakeful state; there time is definite. The past becomes future, and the future becomes past in your dreamland; it is not so in the wakeful state. You may have heard of Mohammad, who in his dream spent a lot of time in ascending to the eighth heaven, but when he woke up, he found that only two seconds had passed.

Similarly the things of your wakeful state are different, not in kind but in intensity, in degree, from the things of your dreamland state. Oft-times Rama wrote poetry in dreams, but when he got up and looked at that poetry, the lines did not scan and it was not coherent; there was a want of continuity, unity. The reasoning of the dreamland is related to the reasoning of the wakeful state as the subtle body of the river is related to the gross body. The space of your dreamland is related to the space of your wakeful state in the same way. Space is rigid, constant, invariable. Now you will ask how it is that in our dreams we always see the same things which we see in our wakeful state? Our dreams are only the reminiscences, are only the remembrances, of our wakeful state. Rama says, "What of that? Let it be so." What is the seed? Out of a seed comes up a beautiful sapling; it is changeable and fickle, and out of this changeable, fickle sapling grows out or develops forth a gigantic, strong, rigid tree. All right. Again out of this rigid tree come some more seeds, the same kind of seeds as gave rise to this tree. Now in the seeds the whole tree is contained. The tree has put all its essence and all its power back into the seeds. Then should we argue that the tree did not spring from the seed? Have we any right to argue that the tree did not come out of the seed? No, no we have no right to argue that way.

Similarly Vedanta says that the *shushupti*, the deep sleep state, is like the seed. Out of that comes the dreamland, and from that flows out or develops the wakeful, gross body. Again if your wakeful experience can be condensed back into your sleep, it is but natural. If your wakeful experience can be condensed or forced into your dreamland, into your dreaming experience, it does not contradict Rama's statement. Let it be. Still that will not entitle you to say that your wakeful state did not develop out of your subtle body or the dreamland. When the whole tree is condensed and put into the seed, this does not entitle us to say that the tree did not spring from the seed. If in your dreams you usually have the reminiscences of your wakeful state, that does not entitle you to gainsay the statement made by Rama that out of time, space and causation, out of the differentiation of the dreamland, or the dreaming experience, was developed, or evolved, the wakeful experience.

The Vedanta philosophy says that the dreamland and wakeful experience originated from the nothingness, or chaos, of your deep sleep. When the Hindus say that the world is nothing or the world is the result of ignorance, they mean that the deep sleep state in which you had a kind of nothing, a chaos, that chaos or nothing of your deep sleep state, is ignorance, condensed ignorance. If you want to say ignorance per se, there the deep sleep state is the ignorance per se, and out of that ignorance, or darkness, comes this world, comes this differentiation and change, and that ignorance is changeable. You know that in your dreamland you have two kinds of things, the subject and the object, according to Vedanta the subject and object make their appearance simultaneously. There in your dreams you become the seer on one side and the object seen on the other side. If you see a horse and the rider in a dream, both make their appearance together; if you see a mountain in the dream, the mountain is the object and you the seer or observer. There the object and the subject make their appearances together. There by a kind of time the past and future of the dream is also simultaneous with the object; the past, present and future of the dream, the causation of the dream and the subject and object of the dream, all these make their appearance simultaneously.

Similarly Vedanta says that in your wakeful state also you are the object seen, and you are the seeing subject. You are the friends and foes on that side, and you are their observer on this side. You are the enemies on one side, and you are the friends on the other side. You are everything. However, all these apparent phenomena of the dream, phenomena of the deep sleep state, phenomena of the wakeful state, all these phenomena are mutable, changeable, fickle, uncertain, indefinite. The real Self, which was compared to the sun, the real *Atma*, shines upon the three bodies in the same way that the sun shines upon the three bodies of the river. That *Atma* is immutable, unchangeable. That *Atma* or sun shines upon the glacier of your deep sleep state. By your *Atma* or sun is the deep sleep state illumined, and by that *Atma* or sun is your wakeful experience illumined.

You see again that the sun shines not only upon the three bodies of one river, but the same sun shines upon the three bodies of all the rivers in this world in exactly the same way. Similarly what if the river of this body is different from the river of that body? What if this river of life flows in a different way from the river of life in that case? All these rivers of life, all these streams of existence have the same eternal, immutable, constant *Atma*, or the Sun of suns, the Light of lights, shining over them at all times, under all circumstances, unchangeable, immutable. That you are; that you are. That is the real Self, and your real Self is the real Self of your friend, is the real Self of each and all. Your real Self is not only present with you in the wakeful state, it is equally present in the deep sleep state; it is equally present under all changes and circumstances.

Realize that real Self stands above all anxiety, above all fear, stands above all tribulation and trouble. Nobody can harm you; no one can injure you.

Om! Om! Om!

AIDS TO REALIZATION—PRANAYAMA

March 8, 1903

U.S.A.

My own Self in the form of brothers and sisters,

Today Rama will discourse on certain matters which will be of great help to those who have listened to his previous lectures. We will take up *pranayama* first. *Pranayama* literally means "control of breath." The Hindu books on yoga give eight principal methods of controlling the breath. Rama will lay before you only one method known as *pranayama*, a very important method of controlling the breath. You will put the question, "What is the use of controlling the breath?" In answer to that Rama simply says, "Learn this method of controlling the breath, and put it into practice, and your own practice will show that it is extremely useful, highly beneficial." Whenever you feel dizzy, whenever you feel in dumps, in blues, dejected, crest-fallen, whenever you feel put out, practice *pranayama* which Rama is going to lay before you, and you will see that immediately you are rested. You will find the immediate use of controlling the breath this way. Again when you begin to write on any subject, when you begin to think on any subject, and you find that you cannot control your thoughts, practice this *pranayama*, and immediately you will marvel at the powers you attain. Everything is in order. Everything is put in the most desirable state. These are the benefits of *pranayama*. It will cure you of many physical diseases. You will be cured of stomach ache, heart ache, headache by *pranayama*. We will now see what is that. In this country people are trying to control the breath this way or that, but

Rama lays before you a method which has stood the test of time, which was practiced in India in the most ancient days, and which is practiced there even today. All those who have practiced it from the most ancient times to the present time have found it highly beneficial.

In order to practice *pranayama* you must sit in a most comfortable, easy position. To sit cross-legged is the most comfortable posture, but this posture will kill you, a West Indian, so you may sit in an easy chair. Keep your body straight, backbone stiff, head up, chest out, eyes front. Place the right hand thumb on the right nostril, and inhale the breath slowly through the left nostril. Go on inhaling slowly, until you feel at ease; go on inhaling as long as you conveniently can. While inhaling, let not the mind be vacant. While you are inhaling, let the mind be concentrated on the thought that all omnipotent, omniscient, omnipresent divinity is being inhaled, that you are drinking divinity, the godhead, the whole world the whole universe. When you think you have filled in the air to your best, then using a finger close the left nostril, through which you were inhaling. Thus when you stop both nostrils, let not the breath escape through the mouth. Keep the inhaled breath within you in the lungs, in the stomach, in the abdomen. When all the cavities are filled with air, the air which you have inhaled, and when the breathed air is in you, let not the mind be vacant; let the mind be centered in the idea, in the truth that you are divinity, the Almighty God that fills, permeates and pervades everything, every atom and molecule in the universe. Feel that. Put forth all your energies to realize that idea; apply all your strength to feel your divinity. When you think that you cannot hold the breath any longer, then keep the left hand nostril shut; open the right hand nostril, and through the right hand nostril, slowly, gradually exhale. There let the mind not remain at rest, let it work; let it feel that just as the breath goes, the impurities of the stomach are being driven off. So is all impurity, unchastity, all that was unclean, all that was wicked, savoring of wickedness, all ignorance exhaled, driven off and deserted. All weakness is gone; no weakness remains, no ignorance, no fear, no anxiety, no pain, no worry, no troubles. All have ceased, have gone, have left you. Go on exhaling so long as you conveniently can, and when you think that you cannot exhale any longer, then try to keep all air shut out with both nostrils open. Take off the hand from your nose. Do not allow the air to come in for some time, for so long as you can, and while by your efforts the air is not allowed to enter the lungs through the nostrils, let the mind be again at work, and let it feel; let it be exerted to its full power and strength in realizing that this is the unlimited divinity. All time and space is conceived by me as my own real *Atman* Self. Feel that this divinity is beyond time, space and causation, is not limited by anything in this world. It is beyond imagination, beyond thought, beyond everything. Feel that.

Thus you mark that in this *pranayama*, as laid before you so far, there are four processes, both physical and mental. The first process was inhaling. The inhaling part was the physical process. The idea, the way of feeling and thinking and applying your mind and exerting your energy to realize that divinity, that divinity am I, this idea was the mental process connected with it. Again, while you kept the breath in your lungs, there was a double process, the physical process of keeping it in your lungs, and the mental process of feeling that you were the whole universe. In the third process you exhaled through the right nostril and threw off all weakness with firm determinations to keep yourself rooted, established, seated in the divinity, never to allow any weakness or any demon temptation to approach you. Then there was the fourth process of keeping the breath outside. Thus the first half of *pranayama* is completed by this fourth process. After going through this fourth process, you may take a little rest. Then allow the breath to fill your nostrils, as it may. Inhale and exhale just as you inhale and exhale rapidly after taking a long walk. This natural inhalation and exhalation, which will go on very rapidly, is *pranayama* by itself. That is the natural *pranayama*. So after taking rest this way, after allowing your lungs to inhale and exhale for some time, begin again. Now begin not with the left hand nostril but with the right hand one. Mental process is the same as before. Only the nostrils are changed. Inhale through the right hand nostril, and while inhaling feel that you are inhaling divinity. After inhaling to your fill, so long as conveniently you can, keep the breath within you, and again, when the breath is within you, feel that you are the breath and life of the whole universe, that you fill and enliven the wide world. After that, exhale through the left hand nostril, and feel that just as the sun drives off the mist, fog, cold, darkness, so you are driving off all weakness, all darkness from your mind. No mist, fog, darkness or cold. Then keep the breath outside your nose, and try to elongate and lengthen every process. Altogether we have eight processes in this practice. The first four processes form one half of the *pranayama*, and the last four form the second half of the *pranayama*. Try to lengthen every one of these processes as long as and as much as you can. Here is harmonious motion. Just as a pendulum has double oscillation, so here you have to make a pendulum of your breath. You will see by your own experience that you gain immense strength. Most of your diseases leave you; consumption, diseases of the stomach, blood diseases, almost every disease will leave you if you practice this.

Rama finds that when people begin to practice *pranayama*, most of them fall sick. The reason is that they do not adopt the natural course. They begin to inhale and exhale for such a long interval that it makes them sick. Be natural in every part of this breathing process. Make efforts; do your best to lengthen every process, but do not fatigue yourself. Do not work much yourself. If after performing only the first two processes, say, the inhalation and keeping the breath in your lungs, you feel tired, stop. Stop. You are under no obligation. The next day be more considerate, and while performing the first process or the second process, try to keep your energies reserved, so that you may be able to continue the remaining processes; be judicious.

This is the only favorable method of controlling the breath. This is a kind of physical exercise. Those who think that this *pranayama* has something mystical, some divine meaning in it are mistaken. Those who think that the highest realization culminates in it and that there is nothing higher than it are mistaken. *Pranayama*, or this control of breath, has nothing supernatural in it. It is an ordinary exercise. Just as you go out and take physical exercise, so is this a kind of exercise of the lungs. There is no real significance in it, nothing mystic about it.

One thing more ought to be said in connection with *pranayama*. When you begin to inhale or exhale, keep your (you will pardon if Rama uses that word) abdomen, or lower part of the body, drawn in. That will be of great use to you. Again when you inhale and exhale, let the breath reach and fill all your belly. Let not the breath simply go down to the heart and no farther. Let the breath go deeper down. Let every cavity of your body, all the upper half of your body, be filled. Well, this will do for *pranayama*, and those who want to concentrate their minds on Vedantic lines, will find it a wonderful aid to practice *pranayama* before they begin to chant Om, before they begin to concentrate their mind on any method they have read in the Vedantic literature.

Now will Rama lay before you another method of concentrating the mind. This is a form of prayer. It is not a prayer in the sense that it begs, asks or seeks anything from God. It is a prayer in this sense that it enables you to realize your divinity. Sit at your ease. Sit in the same way as you were asked to sit when practicing *pranayama*. You may close your eyes, begin in a prayerful mood, or keep your eyes half closed, just as you wish. Then say, reading from the paper I gave you, "There is but one reality, Om! Om! Om! There is but one reality." You know that that is the truth. All those who have taken interest in Rama's lectures know that that is the truth, and when you are convinced that that is the truth, feel it. There is but one reality. Say that in the language of feeling, say that with your whole heart; melt in the idea. "There is but one reality, Om! Om! Om!" Now see that after this verse, "There is but one reality," there is written opposite to it, Om! Om! Om! What does that signify? That signifies that when you have filled your heart and saturated your mind with the idea that there is but one reality, instead of reading out all these words, "one, two, three, four, five," say only one word, Om, as this one word represents the whole idea for you. In algebra, we represent big quantities by x or y, a or b or some other letter. Just so, when you have read out this thought, "There is but one reality," this name Om, which is the holy of holies, this name Om, possessing the highest powers of divinity or God, should be chanted, and while chanting it feel the idea that there is but one reality. While your lips are chanting Om, your whole soul should feel the idea that there is but one reality. At present to you the words, "There is but one reality," are most probably mere jargon; they convey no sense to you. But if you have heard Rama's lectures, you must know that there is but one reality. It ought to have a concrete meaning for you. It means that all this phenomenal universe, which dampens our spirit and mars our joy, all this phenomenal universe of difference, is no reality; the reality is only one; all the circumstances are no reality. This is the meaning. Those who have not tried this experiment and have frittered away their energies alone deny the existence of this one reality. It is just as much matter of experience as any experiment performed in any laboratory; it is a solid, stern fact. When you melt your mind, when you lose your little false self in the divinity, what is the consequence? The consequence is (mark these words of Jesus of Nazareth) that if you have a mustard seed's worth of faith and bid the mountain to come, it will come. Live that reality; feel that reality, and you will see that all your circumstances, all your imminent dangers, all the troubles and anxieties that stare you in the face, are bound to disappear. You put more faith in the outside phenomena than in the divinity; you make the world more real than God. You have hypnotized yourself into a rigidity with regard to outside phenomena, and thus it is that you involve yourself in all sorts of sickness and trouble. Take up this paper whenever you are much dejected, and feel that there is but one reality. See that this one statement is a higher statement than all the so-called truths insinuated in you through the books. All the so-called facts which you believe are simply an illusion, a delusion hypnotized into you by the senses. Be not dupes of the senses. Somebody comes and finds fault with you and criticizes you; another comes and abuses you; another comes and puffs you up and flatters you. All these are not facts; all these are not reality. You should feel the reality, the stern fact. When chanting this, drive out and expel all the beliefs that you have put into the outside phenomenal circumstances. Put forth all your energies and strength on this fact, "There is but one reality." Feel that. "There is but one reality." Om! Om! Om!

Oftentimes you will see that reading out for the first time the idea "There is but one reality" will make you cheerful and happy, will keep you above all pain and difficulty. If you feel inclined to read further, you may. Otherwise it is enough if you can put into practice only one sentence of that paper in your pocket. If you think that you require more strength, read the next sentence, "That reality is myself." Now it comes nearer home. "Oh, my neighbor is not different from me; I am present there also. That reality is myself. Om! Om! Om! Mark;

some people say that when you are chanting Om you should keep your hands closed or do this or that. There is no restriction of any kind. Feel the idea. It is not necessary when concentrating to throw yourself in any definite position. No restrictions. When you are feeling, feeling and trying to breathe in, take in the idea, then care not about the body; be not concerned about what the people will say. If you are inclined to sing, go on singing. If you are incline to lie down, lie down on the floor. Feel the idea. If your hands strike that way, let them strike. No restrictions as to the body; feel the idea. Here comes the idea "omnipotent"; dwell on it. This paper is for those who have attended the lectures. Those who have not will of course not find it of much interest. Those who have attended the lectures will know that the real *Atman* is all power; the Self supreme is omnipotent. With regard to that, everything in this world is being done through the *Atman*, just as through the sun is everything being done on this earth. The wind blows on account of the sun; the grass grows on account of the sun; the river flows through the sun; people wake up on account of the sun; the roses bloom on account of the sun. Similarly it is on account of the *Atman*, on account of the omnipotent Self supreme that every phenomenon is taking place in the universe. Omnipotent, omnipotent, Om! Om! Om! Thus all the doubts which weaken and baffle you, all the misunderstandings which make a coward of you have no right to make their entrance into your holy presence. Feel that you are omnipotent. Just as you think so you become. Call yourself a sinner, and you must become a sinner; call yourself a fool and you must become a fool; call yourself weak, and there is no power in this world that can make you strong. Feel that omnipotence, and omnipotent you are.

Then comes omniscient. Take up this idea; let the mind dwell on that thought. Sing Om. The word Om stands for omniscience, so chant Om. Omniscience, Om! Om! Om! Proceed this way, and let those wrong notions which hypnotize you into ignorant fools be dispensed with. The most direct road to godhead is that.

Take up the similar idea "omnipresent." Feel that you are not finite, not this little body; you are not this little self, this *jiva*; this ego you are not. That which permeates and pervades every molecule and atom, that is your Self. Bear in mind not the least doubt about it. "Omnipotent, omniscient, omnipresent, that I am; that pervades everything, all bodies are mine. Om! Om! Om!" Well, Rama need not dwell on the remaining sentences, they will simply be read out to you. Practice this method and Rama is wrong if you do not realize divinity and truth in one week. "Perfect health is me." If that body which you call "mine" is sick, leave it aside; do not think of it; feel that you are health itself; perfect health is yours. Feel that. The body will immediately become healthy of its own accord. This is the secret. Try, and you will see whether it is a fact or not. Despite yourself the body will get well. You should not care for this body—"O God, make me well." There is a beautiful *mantram* in the Sanskrit scriptures which states "This truth cannot be found by the weak." When you go to the president of the United States or to a king, you are expelled if you go as a beggar; you are not allowed to enter his presence. So when you approach God in a beggarly state, you will be knocked out. Feel that you are health; do not ask anything. Say I am health, and health you are.

Then comes the next idea "All power am I." Keep that in your mind and chant Om! Om! Om! Thus say "All power am I." Then the next idea, "All the universe is but my idea." Believe that, and while reading it call to mind the arguments which the Vedantins advance to prove that fact. Call to your mind all that you know to prove that fact, and if you have not read anything or if you have not heard anything which proves that the whole world is my idea, believe it, and you will see that the world is your idea. The world is my idea; chant Om and feel that. Similarly all the rest—

All Joy I am.	Om! Om! Om!
All Knowledge I am.	Om! Om! Om!
All Truth I am.	Om! Om! Om!
All Light I am.	Om! Om! Om!
Fearless, fearless I am.	Om! Om! Om!
No attachment or repulsion, I am the fulfillment of all desires.	Om! Om! Om!
I am the over-soul.	Om! Om! Om!
I hear in all ears,	Om! Om! Om!
I see in all eyes.	Om! Om! Om!
In all minds I think.	Om! Om! Om!
Sages aspire only to know the truth which is myself.	Om! Om! Om!
The life and light that shineth through the sun and stars am I.	Om! Om! Om!

NON-DUALITY*

Here are a few couplets from a saint of Punjab:

O Devotee! when the sense of ego is purged, there is no fear of being let down by anyone from any quarter.
You are prepared to dive deep into the sea in order to find out a small pearl, but you refuse to identify your own self which is manifest like a high mountain.
What an intoxicant have you drunk which has delayed your enlightenment so far?
The source of light that sheds effulgence is within you. Alas! your eyes are blind to it.
You are the Master of the Universe, and the three worlds are adorned by you."

O the waves of the ocean of non-duality! Dear human face divine, thou art manifest in the laughing outbursts of jovial persons, in the warbling of the nightingale, in the challenges of Rustam, in the heartrending wails of the oppressed, in the blooming of buds and in the coquetry of women.

Lo! the din and bustle of the market, the fragrance of the flowery garden, the chill penury of the beggar's bowl and the splendor of the king's crown all pine for appearance before your exalted Self.

The voice of the blooming faces and the songs of the nightingales are eager to win your favor. You have endowed pleasant fragrance to the musk and the pungent smell to the onion. You have gifted this death-dealing† quality to a diamond and also loveliness to the lips of damsels.

Says a Persian Poet:

* Translated from the Urdu.
† It is said that when diamond is licked, it causes death.

> The fact is that the wine gets intoxicated through me and not that the wine intoxicates me. Likewise the tune in the flute and the fragrance in the flowers have their origin in me.

And thus says an English poet:

> Ye glittering towns with wealth and plenty crowned,
> Ye fields where summer spreads profusion round,
> For me your tributary stores combine
> Creation's heir the world, the world is mine.

(1) The part of the universe which is experienced by the sense of hearing is ether (2) that which is felt by the sense of touch is air (3) that which is known by the sense of eyes is light (4) that which is realized by taste through tongue is water and (5) that which is known by smell is earth; all these five elements owe their existence to thee, O beloved!

A Persian poet said:

> None exists in this universe except thy own Self. It is immaterial whether thou doth agree or not.

The rays of your consciousness emanating from your eyes create the diverse objects. The waves of your creative power produce voices both sweet and bitter. O, the support of the high and the low! the morning breeze fortified by your power blows about sportingly.

> The Brahman at whose instance the wind blows and the sun shines (the gods of fire and rain remain alert and the god of death is on his heels) is none but your own Self.
>
> Yajurveda, *Taitrya Upanishada*

Says a Persian poet:

> It is not my eyes alone which shed the glories of thy hallowed face; the moon and the sun also reflect the same.

The ancient sage Vashista says:

> All that is apparent is God's own manifestation in the various forms and names. That is

> not only His creation, but His own Self is permeating all.

Also says an Urdu poet:

> It is paradoxical that He shines in the form of midday sun in full bewitching splendor yet conceals his glorious face behind the curtain.

The flames of fire may burn wood and stone but they do not harm fire itself. The wrath of an emperor may cause terror among the ministers and courtiers, but he himself is never afraid of his own glory. The roar of a lion and the challenging demeanor of a valiant man, the sharpness of the sword, the hiss of a serpent, the reprimanding of the priest and the scolding of the presiding judge are your glorious manifestations. Why should one get panic stricken by them? Why should one waver?

Says a Persian poet:

> The death-dealing sword of eyes and the arrows of endless coquetry are the reflections of your own face. But why should they confront you?

O dear, have a peep inside your own Self. Why fear? Why get terror stricken? Why bewail your lot? Gloom and anger, pain and sorrow should find no place in this setup. Says a Persian poet:

> I roam about listlessly like a madman full of ecstasy. I am free from fear or sorrows; I tread on the path of endless bliss, and I am the sole monarch of the heaven. Time does not worry me. All bliss, all joy. One who has realized the joy of the soul is free from all fear and doubts. *Taitriya Upanishada*

Day in and day out you are engrossed in monetary affairs, in the fine intricacies of logic and philosophy, in the meshes of mathematical and scientific problems. You also indulge in unnecessary argumentation and critical analysis, yet it is a matter of wonder that you are incapable to discover the invaluable genuine pearl in your own Self. Says a Persian poet:

> That secret which is clear like the flame of a candle light cannot remain concealed. The idea being that the hidden thing which is manifest publicly cannot remain a secret.

O my dear, if you just discover the lost ring* you are the lord of the world and heavens. Says a Persian poet:

> O Solomon, activate your ring and make the celestial beings and the fairies your captives. We are sick of this worldly water from the wells. Allow your stream of heavenly bliss to flow so as to reveal the hidden faces and enlighten our physical frame.

Oh! You, the advocate of morality, how long will you act as the guard of humanity with your cautions.

How long will you repeat, "Who comes there?" How long will you terrorize people with the agony of hell and sufferings of torturing jails? How long will your blackmailing continue? Even in spite of your strenuous efforts, if the darkness of ignorance is not removed, the evils of pilferage, fraudulent practices, gambling and drinking shall not be eradicated.

> Deeds of darkness cannot be avoided in the dark.

Let the sun of true knowledge rise in full glory; the sins and evils will vanish along with the darkness. Aristotle has well said that "knowledge is virtue." This means that the path of truth alone is to be treaded. In the face of the sun's light, the light of ordinary lamps cannot be perceptible. An enlightened man in whom the sun of truth shines in full glory can never be attracted towards the feeble lamp of sensual pleasures. The sweet but deceptive voice of 'Siren can have no comparison with the divine music of Orpheus.

* The refernece is to the Persian version of Solomon who had lost his ring.

What woman will you find,
Though of his age the wonder and the fame,
On whom his leisure will vouchsafe an eye
Of fond desire?
How would one look from his majestic brow,
Seated as on the top of virtue's hill,
Discountenance her despised, and put to rout
All her array.

Milton

The light shed by a colored candle will brighten even the black iron plate. Similarly, the eyes of the lover falling on the physical form of his beloved shall make her effulgent.

A thing giveth but little delight
That never can be mine.

Wordsworth

The man of divine knowledge, who has realized the eternal beauty and grandeur of the Self, is the Light of lights. How can the fireflies of sensuousness stand in the face of His divine effulgence?

O dear one, the sun is your own self. Open your eyes and it is before you. Why do you close your eyes and live in the darkness of ignorance?

Here is a dialogue based on the following quotation from Lilashuk—

Krishna	Mother! Mother!
Yashoda	Yes my child, what's it?
Krishna	Give me a cup, quick!
Yashoda	What will you do with it? Cup is not a thing of play. Here are the toys; play with them.
Krishna	I do not ask for it to play with. I wish to drink milk.
Yashoda	My darling, no milk is available. Nor is it time for it. In the absence of milk what

will you do with the cup?

Krishna (In a mood of annoyance) Oh, Oh, when shall I get milk?

Yashoda Presently you have butter. Let night come, and then you may have fresh milk to your fill.

Krishna (Tightening his lips) Oh, when will the night come?

Yashoda When it is dark.

Upon this Krishna instantly shut his eyes and started saying loudly with extended hands, "Let me have milk. It is now dark; give me milk. It is night now."

Seeing the cleverness of the child, mother was at her wit's end. She burst into laughter and was lost in joy. She pressed the child to her bosom and caressed him.

The same Lord Krishna, the Soul of the universe, who played the trick of making day into night by shutting his eyes, the lord of the ocean of milk,* who cried and begged for a cup of milk, is constantly permeating your head, eyes and heart and making all the frolicsome sports. That head of the thieves† seated in your mind and inner recesses of your consciousness is constantly guiding your senses. That Krishna is the master of your soul. In fact He is your own self. Please realize it and give up the mockery of making day into night by closing your eyes like a child. Says an Urdu poet:

O blooming flower, this mockery
With me does not become thee.

* In the Hindu scriptures God has allegorically been described to be in the ocean of milk, the symbol of prosperity and affluence.

† Krishna was called the head of the thieves because he quietly stole the hearts of others by his charming divine personality.

Why this fun of laughter? O Lord Shiva, Your indifference has encouraged the passions in the form of lust (Kam-dev) which is making you the target of its arrows. Open your third eye (of divine knowledge) and destroy the god of lust outright.

> Had you killed and reduced to dust your carnal desires, it would have been transformed into elixir of life. O alchemist, it cannot be called an extraordinary deed if you have transmuted mercury into gold.

You are the Sun of suns. Do not let the clouds of ignorance cover and conceal your light. Why do you not shed effulgent light all round? O seeker of truth, the forest of the world should get saturated with your ecstatic fragrance.

There should be peace on earth, and the entire world should get perfumed with your good will and light all around. The lusty passions in men and women and the impulses of jealousy and revenge should automatically be dispelled by your mere presence. The glimpse of Dattatreya even from a distance changed the life of a prostitute and transformed her into a pure one. The very sight of the saint produced a soothing and peaceful effect on the heart of the fallen woman, as if a violent tornado had subsided and the duststorm of her inner conflict had settled down. Says a Hindi poet:

> The lamp of divine knowledge is forever lighted in the minds of the wise men. Whenever indolence creeps into their hearts, the light of the divine knowledge keeps the darkness of ignorance away from them. The moths of carnal desire are burnt by the flame of divine knowledge. The selfless deeds are the flames of the divine lamp. The oil of love keeps that lamp burning. Such a lamp is lighted only in the hearts of the most fortunate men.

A Persian poet says:

> O you bright pearl of the ocean of purity, bear in mind that you are both hidden and manifest. It is nothing but you.

If you put a blue cloth near a transparent crystal, the crystal will appear as blue. When a piece of yellow cloth is kept in the background, it will look yellow, and it will appear to be red when it is close to a red object. In fact, the transparent crystal is colorless. Any liquid or gas will take the shape of the container in which it is kept. It will be flat in a flat pot and cubical in a cubical vessel. A long iron rod when heated in fire will make fire appear long. A round plate when red hot will make fire appear round, and so on and so forth. As a matter of fact, fire has no definite shape of its own. This is accepted by all persons who can see.

The science of optics has proved that whatever we see, the palatial buildings, the gardens and all, are nothing but light. The entire world is contained in the rays of light. This is the play of the three original colors—blue, red and yellow. In fact, light has no color of its own. Just as a crystal, liquid, gas, fire and light adopt a variety of colors and forms on account of their property, so to, the Light of lights, your own Self, is manifested in diverse forms and shapes:

> As one energy permeating the entire universe takes up various forms, so too, the One Soul, which is enshrined in all the creatures, presents the phenomena of unity in diversity. *Kathupanishad*

A poet says:

> I see my Beloved everywhere;
> I see Him as the Master here and as a slave
> elsewhere.
> He is manifest in the blooming flowers
> And in the twittering nightingales.
> He is resplendent as a king on the throne here

And wandering as a beggar with his bowl there.
He is a faithful devotee here and a preacher there;
Elsewhere He is the leader of the band of drunkards.
Somewhere He is declaring Himself as God and
gracefully climbing the scaffold;
He sees His own Self, hears His own Self;
There is none besides Him.
It is sheer bunkum to claim
That one has seen or heard Him.
If light, it is He; if fire, there is none but He.

He pervades one and all, yet His apparent splendor is fake and unreal. In His real state He is pure, sublime and absolute. Agreed that the intellect and life are like bubbles in the vast sea of creation or as a rope mistaken for a serpent, yet He remains untarnished, unattached and pure. He is neither body, mind nor intellect. He is beyond all these.

It is, however, very strange that despite the fact that He is unattached, He appears to be the same with whatever comes in His contact like a transparent crystal, liquid, gas or fire, as described above. Identifying with the body, He says, "I am going on pilgrimage to Badrikashram, and I have already performed that of Amarnath and so on." Identifying with the mind, He says, "I am feeling thirsty or hungry. Give me milk." When He identifies Himself with the intellect, he accepts all the deeds of the intellect as His own. "What a fine argument have I thought of. What a nice essay have I written" and so on.

O ignorant man, beware; do not practice the dictum, "Follow whosoever meets you." Give up the evil companionship of desire, mind and intellect. Pray, do not tarnish your absoluteness.

A poet says:

Do not go unclad on the roof in moonlight;
The light of the moon may soil your body.

It has been said in Brahma Namawali:

> I am unattached; I am unattached. I am all absolute. I am truth, knowledge and bliss. I am immortal, unchangeable and immutable.

You are definitely immortal truth, supreme knowledge and bliss. Why do you then identify yourself with your body, mind, etc.? Why do you call yourself inert, miserable and helpless? O dear, why do you commit this sort of spiritual suicide? Why do you identify yourself with this dirty body, containing "blood, sweat, semen, excreta, urine, etc." This is really very surprising.

A Persian poet says:

> Alas, you are shrouded like the moon behind the clouds. You should tear open the cloud of this body and rise in your pristine glory because you are the moon and the embodiment of absolute beauty.

Pupil — I am not able to follow you at all. How can we, the ordinary human beings and sinners, claim to be truth, knowledge and bliss. We cannot be immortal, omnipresent and omniscient. This is sheer heresy. The entire creation of God proclaims loudly that we are dependent, have limited knowledge. Your talk of godhood is unjustifiable. Oh! What a sin! O God forgive us! Be kind to us!

Master — O dear, believe me. It is wonder of wonders that you are nothing but God. You are indivisible God (Brahman). Why should you persist in denying this truth? Every individual being is announcing at the top of his voice that he is pure, eternal bliss, immortal and consciousness absolute. Still you do not accept it. "O dear, it is a huge joke to try to ignite water with fire."

Pupil — It sounds more strange still. Barring others I affirm most faithfully that I have never professed to say that "I am Brahman (God). Tell me when have I put forth such a claim?

Master — In this battlefield of life everyone, including yourself, is in actual practice chanting ceaselessly the mantra, "I am Shiva! I am Shiva!" (I am God, I am God!) through actions, though it is denied verbally. Yet, as you know, actions speak louder than words. A young man was lying dead drunk. His father came and reprimanded him. The young man flatly denied that he had ever touched wine. Be that as it may, the drunken state cannot be concealed! His eyes revealed the real situation. The offensive smell was loudly falsifying his statement. And look, while he was denying, he started vomiting and the whole truth came out. How long could it be suppressed!

> The sweet beloved cannot be kept hidden behind any number of curtains like the fragrance of roses.

Your tongue does not disclose the truth, but in fact your outward behavior and actions do reveal that you consider yourself as God.

O dear, your real Self is the center of unbounded joy. The more you try to hide this truth, the more it will reveal itself.

A quotation from Mahabharat:

> A question was once put to Yudhishtar, the king of the Pandavas, as to what was the most wonderful thing in the world? He replied: 'Day in and day out we see numberless persons dying, but the wonder is that even then the people do not realize that they

have also to die one day. They are still enamored of
this life. Is it not a wonder of all the wonders?

The underlying idea is that we see and hear every day that persons are dying or passing away, and we also know that one who is born is to die, yet we remain indifferent to death. It comes to our knowledge after an age that life is death. Man comes into being only to melt away into nothingness. Even then one does not think that he would ever die. He wants to live forever. We may sing songs of death every now and then:

> This show of our world is only for four days
> and none has to live here forever.

But in our practical life we do not at all give the idea of death any serious consideration. We continue to remain entangled in the worldly affairs, as if we shall never die. Completely regardless of the coming old age and loosening of the worldly ties, we continue to add to our worldly desires, thinking that death will never come to us. What can be more wonderful? A Sanskrit couplet says:

> The hair and teeth of old men wither away,
> But the lust of life and greed for wealth continue
> To hold their sway.

A Persian poet says:

> The proud men do not care about death,
> though the form of their neck gives the
> appearance of scissors (which cut the cord of life
> incessantly).

After all what is the secret behind this? There is no doubt about the dissolution of this physical body some day. Why then do people not believe in the inevitability of death?

O dear reader, this evidently means that there is no death to your real Self. Your *Atma* (Self) is immortal and timeless. You are truth personified. A quotation from the Gita:

> By destruction of the physical body the real Self or the Atma (soul) is not destroyed.
> Death hath not touched it at all,
> Dead though the house of it seems!

A Persian poet says:

> The Soul is the weaver of the garment of this body.
> The thought of its destruction is meaningless.

You are never to die. Why should you then have any practical belief in death in your daily life? Each one of your actions proclaims at the beat of drum that "you are immortal." Let me add further. Outwardly we are not tired of repeating with all humility, "I am a sinner. I am sinful." On occasions this unsavory thought is covered under the sacred feeling of love for God. For example, says a Persian poet:

> O Lord, I have brought four gifts to offer to you. These are humility, helplessness, self-surrender and sinfulness.

But in practical life, people boastfully declare that they are pure, incorruptible, unattached and holy. After all how long can we suppress truth? It has got to come out in some form or the other.

> Truth invariably succeeds, not falsehood.
>
> *Mandukupanishad*
>
> O Nanak, the untruth never stands, and truth is eternal.

Whenever even a small mistake of ours is pointed out, it is very painful to us. It becomes intolerable. If our guilt is brought to our notice, we are apt to take it ill. It is damaging to my honor, we exclaim on such occasions. Whenever we hear unfavorable remarks by others about ourselves, the person concerned is warned to withdraw his statement; even a suit of defamation is threatened. Even if a small child is charged for some lapses, he will resent it.

Whenever even a lowly paid servant is accused, he murmurs and gets annoyed.

From the above it is evidently clear that each one is pure from the standpoint of his real Self. He is unvitiated. As a result of crimes committed by the body or mind, the Self is not to be held liable. A water duck does not get drenched whether it lives in a dirty pool or in the Ganga water. Likewise, the soul, the *Atma*, whether enshrined in a body with a pure or impure mind, remains ever pure and unaffected.

A quotation from Shankaracharya:

> The sun cannot be affected at all, whether its reflection falls in the Ganga water or in the drain water in a gold vessel or in an earthen pot. The reflection of the sun will be all alike. In the same way, why should one have misgivings about the primal soul, which is the embodiment of eternal bliss and the unbounded sea of knowledge? Why should we discriminate between a Brahmin and a low caste sweeper?
>
> Shankar Manisha Panchak Stotra

The sun neither gets more sanctified when its reflection falls in the Ganga water, nor does it get polluted when it falls in wind. By the same analogy, the Soul (one's real Self) is not contaminated when its body and mind are debased, nor is it in any way further evolved or enlightened by the skillful development of the same. That man who knows this truth and is firmly established in his own Self is truly immortal and has risen to the spiritual heights, "where the passions, greed and desires fear to tread."

Why not then realize your real Self and own this kingdom of spirituality? Your life has been wasted in reading, writing and listening to the teachings of others. Now you must also pay attention to listen to the inspiring voice of your inner Self—the voice which is resounding ceaselessly and the dictates of which are unconsciously being followed by you in your practical life. Please ponder over it carefully.

Does anyone accept a guilt against himself willingly? Even the person against whom the guilt has been fully proved tries to shift the blame onto someone else. He pleads "not guilty." He will cry at the top of his voice, and assert that he is innocent and free from any criminality. In the courts of law where the learned judges are appointed to do justice, you can see things for yourself. When the judge questions the accused "Are you guilty of committing such and such crime?" the accused invariably says, "No sir, not at all." Even if sufficient circumstantial evidence and proof against the accused are forthcoming and he is charge-sheeted, he continues to plead his innocence. If, however, an appeal is filed, and the appellate court also holds him guilty, then he will say that bribery and favoritism have had their full play. Even if he is sent to jail he will continue to say that he had wrongly been convicted and that there was no justice even in the High Court. In spite of overwhelming proof against him, he would plead not guilty. He would say, "even if the whole world calls me bad, I am guiltless, and the entire world is mad like a Hydra-headed mob."

Aye! convicted person, you are in essence really blameless and free from any guilt. An owl may be able to face the sun, but sin cannot vitiate your sacred Self. The wrong lies in the fact that due to utter ignorance you are oblivious of the innocence of your pure Self. You treat your gross body and mind as your real Self. Nay, ignoring the inner voice which constantly reminds you that you are sinless and immortal, you give it a wrong interpretation.

Your true nature rebels against the idea that you are a sinner. There is natural repugnance to the idea of being low or polluted. The advice of the inner voice is that "you are pure and free from sin. You are not this body. The physical body (container of waste matter and night soil) cannot become pure and sinless, even though you may wash it in Ganga water for thousands of years."

Says a Hindi poet:

> This gross body cannot be purified even though
> it may be washed in water,
> Onion cannot be turned into saffron,
> even if it is grown in Kashmir.

From your inner impulse the following gospel is constantly whispered:

> You are the holy truth. You are not this body. You should give up for good the idea that you are limited to the body and mind. Wake up in your pristine glory.

But alas! Due to perversity of understanding, you act deaf. You persist in identifying yourself with your body. How can you then call yourself sinless, when you consider yourself to be body, mind or intellect. In essence you are *Atma*, the sinless Self, the same today, tomorrow and forever. If you rise above your body and mind consciousness, you are the master of the universe. The inner voice of your real Self directs you to free yourself from the limited considerations of your body, mind and intellect and to establish in godhood your real Self. But like Farroha and Namrood you are engrossed in love for gold and worldly possessions. How then can you be great?

> Namrud was subjected to shame and degradation because he was narrow-minded. Such a vanity and limited vision does not become me because I am all pervading, like God.

Seeing your conduct and way of life, divine Light, the

real Spirit is instructing you not to consider yourself as this body. You are not the body. You are the Soul, immortal and all-pervading. The substratum on which you stand is very sacred. But the wonder is that you want to cover the Holy Spirit, the sacred Soul, the *Atma*, with leather shoes (the body).

There is a saying, "Flattery is loved by all from an ant to God." "Whoever is praised is enamored of it." The question is "Why is it so?" The praise brings to us the fragrance of our lovely beloved, *Atma*. It brings a message from our inner Self, "I am the Prime Soul—the Great One." It gives us the clue of God within and conveys the happy message to us.

A poet says:

> You are the heavenly star to the eyes of Moses on the mountain of Taurus; you are the embodiment of the God's message meant for His creation.
> Alas! You drown this sublime message in the wine of ignorance, treating it as meaningless. This official letter is fit to be drenched in first class wine.

If, however, you are enamored for a while of the beauty of its outer cover and, without going through its contents, throw it in the waste paper basket, it will mean that you attach more importance to the body than to the soul.

Had you cared to see the subject matter of the glorifying message after opening the cover, you would have found the message of God, the center of eternal bliss.

Being overjoyed and filled with ecstasy, the envelope would have fallen from your hands. It means that you would then give up the habit of flattering or praising others. Under the outer cover, you would find the glorious picture of the Beloved.

A poet says:

> What peace would it be, if I get a picture of Thine
> And sleep, keeping it close to my heart.

One would feel that not only his picture but the Beloved is saying:

> Thou art close to Me, do not feel that I am afar,
> Thou art by My side, do not depart from Me.

O! Students, public servants and others, please say on oath how strongly you covet for a holiday. It is not actually a holiday but freedom that you pine for. Freedom, freedom, the entire world pines for freedom.

> O Liberty!
> Thou huntress swifter than the moon! Thou terror
> Of the world's wolves! Thou bearer of the quiver,
> Whose sun-like shafts pierce tempest winged error,
> As light may pierce the clouds when they dissever
> In the calm region of the orient day!
>
> The voices of thy bards and sages thunder
> With an earth-awakening blast
> Through the caverns of the past;
> Religion veils her eyes; oppression shrinks aghast,
> A winged sound of joy and love and wonder,
> Which soars where expectations never flew,
> Rending the veil of space and time asunder.

Freedom is your natural state. You are already freedom absolute. That is the reason why holidays, festivals, shows and fairs are most welcome to all. They restore freshness to you like the fragrant garb of lost Yusuf. They lull those into gentle sleep who are handicapped with limitations and pass their days restlessly in ignorance. They afford some relief from the pangs of slavery. The ignorance is the bed of thorns. They will pinch you. You cannot enjoy the benefits of freedom so long as you are steeped in ignorance. The worldly pleasures and sensuous joys, relaxation, marital relationship, etc. are palliatives which give only temporary relief like narcotics and tranquilizers.

It is not safe to follow this way of life.

A poet says:

> I was an angel, and the beautiful heaven was my abode,
> But Adam misled me to this heinous temple of the world.
> I laugh at the man's folly;
> He is responsible for his sins,
> But strangely, he blames Satan for his misdeeds.
> Fill the bright goblet, spread the festive board;
> Summon the gay, the noble, and the fair;
> Through the loud hall in joyous concert poured
> Let mirth and music sound the dirge of care,
> But ask thou not if happiness be there;
> If the loud laugh disguise convulsive throe,
> Or if the brow the hearts true livery wear;
> Lift not the festal mask. Enough to know,
> No scene of mortal life but teems with mortal woe.

If you wish to get rid of the pricking pain of the worldly thorns, do away with ignorance and you will realize that you are the source of freedom, peace and bliss. You will then need no sleeping drugs (worldly objects like wealth) for attaining the blissful state.

A poet says:

> I am hand in hand with God. I need no mediation of any prophet.

Yet another poem about such a state of God intoxication says:

> Day and night pass in pleasure and joy;
> The river of wine is in happy mood, and there is full freedom.
> The colored flower has bloomed in glory,
> There is happiness all around;
> When the river of love is in floods, there is peace all over
> Every night is full of new joy, and all the days are fine.

My dear, you had had enough of sufferings in the worldly attachments. Now enjoy the infinite bliss of divine life of freedom and ecstasy. Give up chanting the following lines:

> O hunter, although there are limitless joys of freedom,
> Yet the thrill of restlessness under the net is something unique.

The discoveries of knowledge and science emanate from the one supreme power, the repository of all knowledge. That sovereign (Ram), the all-pervading entity from which the entire knowledge of the universe radiates, is none but your own real Self. You are not this limited body or intellect. You are he. Newton's mind was but a flash of the light within yourself. The Bhagavad Gita was a pencil of the same light, and so are the sacred Quran and Bible the waves of the ocean of your own universal Self.

In the *Kaivalya Upanishad* it has been said:

> I am subtler than subtlest and also bigger than the biggest. This wonderful world of name and form is nothing but My manifestation. I am the most ancient and the eternal being. Also I am the most effulgent and merciful lord. Though I am without hands and feet, yet my power is unlimited. I see without eyes and hear without ears. Though I appear in different names and forms, I am not limited to them. There is none who can fathom Me. I am the eternal consciousness, knowable through the Vedas. The knowledge of Vedanta originated from Me, and I am the sole knower of Vedas. I am above virtue and sins. I am free from the bondage of birth and death. Body, mind or intellect cannot limit Me. My pure and sublime Self is not constituted of earth, water, fire, air and ether. I am the absolute supreme law.

Said the Lord in the Bhagavad Gita:

> I witness My nature to create this universe. I am the primordial cause of the creation of the universe.

Disciple — If the original cause of the whole universe is the same, why are there differences in the intellect and the bodies of men? One man is learned like Lord Colvin, while the other is quite illiterate. At one place someone feels uncomfortable even on velvet cushions, while the other is not permitted even to sit on the pavement. Someone is the champion wrestler, while the other is a born imbecile. There is complete lawlessness, exploitation or injustice all around.

Preceptor My dear, it is unfair on your part to apprehend such disparities. It would really be a terrible injustice if these disparities were to be perpetrated by God, the supreme Lord. It would indeed be a great cruelty. The truth is that there is nothing big or small, high or low. One who is a beggar here rules as king there. One whom you see as a sick man here is a heavyweight champion there. The uncultured fool here is the great sage, Vyas (compiler of the Vedas) there. Since one and all are the different forms or manifestation of the Divine Being, there is no question of injustice or confusion. In this creation, right from ant to elephant, the one indivisible Force permeates all. One starving with hunger here is fed with fruits of Kashmir there. The uncivilized man here rises up as sage Yagyavalka there.

In Avdhut Gita, it has been said:

> You are the same Brahman. This description is given of the soul in the scriptures. From the spiritual standpoint, therefore, you are divine. Barring the limitations of body, mind, etc., the same Brahman permeates all

> and is omnipresent. As such, why should you bewail your lot? You are He Himself.
> Bondage or freedom have no hold on you, and unity or separation do not affect you. Reasons and arguments do not limit you. None, whatsoever exists, binds you. As such why should you bewail your lot?
> The divine nature is the same everywhere, free from pleasure or pain, removed from joy or sorrow. The idea of relationship between preceptor and disciple is unknown to the supreme divinity. As such, why should you bewail your lot?
> The supreme Self is neither subject to limitations of birth or death nor concerned with blessings or sins. He is neither solid nor hollow. Then why should you bewail your lot?
> The various sacred scriptures have averred that the heavens, etc. are mere forms and names, illusive like mirage. When the supreme Self is present everywhere alike, why should you bewail your lot?

A Persian poet says:

> Blessed ones! I was present even before the birth of Adam. Even when Eve did not exist, I was present. In short, prior to the creation of this world, was I. I am the most ancient of all the lovers.
> The savior of Noah's Ark was none but Myself, sitting by his side; I was the protector of Yusuf hiding in the depth of the well. I was in the life-giving force of Christ. I am the most ancient of the lovers.
> When in the battle between Moses and Firoon, the evil-minded Firoon was drowned in the river, I was there. O dear ones, I am the most ancient of all the lovers.
> When the great Mohammad in his spiritual flight passed over the fifth, seventh and the eighth heaven, I was there on the eighth heaven. O dear ones, I am the most ancient of all the lovers.
> O sun, do not boast of thy brilliance; restrain thy heat. Be sober, as I am the most ancient of all the lovers.
> I am the king of righteousness, i.e., I am the Supreme Overlord and the endless ocean of wisdom am I. God is non-entity before Me. I am the most ancient of all the lovers.

Disciple — I am of limited means. God is supreme overlord. My power is restricted. God is the supreme divine. There can be no comparison between this humble servant and the great overlord. What relationship can there be between the lowly dust speck and the supreme being?

Preceptor — Why do you think so lowly about your powers? After all, you have the power to do something at least. Speak out what you do. From that I shall be able to analyze whether your powers are limited or unlimited.

Disciple — I get up early in the morning. After daily routine I take a bit of exercise. Thereafter I do some reading and writing. After the morning meal I go to my office. On return I take milk and go for an outing or for meeting friends. Then I read the newspaper. Thus passes the day. In the night I sleep.

Preceptor — You do certain other things in the ordinary course.

Disciple — I do carry out daily routines and attend to other personal affairs. I also keep waiting for the magazine *Alif* (a periodical) at due time. Besides these I do not recollect anything more.

Preceptor — Why this denial? You do innumerable other things beside the above. You have failed to mention them. You pretend to be quite innocent.

Disciple — Innumerable things! No, certainly not. It is rather unbecoming of a high souled person like you to say that.

Preceptor Just hear me. Is this body yours?

Disciple Of course! It is mine; who else can claim it?

Preceptor In the morning you take your meals, you breathe and see. In the evening you go out to the fields to answer the calls of nature. Then you also go to sleep. Is it not so?

Disciple Yes, sir. That is right.

Preceptor Who digests the food in the stomach?

Disciple I, myself.

Preceptor And do not forget that you cause the blood to circulate in the arteries and veins of your body. You produce saliva in the mouth, move the kidney to produce urine. You make the hair grow and lungs breathe. The bile in your liver is produced by no outside agency other than you. You supply energy to the optic nerves. The cerebrum is activated by you, and the intellect is sharpened by you. Besides you are responsible for all the physical and chemical processes going on within you. How do you, then, say that you had not done anything more? Even in sleep when apparently your mind and intellect are not functioning, your activities do not stop. You digest your food during that state; the hair and nails, etc. continue to grow. Why then call it a sleep? You are always awake. A poet says:

> I am never a victim of sleep; I ever keep wide awake.

When the body of yours was born, and your mind and intelligence were immature, you were the same as today. In sleep you are the same as when awake. You activate the mind and cause circulation of your blood for the general growth of your body. So, too, you function in all other forms. Every leaf radiates your light. How then do you say that your power is limited? In the *Prashna Upanishad* it has been said:

> O dear one! Whoever identifies himself with the eternal knowledge and the immutable divinity which is the origin of all life and the elements is the knower of all and is in fact all.

This is the very essence of the real knowledge. One needs nothing else. Now please listen to me as to why you call yourself limited.

The young child of a king was fond of a small painted plate. Whenever some edible was served, he would insist on taking it in this very plate. Even when food was served in a bigger or more beautiful tray, he would kick it off. He would become wild by crying aloud. If someone asked him as to who else was the owner of the variety of the beautiful dishes of gold and silver, he would not listen to anyone and would continue to insist on his demand most obstinately. Likewise, O true sons of the Almighty, you are the owners of unlimited wealth, but whatever little is contained in your intellect (the small plate as in the above case) is accepted by you as your own, disowning the rest of the treasure, i.e., your own *Atma*, your own Self. You spurn it unknowingly. Even when it is suggested that the unbounded and unlimited legacy is all yours, instead of appreciating it you get annoyed at it.

Whatever is perceptible to you through your senses

or intellect is accepted, and the rest rejected by you. This means that you identify yourself only with your body and the mind. This degenerates you to the state of *jiva*, the little self. But you are not the *jiva.* Just ponder over it. You are *Atma*, the immortal, all-pervading, the Light of lights. Why should you degrade yourself? What right have you to commit suicide in this way?

There was a narrow-necked jar full of parched grams stuck in the earth. A monkey put both his hands in it and took grams by handfuls. But his hands full of grams could not be taken out of the narrow-necked jar. He tried his best but with no success. Though his hands were stuck up inside the jar, he would not release grams from his hands to help him extricate them. Who can help him under such circumstances?

Similar is the case with you, my dear. There is none to bind you, none to keep you in shackles. You are yourself firmly tied to your body and mind. You have limited yourself to your egoistic self and made yourself virtually a prisoner, a helpless and a dependent being known as *jiva*, the little self.

Emerson has quite correctly said, "Every man is God playing the fool."

A poet has said:

> When the supreme consciousness desires to indulge in wasteful pursuits, it is led away in the waterless stream of mirage.

Relax your hands. Get rid of the evil temptations in respect to your body, mind and intellect. Why do you limit yourself only to one body, one mind and one intellect? Open your fists and be free. You are the friend of all. Your good will towards the entire creation shall remain undiminished even if you are stabbed or attacked by sword. Open the fist, untie the knot, give up the worldly desires which ensnare you; establish your oneness with the entire universe and be wedded to nature.

> When I relinquished the sense of ego,
> The veil between us was removed;
> The veil-wearer has come out of the Purdah,
> And none remained besides Him.

A Persian poet says:

> The One who built his abode out of mud prepared by my soil kept Himself aloof and made me an excuse. (The idea is that He is the real doer but He has made us responsible for all that happens.)

The *Mandukya Upanishad* says:

> When we identify with the supreme being, all the knotty problems are solved, and all the actions are rendered infructuous.

In the sacred fire of divine knowledge throw all the desires due to the senses and the mind as an oblation to the supreme Lord, who is the controller of all beings, human and animal. Purge the annihilating sense of duality, and accept only the supreme being, who is the support (rock) of all the senses, life and power. Destroy the limiting intellect, and merge it in the universal Self, the primordial cause of the sky, the earth and the sun, which are trembling under his supreme command. Turn your face and look to your inner Self. You are the supreme divine power which imparts grandeur to the Himalayas and vastness to the blue seas.

In the *Rigveda* it has been said:

> The snow-clad peaks proclaim his majesty,
> and the oceans reveal His all-pervasiveness:
> Thou art the supreme nature.

A couplet says:

> They raise their arms in thy prayer;
> Thou art the prime soul, master of the three worlds.

A Persian poet says:

> Though thou art on this earth as a material body, yet thou art purer than distilled water. Rise above ego, identify with the real Self and realize that thou art the supreme lord.

Disciple That will do, O master. My delusion is destroyed by your kindness. My sense of hearing is satisfied beyond measure A poet says:

> My heart said, 'I thirst for spiritual and material knowledge. If you are possessed of them, teach me.' My reply was '*Alif*' (the first letter in Persian script). It further asked if there was anything higher than that. I said, 'No.' If there was anything to be cherished in the inner recesses of the heart, it was the one letter *Alif* (monism) complete in itself.

Indra, the rain god, continued to ponder over the teachings of Brahma (the creator-God) for thirty-two years. So, too, I will ponder over your teachings daily for at least thirty-two days in solitude and then again present myself for further lessons. (The disciple respectfully touches the feet of the preceptor.)

Preceptor O God! How is it? You have forgotten the teachings so soon. For God's sake, do not take me for this physical form, nor consider yourself subservient to this body. What a strange disciple you are. You have made me limited to this body. O dear, I am ever present with you; I illumine your heart. I am an honored guest in your house. Embrace Me lovingly; merge into Me and become One. Having the guest in your house, it does not become you to wander about seeking him in the market. A poet says:

> O dear seeker! Do not be disrespectful to Me. Rama resides in your heart. Look deep into it. Why do you turn your face from Me? I am ever present in your heart.

Just remove the veils of name, form, body, intellect and other illusions, and attain immediate identification with Rama.

Om! Om! Om!

THE IMPORTANT DUTY OR SELF HELP*

The Vedas say, "*Shreya* is different, and *Preya* is different," i.e., duty demands something but your selfish interest pulls you in a different direction. *Shreya* tells you to give and to renounce, but your selfish interest tempts you to take and to accept, saying, "This is our right. This is due to us. This is reasonable and just for us." It is common and also easy to assert your right, but it is difficult and also distasteful for a man to stick to his duty. If we go deep, we find that duty and right have the same relation which a seed of a tree has with its fruit. It is really very surprising that everybody wants to enjoy the fruits, but nobody is prepared to take the trouble of sowing the seed, nourishing it and taking its care till it grows into a tree. The fact is that when we go on performing our duty, the right will accrue to us automatically. On the other hand, if we only care for our right without doing our duty properly, we shall only be disappointed. The law of nature is like this.

There are four kinds of duty. The first is duty towards God; the second is duty towards humanity; the third is duty towards your own country and the fourth is duty towards your own self. All these duties ultimately merge into one duty. What is it? It is your duty towards your own Self. If it is properly taken care of, the rest of the three duties are automatically performed.

It is said that there are three types of kindness: kindness of God, kindness of the preceptor or the guide and kindness of one's self. In other words, it means God'

* Translated from the Urdu.

grace, attention of the guru or the guide and the determination of one's own self. God's grace is showered on one in whom the preceptor takes interest, and the preceptor gets interested in the man who is determined to help himself. Take, for example, a school boy. If he does not study well or does not care to help himself, his teacher will not come forward to help him further. It is well known that teachers are pleased with good students, and that they willingly pay special attention towards brilliant students. Ultimately those who are favored by the teacher get the grace of God automatically. The whole thing boils down to the conclusion that self-help is the foremost duty of a man. Without self-help neither the preceptor nor God will be prepared to help us. There is a well known saying that "God helps those who help themselves."

A Persian poet says:

> If an impious man talks of wisdom, people would not be reformed but, if there are pious men, even though they may only sit quietly, all will be inspired to draw good lessons from their saintliness.

Sir Isaac Newton never thought that he would be serving the world. He was running in pursuit of knowledge, as the moths run towards the burning candle. Because he was doing his duty properly, because he tried to help himself, he ultimately proved himself the benefactor of the world. If a man stands at the top of a high tower or a mountain, he can see up to a far greater area. Rama was once going with a few companions to Gangotri in the Himalayas and lost the way. Their bodies were scratched and bruised by thorns and shrubs. They were all scattered, and no one could hear the call of the other. When, with difficulty, Rama reached the top, he raised his voice to call them, and as a result, they could hear him and assemble together. Similarly, so long as we are fallen nobody will hear us, but when we speak from a higher level, all will be able to listen to us.

If you want to move the whole world, you should do so by moving the nearest part of it, i.e., by moving your own self. If you can uplift yourself, the whole world will be lifted up. I dare say that you can move the world to the extent you can move your own self. Some people are engrossed in preaching reform day in and day out, but they do not achieve any success. On the other hand, there are some who achieve so much success that people remember them forever. In order to perpetuate their memory, people construct memorials to themselves in the form of colleges, societies and associations, etc. Why? Because these saints were their own reformers first. There was in Greece a great mathematician, Archimedes. He used to say that he could move the whole world if he could only get a point to act as a level. O dear ones! that point through which you can move the world is your own Self. When you are fully established there, you are sure to move the whole world.

When the air is heated by the sun, it becomes light (less dense) and rises up, creating a vacuum. The air from all around automatically rushes to fill up the space, sometimes causing storms. Similarly, the man who acquires godly qualities is sublimated and becomes the automatic cause of elevating and uplifting the people around him. Is he not a wonderful reformer?

Now I will try to prove how a man while doing his duty for himself can fulfill his duty towards God. There is a story in Muslim mythology. There was a seeker after truth. He was wandering from place to place in his love of

God in search of a learned man who might satisfy his thirst for knowledge of God. During his wanderings he reached a jungle, and in disappointment, resolved not to eat or drink anything and even to give up his life till his doubts were clarified. According to an Indian poet:

> I am sitting at Thy door with a resolve to leave it only after gaining something. Either I must meet Thee or I must die.

During those days there was a man named Juned, who was famous for his religious studies. That day Hazrat Juned was going to the river Dajla to make his horse drink water. However the horse was not advancing towards Dajla in spite of his efforts. Seeing this he thought there must be some good in it and allowed the horse to go his way, saying, "Go, wherever you like. All around is the country of my God. There is no foreign land for me." The horse ran away and reached that particular spot in the jungle where that seeker after truth was lying hungry and thirsty in search of knowledge of God. Hazrat Juned alighted from the horse and enquired of the man the reason for his sitting all alone in the jungle. In a short time, the seeker was fully satisfied in the learned discourse with Juned. When Juned was leaving he said to the man, "If you ever have any such doubts again, you can come to Baghdad. I live there. My name is Juned. Any man will direct you to my house." The man replied, "Did I go to call you this time? Now I have discovered the secret. I will not go anywhere now. In future if I need the help of anyone, you or somebody else will perforce come to me to remove my doubts."

A poet says:

> If there is any effect in my love, my beloved must be attracted towards me. I do not mind if for the present he is indifferent to me."

Another poet says:

> Why do you unnecessarily run after God? If He is God, He must come to you of His own free will. Love is first created in the heart of the beloved. The candle burns first before the moth falls in love with it.

Yet another poet says:

> O Ghani, concentrate on your own Self. How long will you continue to go round Kaba*? On the path of God there is no guide better than your own inner Self.

God is omnipresent, but self-help or self-effort is that force which can draw God from the seventh, the fourteenth, or the thousandth heaven, from Gau-lok or from anywhere to be materialized before you. But mind you, your will force, thought power or the intensity of your devotion must be strong enough.

A poet says:

> You will come per force without any resistance. You will then have no reason to say that the concentration of my mind has no effect.

Another poet says:

> There is no problem which cannot be solved. What is it that a man cannot achieve, if he has a will to do it?

Yet another poet says:

> A small insect can bore a hole even in the stone. Cannot a man win the heart of his own beloved?

O man! You have got within you the great wealth and unlimited power, the right use of which can please not only the country or the world but God Himself. O you, the beautiful rose of spring! You must first be firmly established in your real Self, and then you will see that by discharging this duty concerning your own Self all the rest of the duties will be performed automatically.

* Kaba is a place of pilgrimage in Arabia for the Muslims.

A poet says:

> When you are yourself the source of eternal bliss, why should you seek the obligation of wine or alcohol?
> Howsoever exacting the labor may be involved in our profession, we should not grudge it in the least. If the pole star were to shift from its position, if the Himalayas were to move by the force of wind, if the ocean were to be burnt up by the fire of fireflies, or even if the sun were to come down without going up, a courageous man must not feel dejected or depressed.

If you think of a flower, your mind takes the shape of a flower. And if you think of a restless nightingale you are a nightingale for the moment. If you think of sorrow, you are sure to become sorrowful. And, if you think of goodness for all, you will be "All."

Now please reflect on this principle attentively. The evil which we attribute to others must first find its place in our mind. Rama says that in order to help ourselves, we must give up the idea of criticizing others. It will be in the interest of our own uplift. Also we must not allow any thought other than goodness and purity to enter our minds. Just as in a dome, our sound is echoed back to us, so too, under the dome of this blue sky our own thoughts are reflected back to us in the form of our luck.

A poet says:

> If you listen to my advice, do not think ill of others under this sky because under a dome a man has to hear only what he utters.

Entertain only good thoughts for your own good. Do not blame your luck, like children, because you yourself are the architect of your own fortune. Whatever you sow, you will reap. Your luck or fortune is in your own hands. It does not come from anywhere outside. Had it not been so, our scriptures would not have ordained in respect of "dos" or "don'ts." Had the scriptures known that nothing is in your hands they would not have ordered you to do this or not to do that. Why? Why have they fixed the responsibility of your deeds on you? A poet says:

> In the midstream of the river you have left me tied to a plank, and then you command that my clothes may not get wet. How is this possible?

Rama says that no outside personality is responsible for your good or bad luck. It is you and you alone who can mold it in any way you like. You have got unlimited power within you. You can do whatever you like, make or mar your future. To speak the truth, Rama says: "I do admit that God has created this universe, but, so far as I am concerned, I am that creator who has created God Himself."

A Sanskrit shloka says:

> Success is attained by courageous efforts. The wise men carry out their daily business with dauntless efforts. The word luck, lot or furtune is only to console the weak-hearted persons.

God helps those who help themselves. This is a law of nature. This is an immutable law. When a man with his own efforts is fully deserving, his "right" will automatically search him out. For example, fire is burning here. In order to keep it burning oxygen will automatically be drawn towards it. There is a saying in English, "First deserve and then desire," but Rama says, "Deserve only and you need not desire." If you really deserve, all your desires will be realized of their own accord.

A poet says:

> Hundreds of thoughts are present before me waiting with folded hands to be accepted by me because I have earned my right over them.

A quotation says:

> The stone that is fit for the wall cannot be found in the way.

As I have already said before, you will achieve your object without delay when you will fully deserve it by your own acts. You need not waste your time unnecessarily to gain your object without deserving it. Work hard to justify your right. You have to earn your right.

A poet says:

> After lifting myself above the desires, all my desires have been accomplished. The desires themselves were my obstacle in achieving them.

Nobody gives a lift to the beggar. On the other hand the desires of the man who discharges his duty properly and contentedly are fulfilled by themselves.

A poet says:

> Why are you imploring and requesting others? If you make yourself deserving, others will run after you in their own interest.

I have seen in Japan three to four hundred year old trees which are hardly a span or so in height. You might enquire the reason for their stunted growth, even during a period of centuries. When I enquired I was informed that they did not touch their leaves or branches, but they only continued to cut their roots from time to time and did not let them penetrate deep into the soil. As usual, the tree would not grow high if its roots did not go deep below. There is thus a definite relation between the height of a tree and the depth of its roots. This law holds good not only in the case of trees, but also in that of men. Those who want to go up or be prosperous in this world must dive deep in their soil, the Self. If your roots will not go deep, you will not prosper outwardly. A poet says:

> The deeper you blow your breath in the flute,
> the higher the pitch of the tune.

A poet says:

> Someone asked Mansoor the way to the Beloved. In reply he pointed his finger towards the sharpened end of the death pole (sooli). He meant thereby that sacrifice is the only way.

Yet another poet says:

> I have pierced my mind like the thread in a rosary of a hundred beads. But I could get peace and tranquility only when I realized my real Self.

According to Rama self-help does not mean self-praise, self-aggrandisement or selfishness. It means spiritual training. The most important factor of self-help, or spiritual training, is to develop large heartedness, or purity of heart. It is to be expanded to such an extent as to make our own conscience the conscience of the whole country or that of the world. Our heart should become the mirror of the world. We must feel the needs of the whole world as our own need. We must take it as our own work, when we are in the eyes of others doing good to the country or to the world. Accordingly we must evolve ourselves to such an extent as to make our individual self the self of the whole nation. This is personal evolution or self-help. In short, we must feel our oneness with the whole nation.

Another poet says:

> The petals of a flower felt the shock of the morning breeze so much so that they dropped tears of dew from their eyes.

This "oneness with all" is the essence of the expansion of the self. The will force of your little self is really the strength or the will force of God Himself. Your own self is the Self of all, and in reality it is the Self of God. Feel it; be conscious of it and realize it. This is the ultimate goal of one's life which cannot be attained without self-help.

A poet says:

> In the temple of this body, we are the light of God.
> In the canal of this body, we are the water of life flowing into it.

These forms and names are like transitory shadows of the real Self. Whatever work we do individually, with a feeling of separation, as a separate name or form, is due to our narrow-mindedness or selfishness. It results only in pain, suffering and deception. Whatever is done with the feeling of oneness with all is not selfish. It is godly. Its result will always be success, relief, pleasure and peace.

The ultimate aim of this lecture is to inculcate in you a natural habit of viewing all the worldly connections not with selfishness but with godliness. Instead of considering yourself to be limited only to your name and form, you must be fully established in your real Self or Godhood.

> The house of God is more durable than your own house in this world. You must, therefore, take out your treasure (the soul) from here and keep it safely there.*

The man who transacts his business for his narrow selfishness based on his transitory name and form is building a castle in the air. He alone wins the laurels who regards the worldly success and prosperity or humiliation and failure as unreal like the foam of the waves, and does not trust them.

A poet says:

> Shadow is always light, even though it is that of a mountain.

He alone possesses the true eyes who can see the reality clearly, ignoring the worldly promise or denial and

* A couplet from Swami Rama's Urdu poem.

the threat or praise. "There is nothing but Allah. Only Brahma is real. All else is unreal." He alone is wise who always appreciates absolute goodness, extreme beauty, and the real Self. He sees the all with an ecstasy of wonder, "See Me, see Me, you will be all amazed. The man who has been deeply impressed by My unlimited beauty is lost in wonderment."

Somebody got a treasure in his dreams. On waking, if he regards himself to be a rich man on the basis of that wealth, he is a fool. So too is the man who trusts the objects of this dreamland world. He is only a living-dead. The greatness of self-help is to merge yourself in eternity, in God. Efface your selfishness to such an extent as to leave no sense of duality in you. There must not be left any trace of this limited selfishness within you.

A poet says:

> There must not be any limited "I." Do away with your narrow-mindedness and selfishness for good. This is the only condition to realize the Self.

Another poet says:

> You are yourself your own obstacle. Remove it from between yourself and the reality.

Unless you sever all your connections and detach yourself from all worldly attachments, like a flower from its parent plant, you cannot reach Him at all.

Someone enquired of the flute the reason for its being so much loved by Lord Krishna who governs the whole universe. "The great emperors like Arjun and Yudhishtira are anxious to touch His feet. The dust under His feet in Bindraban is even now being respected and put on the heads by the great Kings and other devotees. The great beauties of the world pine to have a glimpse of His smile. That Krishna who is All in all puts you, flute on His lips and kisses you with love, licking again and again. Why? You are just a small and thin bamboo piece. How could you manage to win so great a Lord? Whence did you get this power to perform such a miracle?"

The flute replied, "I have made myself hollow from head to foot (by destroying my egoism and selfishness). The result is that Lord Krishna Himself comes and kisses me. He kisses me with fondness. Why should I not give out pleasant and melodious tunes? I have within me the life and breath of Rama. My tune is His tune. I have harmonized myself with Him."

A poet says:

> Empty yourself from top to bottom like a flute otherwise it is not easy to get the loving kisses from Murli Dhar (God).

After detaching themselves from the worldly attachments the Arifs, the wise men, attain Eternal Life.

Om! Om! Om!

A MESSAGE FOR THE INDIAN PEOPLE AND THE WORLD*

Rama urges no law of theories but the logic of events. Wherever you hear the statement, "The law allows it," remember that the fellow is up to mischief. Whoever lives in love lives above law as law. The only lawful law is love. To live in love is to live true to yourself. The real law is myself. To dictate law to me is to sever it from me. Should any laws be laid down for the child commanding him to breathe, to grow or play and live? Is not his very life law? Like a free bird, a child is seen singing, laughing and talking spontaneously. There come up the officious visitors soliciting him to sing, talk and laugh. Immediately the child stops. The playful expressions which were so natural for him turn unnatural the moment the consciousness of being alien to those expressions is brought home to the child. Whoever lives a free life, true to the Self, a life of divine recklessness, all the laws of the world are true to him, being identical with him. He abhors nothing. He curls up from nothing. He shrinks from nothing.

What is disease? Contraction due to lack of love, shuddering at the flutter of shadows, crying at the day-dreams of danger. In reality there is nothing to be afraid of. All around, in all future, in all distance, there is but one Self supreme existent, and that is my own Self. Of whom shall I be afraid? Night is just as good as day. Storm is just as necessary as sunlight. Often whole nights

* The following are some of the letters originally written to Swami Narayana and afterwards enlarged and edited by Swami Rama himself for publication. These excerpts have been translated from the Urdu.

pass away without a wink of sleep, and yet Rama is as fresh in daytime as ever because weariness comes from worry for sleep, and not so much from lack of sleep. How happy are the vigils when Lord Love keeps us awake! When the system requires hearty meals they are enjoyed, but often no inclination to eat being felt, fasting is enjoyed equally well. Rainstorms of tears bring floods of joy because Love rides the storm. Streams of laughter flow free and the joy involved in them is neither less nor more than the joy of tears. What shall Rama resist? What shall Rama escape from when all is his Self? Oh, what a supreme recklessness!

Rama frets not when fever would pay a visit. Rama receives it as a friend, and spiritual truths flash which could never otherwise be disclosed. All is health. Wakefulness is one kind of health; sleep is another form of it; gentle calmness is beautiful, but the storm of hot fever has a charm of its own. True religion means faith in *good* rather than faith in *God.* There was never yet such a storm, but it was aeolian music to a healthy and innocent ear.

With the rumble of thunder let it be proclaimed, "So long as any trace of external obligation and categorical imperative, 'Thou shalt' and 'Thou shalt not,' is in play there can be no room for spiritual growth of true purity." The imperative mood, second person, keeps alive in us the limited personality, and wherever there is limitation there is no bliss nor any escape from attraction and repulsion, no salvation from attachment and hatred, no freedom from vacillation and temptation. So long as there remains a limited body in space surrounded by other bodies, how could it give gravitation the door, throw dust in the eyes of the laws of attraction and repulsion, cheat nature and escape outside influences? The man in regard to his single body lives in the consciousness of unity of Self; despite the seeming differences in the functions of different organs the same "I" sees, hears, walks and so on. So in regard to the whole world the free-man lives in the consciousness of unity of world-self, and the differences take care of themselves even as the assimilation of food, growth of hair, etc., take care of themselves in a single body. It is through realizing one's infinity, conquering all sense of difference, feeling our oneness with all, realizing the stars, landscapes, rivers and all as my own and through love owning all that temptations lose their power over us.

When the great sun is shining, what light can the little glow worm cast? When all is beauty to me, and I am that, what shall I run after? What is there in the whole range of the world's possessions to attract a man just one with all objects of attraction?

What mischief does not, or will not, the stingy thief commit who wants to hide the Light of lights behind the bushel of lies, the suicidal playing false to the supreme Self, thinking oneself other than God?

No physical action, good or evil,
No mental action, virtuous or ill,
No shame or fame, no praise or blame
Could taint me e'er, no kind of game,
Nothing but the flood or glory!
To whom shall I give thanks,
To whom shall I turn and look up,
When bliss absolute,
When light immeasurable
Is manifest even in me?

LABOR AND LOVE

Give the poor laborer food for the soul; give him love, and he will work for you even without asking any food for the body. Love you the workman; the workman shall love your work. Labor actuated by love, can it be called labor? Nay, it is entertaining play.

What is art? Bringing out beauty in what we touch. What on earth or in heaven is that which draws out and unveils beauty? Why, what else could it be but love?

Thus the spirit of love shining upon our labor makes industry artistic and produces what are called industrial arts. Why is there no original designing, aesthetic workmanship, no industrial art worth the name flourishing in India these days? Why, because no love is lost upon laborers. The poor working classes, instead of being welcomed in the heart are turned out from their own huts.

Where labor is despised, the result is stagnation, decay and death, and art becomes laborious. Where labor is loved, life and light abide, and labor becomes artistic. Oh, Lord Love! Has it come to such a pass? Love is misunderstood to such a degree that the very mention of the word "love" suggests to the dear people the idea of cupidity and stupidity instead of that divine flame! Sometimes they make big talk about divine love, *bhakti* and *upasana*, but practically it amounts to muttering aloud some Sanskrit hymns and chanting certain mantrams, hardly understanding, not to say feeling, what they say. Vain bullets with no powder! Counterfeit imitation of Chaitanya's genuine burning heart! From temples hymns in the vernacular are often heard, sung with the most perfect music known to them, but not a single sanctifying tear of love!

Blessed Hindustanis! You cannot befool God and win His love by calling yourselves sinners and slaves. Just as you think, so are you bound to become. The inexorable law of karma works with a vengeance and makes sinners and slaves of you when you pray that way. That is not *bhakti.*

Bhaktas of India! You are all very ready to take up the sweetheart of Gopis and Chaitanya, but how many of you have the pure flaming passion of Gopikas and Gauranga? You will be the darling dear of that sweet cowheard when you see Him with divine love in the chandala, in the thief, in the sinner, in the stranger and all, and do not confine Him to mere stone images.

Bhakti (love) is no crying, begging, negative condition. It is an indescribable sense of equality, beaming sweetness and divine recklessness. It is the seeing of the All in all we see. It is seeing your own Self wherever your eyes fall. It is to realize that all is beauty and I am that, *Tat tvam asi* or "that thou art."

Mohammedans! You may slay Rama, but Rama's heart burns with your love. Christians! You may misunderstand Rama but Rama loves you. Pariahs! Sweepers! If no one will enter your filthy, diseased wigwams, you will find Rama there with you. Feigned love, false feelings and assumed sentimentalism is an insult to God. A genuine flame is needed even if it be accompanied with smoke of lower passion. Conventionality, customs, conformity, slavery to shame, name and fame act like a heap of chaff and charcoal, choking down the spark of truthful feeling which may be burning in the innermost heart of a youth, borne down by the dead weight of appearances. Welcome, truth! Thou alone art my relative, friend, sweetheart, lord liege and my Self.

Kings! Laws and communities! Bless your hearts, but you have no power to extract any compromise from

Rama. Spare your threats, favors and frowns. My king, the tyrant truth, is stronger than myriads of emperors, despots and autocrats put together.

There can be no love where there is no truthfulness. Lord Love is the vice regent of the tyrant truth. It may be vice versa. Perhaps both are the same.

> But God said,
> I will have a purer gift,
> There is smoke in the flame.
> Deep, deep are loving eyes,
> Flowed with naphtha fiery sweet;
> And the point is paradise
> Where their glances meet.
> Their reach shall yet be more profound
> And a vision without bound;
> The axis of those eyes sun clear
> Be the axis of the sphere.
>
> Emerson

Roar, ye torrents from the mountains! Roar, oh sea! Roar under the pale stars, O gulf of death! Yawn blackening beneath. Oh! great heart over the forests, the mountains and the seas, o'er the black chasm of death, in spectral haste I know Thou ridest, my Lord Love, and the hungry winds and waves are but thy bounds. Oh tyrant truth! Thou, the eternal huntsman.

In the twilight of Galilee, He saw them (the disciples) toiling and moiling, tugging and towing; hurriedly rowing for the wind was contrary unto them. But there was no toiling and rowing for the Master. Why should not such a man sleep in the midst of the storm, knowing He would walk upon the waters? Oh! Joy! My Love rides the winds and waves.

Foolish moralists! Religious fiends! Hands off! You have no right to dictate to the young folks. The only right anybody has is to serve. Nature, if allowed to have her free course, will never err. The law, or God, that worked up the evolution of man from the tiniest amoeba to the human form divine can well be trusted.

Why are cattle and other animals more regular, cleaner and better behaved in the control of what human jealousy has styled animal passion? The plain reason is that the former are not pestered by "thou shalts" and "thou shalt nots." Service and love, not mandates and compulsion is the atmosphere for growth.

How can we make the flowers grow? By loving them. A woman raised beautiful flowers in a climate most uncongenial for their growth. How did she manage it? She loved them, and the means were suggested of themselves. The genial heat of love is the only incubator. It makes industries artistic and brings about beauty in our work.

Confound not love with attachment. Your wife and children instead of being the circumscribing hedges of your affections, ought to be the center of radiation of love to the whole world. Says Jean Paul Richter, "I love my family more than myself, my country more than my family, and the whole world more than my country." How noble are the words of Lovelace (slightly altered) to Lucaster on going to the wars, "I could not love thee, dear, so much, loved I not the nation more."

True love like the sun expands the Self. Attachment (*moha*) like the frost congeals and contracts the soul. The first law of Moses means, "Thou shalt have no other God but Love." This jealous Lord Love will not allow any idols of cupidity and attachment to usurp His majestic throne.

What is idolatry? To give the forms of foes and friends a sense of personality, individuality and reality to such an extent as to miss the impersonated (masked) individual (indivisible) real Self or law.

Why is it that the sight of woods, landscapes, rivers, lakes and green hills inspires, uplifts, charms and breeds ecstasy? Why? Because it relieves us of the sense of limited personality; it takes off the put-on looks which weigh us down in the crowded streets. The blessed trees and dear water in their impersonal gentleness, nay sweetness, no more force on us any sense of smallness.

Happy is he who turns the whole world into a heavenly garden by seeing the same impersonal breath of life in the throngs of men and women as inspires in the rose garden and oak groves.

BURNING REST

The different objects, big, small, fair, foul, ugly and charming, all are but strange heiroglyphics to the living lover, all indicate the same love, beautiful characters, all meaning my own Self, fine pictures, all representing the beloved Lord, different garbs of beauty, all clothing the same sweetheart—Self.

Oh, what an ocean of beauty! What an ocean of love! The dark tresses of the beloved are just as fascinating to the lover as the bright face. So night is just as welcome to Rama as day; death, as sweet as life; fever, just as welcome as health; the foes, as dear as friends.

How blessed is he whose property is stolen away! Thrice blessed is he whose wife runs away that by such means he is brought in direct touch with the all love. The Mohammedan tradition says that Abraham at one time desired to take a sea voyage. Khizar, or Neptune, offered his services as a humble captain of the boat.

Abraham at first gave his foolish consent, but on reconsideration he begged pardon of Khizar, saying, "My most gracious brother, excuse me please; I would prefer to have my boat without a captain, ferried directly by the hand of love. If you, the Lord of the Seas take the oar, it is safe riding, but, ah me! It is too safe! It will make me rely on you and will bar me from direct dependence on God. Please do not stay between me and God. There is more joy to me in resting directly on God's bosom than even the bosom of my brother Khizar."

Says the desperate and forlorn lover, "Pray, flash on, Oh lightning! Roar on, Oh thunder! Rage on, Oh storm! Howl on, Oh winds! I thank thee, I thank thee, I thank thee. Oh blessed thunder, you frighten delicate love to cling to me for a moment. How infinitely sweet are the bitters of life when out of its grapes we can press the sweet wine of delicious pangs of God love!

Dear blessed reader! Did you ever have the privilege of being lost, nay risen, in love, unselfish love, giving all to love? Then you must be in a position to appreciate sentiments like the following:

> Soft skin of Taif for thy sandals take,
> And of our heart-strings fitting latchets make,
> And tread on lips which yearn to touch those feet.
> O my blessed Lord, accept me as the most humble
> slave of feet.

What office is there that love cannot bless and beautify? There is no great and no small, no low and no high, where love is. The hardest work becomes heavenly when the spirit of love prompts us to it. Selfishness will make the highest position most wearisome and tedious. Whatever your station of life, love makes it sweet. All troubles, storms, pangs and anguish spring simply from the spirit of possession in us. Where is the pain of hell when I love it? All our troubles and turmoils are, so to say, a teasing on the part of love to wake us up to her embraces. These jerks, shakings and pats are from no other than sweet love. God, sweet Hari, wakes you pouring forth His love.

PRACTICAL WISDOM

Whoever walks a furlong without sympathy walks to his own funeral dressed in his shroud.

Wisdom and learning are not identical. They are not always on speaking terms. Learning looks backward to the past. Wisdom looks forward to the future.

Wisdom has been defined as knowing what one ought to do next. Virtue is doing it.

Wisdom without virtue is a weariness of the flesh. As volition passes over into action, science into art, and knowledge into power, so does wisdom pass into virtue. Where thought does not go over into action, there results mental dyspepsia or moral constipation. Men of mere ideas and no legs are no more than intellectual centipedes.

Says an American humorous writer:

> I've thought and thought on men and things;
> As my uncle used to say,
> 'If the folks don't work as they pray,
> Why, there isn't no use to pray.
> If you want something and just dead set,
> A pleading for it with both eyes wet,
> And tears won't bring it, why, you try sweat."
> As my uncle used to say.

The power of safe and accurate response to external conditions is the essential feature of sanity. The inability to adopt action to need is a character of insanity. "Change or perish" is the grim watchword of nature. Keep pace with the advancing times and you can survive in the struggle of life. (India! take note.)

The spirit of all practical wisdom is summed up concisely in the simple and saving advice of Krishna, "Thy business is with the action only, never with the reward or merit accruing from it. Let not the fruit of action entangle thee, nor be thou the slave of inaction."

And live in action! Labor! Make thine acts
Thy piety casting all self aside,
Condemning gain and merit, equable
In good or evil. Equability
Is yoga, is piety.

Be in the struggle; that is your duty. A true hero loves engagement (action) as never a lover wooed his sweetheart. In case of death in the field, you bring glory to heaven or truth, i.e., advance the cause of evolution and cosmic progress by letting the fittest survive, and in case of victory also you let the real power, truth, shine through you. In reality you are the truth that conquers and not this body or that which is consumed in the strife. You are ever victorious. As truth's self, shine out as energy of life.

Either, being killed,
Thou wilt win heaven's safety, or alive
And victor, thou wilt reign earthly king.
Therefore, arise thou, son of truth! Brace
Thine arm for conflict; nerve thy heart to meet,
As things alike to these, pleasure or pain,
Profit or ruin, victory or defeat.
So minded, gird thee to the fight, for so
Thou shalt not sin.

The true gauge of success being of spiritual growth and not outward gain or loss, defeat is as glorious as victory. O happy knight, you happen to be on the play-ground (world); hit on; hit on! A man's strength of character bears a direct proportion to the extent of trials he has undergone.

Waiving all conventionality and superficial mode of talk and appealing directly to the facts of innermost experience, we see that all wise counsels, rules of conduct, authoritative obligations, categorical imperatives, "Thou shalt nots" and "Thou shalts," are only vain efforts to infuse life into one who is not firmly rooted in his own Godhead, whether consciously or unconsciously. These are outside electric charges which can at best but move this muscle or that of the dead carcass, being never capable of inspiring more than a sham life.

"That which is forced is never forcible." Unless love builds the house they labor in vain who build it. It is true that the miracles of genius were always miracles of labor, but what seemed painful labor in the eyes of others was always most enjoyable play to genius.

That lifeless, insipid work which I (personal ego) have to labor out, I better leave alone. If the work does not do itself through you as an afflux of the soul, your strained exertion furnishes but a poor excuse for doing it. Such dull prosaic work, dragged along by the credit-hunting small illusory self (egoistic consciousness) is described by Shankara as the twin of bondage (slavery).

A boy was merrily whistling in the streets. A policeman objected. The boy replied, "Do I whistle? No, sir, it whistles itself."

Let a nightingale or dove be perched on the top of a stately cypress, and full, delicious notes begin instantaneously to flow from the bird.

Let the little self be flung into infinity. May you wake up to your oneness with Life, Light and Love (*Sat, Chit, Anand)*, and immediately the central bliss will commence springing forth from you in the shape of happy heroic work, both wisdom and virtue. This is inspired life; this is your birthright. Says Coleridge:

> From himself he flies,
> Stands in the sun and with no partial gaze
> Views all creation; and he loves it all
> And blesses it and calls it very good.

"It is difficult to find happiness in oneself," says Schopenhauer, "but it is impossible to find it anywhere else."

All great work is done impersonally in spite of the prudent little self, and not by it. The sun simply shines in his native glory as a disinterested witness-light *(sakshi)* and lo! the rivers and unlocked from their snowy cradles; the breezes begin to dance with glee, and nature is set in activity; animals wake up, plants grow on, violets and roses blow on, and even the sparkling flowers of men, women and children's eyes open up at the mere presence of the sun's glorious majesty. You have simply to shine as the soul of all, the source of light, the spring of delight, O blessed One, and energy, life, activity will naturally begin to radiate from you. The flower blooms, and fragrance emanates of itself.

If anybody not knowing the art of swimming perchance falls into a lake, he will naturally be buoyed up by the water, but the losing of calm and his desperate struggling with the hands and feet will make him sink helplessly. "So, the care and anxiety-worn, struggling little ego is the drowning sink for man," says Jalal-i-Rumi.

> Heavenly manna was showered daily to the
> Israelites in the forest, but
> Some graceless scoffers out of Moses' host
> Dared to demand the onions,
> And manna was lost.

What aches the head, bends the back or chokes the chest? It is walking on the head instead of on the feet. Let your feet be on the earth and your head in the air filled with heavenly joy; invert not the divine ordinance; put not the earth on your head, and call it sane living; take not the appearances more seriously than the divine real Self.

They say a man treading the forest in search of mushrooms tramples down oak trees under his feet. Beloved, why should your attention be dead set on petty gains and losses so as to miss the infinite bliss *(Atman)*? Is it the responsibility-ridden, duty-stricken, honor-laden (false) ego that really affects any deed? A flea on the flank of a horse might just as well claim that it makes the horse run and drive the carriage.

Obtrude not the little I *(Ahankara)* in the way of the effulgent outbursts of ecstatic truth. Trust, trust that power. The true Self whose presence caused the poor little amoeba unconsciously to evolve up to your human form divine, that Self supreme, that divine law, is still present. Since that God is neither asleep nor dead, there is no fear of fall.

Says Thoreau, the *Brahmacharin* of America:

> Whate'er we leave to God, God does
> And blesses us;
> The work we choose sh'd be our own,
> God leaves alone.

Trouble and pain is another name for feeling oneself a prisoner and a slave of conditions and circumstances. Shake off all atheistic delusions of isolation. If the ruling Self of outside nature were different from your own inner Self, there was no other course left for you but to wring the hands, hang down the head and be damned.

As it is, thou appearest on the one hand as garrisoned by environments, and on the other hand thou appearest as those environments and conditions. The looking glass is in me, in my hand, and I am in the looking glass.

I heard a knock, a hard blow,
On my door and cried I "Who is it? Ho!"
I wondering waited entranced, and lo!
How soft and sweet love whispered low,
"Tis thou that knockest, do you not know?"

According to the true interpretation of Muslim scriptures even the Archangel was hurled into perdition by refusing to recognize the Supreme (God) in man, and even the rankest sinners inherit heaven through realizing God *(Ahad)* in man *(Ahmad).*

This practical or living perception of "my self as the Self of all others" is the true saving Islam (Shraddha faith). To call it mere belief is doing no justice to it. It is the ultimate science or in Vedanta, *Jnanam*. It is the art of arts. The final test of truth, says Dr. D. S. Jordon, is "Can we make it work? Can we trust our life to it?" You can safely trust your life and all to the fact underlying all phenomena, "I and my Father are one." "That thou art." The law of gravity might even deceive your trust in it, but the law of spiritual unity never deceives. Just feel this unity, and you find all creation behaving as your own body. Gold and silver cannot insure your life, O deluded immortal. Thou it is that lends life to *prana*, lustre to gold and silver, and light to the suns and stars.

People do not make rapid progress because that load of outside opinion and conventionality sitting like the mighty Himalayas on their back (nay, breast) does hardly let a single step be advanced. Free yourself of unhealthy superstition of limitation. In your mind there must be a liquor which will dissolve the world whenever it is dropped in it.

The universal solvent of *Jnanam* (self-knowledge) will hold the universe in solution and yet be as translucent as ever. Provided you think aright, the heavens falling or the earth gaping will be music for you to march by. No foe can ever see you, nor you, him. You cannot so much as even think of him.

In music, the different notes may succeed and precede each other in regular sequence (as cause and effect); the symphony is not understood by examination and comparison of the notes alone but by experience of their relation to the deepest feeling which inspires and sustains the piece, which is the origin of the piece and the result of its performance, the alpha and the omega.

So nature is not explained by dwelling on its surface laws and superficial causation, but by "its becoming the body of man."

Unless you feel all, you know not all. Diving into the reality, sounding below the names and forms, passing free into woods and fields, mountains and rivers, into day and night, clouds and stars, passing free into men and women, animals and angels, as the Self of each and all, this is life, this is self-knowledge, this is practical wisdom.

The whole world is bound to co-work with one who feels himself one with the whole world.

Jnanam, living knowledge of truth, being realized on the causal plane, becomes overwhelming love, that is to say, oneness feeling with the All, an abiding ecstasy, which like the effulgent sun although it seeks no fruit, begs no reward and asks nothing. It manifests itself as renunciation on the mental plane yet reveals itself as wonderful energy and powerful action on the physical plane.

Hence realize *Jnanam,* renunciation through love in action.

THE LAW OF LIFE ETERNAL

Rama lays claim to no mission. The work is all God's. What have we to do with the examples and precedents of Buddha and others? Let our minds respond to the direct dictates of the law. But even Buddha and Jesus were forsaken by all their friends and followers. Thus out of the seven years of the forest life, Buddha passed the last two years entirely alone, and then came the effulgent light, after which disciples began to flock to him and were welcomed. Be not influenced by the thoughts and opinions of well-meaning respectable advisers. If their thoughts had been at one with the law, they might have created ship loads of Buddhas by this time.

Slowly and resolutely, as a fly cleans its legs of the honey in which it has been caught, so we must remove every particle of attachment to forms and personalities. One after another the connections must be cut; the ties must snap till the final concession in the form of death crowns all unwilling renunciations.

Mercilessly rolls on the wheel of law. He who lives the law rides the law. He who sets up his will against God's will (i.e., the law) must be crushed and suffer Promethean tortures. The law is the cross; it pierces the little false self. He who suffers willing crucifixion, to him the world is a garden of Eden. To all else it is a paradise lost. The law is fire, it burns up all worldly attachments, it scorches the ignorant mind, yet it purifies and destroys all kinds of spiritual plague germs.

Religion is as universal and vitally connected with our being as the act of eating. The successful atheist knows not the process of his own digestion as it were. The law makes us religious at the bayonet's point. The law flogs us up to wakefulness. There is no escape from the law. The law is real, and all else is unreal. All forms and personalities are mere bubbles in the ocean of the law. Reality has been defined as that which persists. Now nothing in the world of forms, no relationships, no bodies, no organizations, no societies, could ever persist so tenaciously as this law of the cross.

Why do deluded, short-sighted creatures love appearances (personalities) more than the ideal law? Because through ignorance, persons and other appearances seem to them persistent realities and the law, an intangible evanescent cloud. Though hard knocks and painful bumps they may be saved if they happen to learn the lesson which the grim dame nature intends to teach, i.e., the cross. Shiva is the only reality, and all personalities and objects of affection are passing phantoms, merest shadows, fictitious ghosts. The apparent bitters and sweets, the seeming beauties and monstrosities are only masks put on by the *bihareeji* (the playful one) to open our eyes to His glory at last.

When we believe in the forms of foes and friends as real, they deceive and betray us. But we make the matters still worse when we begin to retaliate and impute to them motives and evil natures. The first faithlessness on their part was due to our assigning through love that reality to them which belongs to God alone. Now that we resent, we intensify our previous error through hatred, assigning still greater reality to their forms and thus inviting more pain. Beware! This perfect renunciation, Shiva, is the ultimate purpose in life. It is a living reality, something more concrete than stones, and well might it be represented by the stone lingam. It strikes harder than stones to correct the forgetful mind. To remember it perpetually is of vital necessity.

Mohammadans and Christians are not wrong in calling this law, or God, *Ghayyur* (jealous) and *Qahhar* (terrible). Indeed, it is no respecter of persons. Let anyone set his heart on anything whatever of this world and unavertedly the wrath of nature must, must, be visited upon him. If people are slow in learning this truth, it is because they have little power of correct observation; usually in matters concerning their own personality, they do not like to see the cause in the phenomenon itself, and they would readily blame others for their own faults and know not to retrospect as a disinterested witness their own moods of passion and feeling and the consequences these entail. Betrayed we must be when we trust the forms or when in our heart of hearts we give that honor to false things and personalities which is due only to the One Reality, i.e., when we let idols sit on the throne of our hearts instead of God. The method of agreement and difference establishes the law of the unsubstantiality of not-God, knowing no exception.

How often are we not the cause of perfect gentlemen no longer remaining as good as their word by setting our heart on their promises and believing in them more than in God? How often do we not bring about the death or ruin of our children by the law-forgetting love for their bodies (forms)? How often do we not make friends faithless by depending on them and placing in their persons that innermost faith which is due to God alone, i.e., the jealous law? How often do we not bring living gurus down from their spiritual heights by making them trust on us and on our faith in them, whereas the law must make us deny them even more than "three times before the cock crows"? How often is not our heart dependence on wives the cause of domestic strife and of far worse scenes? Take anything more seriously than God, and divine love must stab you with piercing glance.

To talk of no unworthy loves, let us take the case of the Gopikas who set their hearts on the fascinating form of God-incarnate, and yet they had to shed bitter tears of blood for their mistake. The embodiment of chaste affection, Sita believed in the reality of the form glorious of divine Rama, yet she, O even she! had to pay for the error in being driven into the hissing forests by the jealous (formless) Rama or the real Rama, her master, the Lord of each and all.

"The Brahman must desert him who sees the Brahman not in Self. The Kshattriya must forsake him who feels the Kshattriya to be elsewhere than in Self. The people (or the worlds) must banish him who regards the *lokas* (the people) separate from Self; the gods must abandon him who looks upon gods as different from Self; the objects or things must give him up who realizes the objects as elsewhere than in Self. Anything and everything must reject him who does not take anything and everything as one with Self. That Self is Brahman, that Self is Kshattriya, that Self is the people, that Self is the gods, that Self is things, that Self is each and all."

Shruti Veda

The seeming objects which attract are apparently equivalent to the innocent form of Krishna. The dragon of mind readily takes them in, but on getting inside they stab from within, pierce the dragon's belly, and people begin to complain, "O, my heart is broken! I am undone! I am undone!" Why did you let yourself be deceived by names and forms? Love the Reality only. Cling to God alone. Take in God, assimilate God, walk with God, be God, behave like God. That is life. Not till you have given them up, you will see the infinite faithfulness and love which is in the things of this world.

Dear Ones! God alone is real and all else unreal. It is true that Mohammad has been misunderstood and often wrongly followed, but anyone who sees the truth must reverently bow before the idea, although only one-sided, of putting an immediate end (by sword) to the lingering, chronic tortures of those who are dying by inches through practical non-belief in the only truth—"There is no reality but God." Christ teaches practically the same lesson; Buddha the same; and, of course, every one of our own rishis in one form or another preaches the same thing. But what of that? Their preachings and teachings could never have survived if they had not found hearty response in the private experiences of those who heard them, and if they had not been borne out, verified and time and again rediscovered by the truthful, the sincere devotees of light in all ages.

The law of renunciation is a stern reality. No flimsy phantom this! Nations could not be all deluded and carried away by the mere chimerical hallucinations of prophets and leaders. Centuries and centuries could not be run away with by the mere fancy of poor cranks.

People, not knowing the real cause of their miseries, which is falling out of tune with the law, begin to fall foul with the outside symptoms of their malady, i.e., the apparent circumstances. Let the good or bad talk or conduct of people be washed out of consciousness even as misty dreams are consigned to oblivion. Dreams may be nightmares or sweet dreams, we do not try to adjust them or quarrel with them; but rather our own stomach it is that is straitened. So good or bad folks that meet us ought to be entirely ignored and our spiritual condition improved. Let not these seeming evils or lucks stand between thee and God. There are no insults and faults immense enough to satisfy me in the act of forgiving them.

Let nothing be prized higher than God, nothing valued equally with God. Compliments, criticisms and diseases are equally fatal if we regard Self as subject to them. Feel yourself God, and sing songs of joy in Godhead. Look upon compliments and criticisms even as Rama looks upon physical ailments merely as footmen from God's Durbar, who with all the authority of the supreme government say, "Get out of this house (body consciousness) at once!" They obey me when I occupy the Durbar throne; they whip me and stab me when I enter into this hovel, the body consciousness.

Even governments whose so-called laws do not conform to the divine law of the cross work their own destruction. Shylock-like laying stress on personal rights, thinking this or that is mine, feeling a sense of possession, saying "the law grants it," is to contradict the real law according to which the only *haq* (right, prerogative) we have is *haq* (God), and every other right is wrong. If nobody else recognizes this principle, the Sannyasin at any rate ought to work it into life.

The law is all pervasive, is the higher Self of each and all and is Rama in this sense. Yet it must kick out and kill out the personal self. It is cruel, but its cruelty is the quintessence of love because in this very death of the apparent self consists resurrection of the real Self and life eternal. He who keeps the false self and claims for it the prerogatives of the king-Self must, as it were, be devoured by vultures on the height of vanity. The freedom of Vedanta is no impunity from law for the limited local Self, i.e., personality and body. This is turning G-O-D into the very reverse. Millions of beings perish every hour through this mistake; thousands of heads are sinking into pessimism, and hundreds of thousands of hearts are breaking every minute by the foolish reversal of the order of the law. The freedom from law is secured by becoming the law; that is the realization of Shivoham.

That dupe of the senses who counts on what are called facts and figures and rests on the foundation of forms, builds on the foam and sinks. He builds on the rock in whose heart of hearts,

> God is Real; the world, unreal,
> and the law a living force.

Let this body be freely called policy player, selfish, vain, proud or anything else; let it be what they call insulted, kicked, killed; what is that to me, the Self of all?

> I am Truth the inevitable,
> I am Law the inexorable;
> To know Me is to obey Me,
> To obey Me is to prosper.
> Oppose Me; it will not annoy Me;
> Ignore Me; I cannot be anxious
> But will calmly destroy him who slights.

This is no empty threat. It is too terrible a truth. Let us have at least as much respect and regard for truth (God, law) as we have for the feelings of persons. If the hearts of persons break by our faithful, innocent loyalty to the divine law, we cannot be held responsible for that.

To us it should by all means be of far more serious concern not to break the law. By yielding to the whims of those we call our dear and near, as against the law, we invite calamity over their heads as well as ours. There is none nearer than God; none should be dearer than God, truth (law).

As a woman of a man, so shall I learn of Thee; I shall draw Thee closer and closer; I will drain Thy lips and the secret juices of Thy body; I will conceive of Thee, O law! O liberty!

Is not Rama married to the truth and law, that other attachments and other connections are still expected of him as of a harlot?

This is no blind impulse, nor is this a selfish policy to harm anybody. Why, what has innocent Rama committed that ye would drag him into narrow limitations of personal relationship? Spare him; pray spare him. For your own safety's sake, spare him. Leave him alone. In this lies the good of your country and of humanity. Do ye suppose that he will die in loneliness without the tender cares of his body on your part? No, God is real, and life in God knows no hardship, and this body cannot drop before it has done the work of God.

It is no good to be meddling with anybody's sacred vows. He will let nothing stand between him and his ideal; no, not even death. Let no one try to shape his career according to notions borrowed from a godless reading of history. Away with your loves and homages to the seeming Rama. These are an insult to the real Rama, the Self of all. Hands off! Wake up from the dream of forms. Shake off the illusion of personalities and body-consciousness even as Rama has shaken off dyspepsia by a life of law. Burn up sense-attachments by focusing the scorching light of Self on them. Give no quarters to worldly impressions in your heart, keeping it all the time brimful of the real Rama. Any other thought besides that of the Beloved let me expel from the city of my heart. Is not God at least as sweet as any sense object?

People hesitate to love God because they think they receive no response from Him as in the case of fictitious worldly objects of love. It is this foolish ignorance that thus deludes them. O dear! His breast instantaneously, nay, simultaneously, heaves with thy breast in responsive impulse. Look not in the apparent friends and foes the cause of their conduct. The real causation rests with your real Self alone. Look out! As a little bird just learning to fly leaves one stone or twig and perches on another similar support, then on another, and another, but cannot leave entirely those ground objects and soar into the higher air; so a novice in *Brahma jnana* while disengaging his heart from one thing or disgusted with a particular person immediately rests on something else, then clings to another similar delusion, does not give up dependence on frail reed or straw, and quits not in his heart the whole earth. An experienced *jnani* would turn the apparent faithlessness of one earthly object into a stepping stone for a leap into the infinite. The art of religion consists of making every little bit of experience an occasion for a leap into the infinite. Deplorable dunce must be he who does not recognize the piercing truth that death of the selfish personality alone is the law of life. The shaking off of personalities is resurrection of life eternal. Live ye forever! Farewell.

Notebooks

The good man confers a blessing upon the world by merely living.

There is nothing that is evil except because a man has not mastery over it; and there is no good that is not evil if it have mastery over a man.

Vice is our name for self-inflicted injury.

True liberty is the accurate appreciation of necessity. I am that necessity and being that necessity am free.

Rights are the condition of individuality. But rights are always wrong.

The merit of originality is not novelty; it is sincerity. The believing man is the original man; whatsoever he believes, he believes it for himself, not for another.

A prudent man is like a pin; his head prevents him from going too far.

Comparison, or drawing contrasts, is the root of all evil.

Some slaves are scourged to their work by whips; others are scourged to it by restlessness or ambition. It does not matter what the whip is; it is none the less a whip, because you have cut thongs for it out of your own souls. The fact so far of slavery is in being driven to your work at another's bidding. Again some slaves are bought with money and others with praise. It matters not what the purchase money is. The distinguishing sign of slavery is to have a price and be bought for it.

A community is adorned not by great men with small views, but small men with great views.

We fear social ostracism a little too much as children fear to go into the dark.

Reputation is an idle and most false imposition, oft got without merit and lost without deserving.

Worldly riches and honors are the fig leaves with which the shamed soul attempts to hide its nakedness.

Growing old is a bad habit.

There is always room for a man of force, and he makes room for many.

Head as high as you please but feet always upon the common ground, never upon anybody's shoulders or neck even though he be weak or willing.

I doubt the wisdom of being too wise; and I see much wisdom in some folly.

A man never rises so high as when he knows not whither he is going.

Hope is the only universal liar who never loses his reputation for veracity.

Truth is tough. It will not break like a bubble at a touch! Nay, you may kick it about all day like a football, and it will be round and sound at evening.

Our concepts and generalizations are like paper money which for the time and under certain conditions may and do represent value, but no more.

All dogmatism is flying off at a tangent from actual facts. The tangent represents the direction of a curve over a small arc, but following the tangent we soon lose the curve.

The views of science are like the views of a mountain; each is only possible as long as you limit yourself to a certain standpoint. Move your position, and the view is changed. In science you select certain details and isolate them from the rest. But in supposing such isolation you suppose what is false and therefore vitiate the conclusion. A man seeing a very small arc of a very vast circle easily mistakes it for a straight line.

He who identifies himself with the unstable appearances and wants to fight for it is unfit to survive.

Pain may be likened to the heat produced in a machine by destructive friction and pleasure to that musical hum which comes from a machine that is doing its work without injury to itself.

The deepest truths we can reach are simply statements of the widest uniformities in our experiences of the relations of matter, motion and force; and matter, motion and force are but symbols of the unknown reality.

When human tongue ceases to speak, then the stones begin to talk.

"I believe," said the rose to the lily in the parable, "I believe that our gardener is immortal. I have watched him from day to day since I bloomed, and I see no change in him. The tulip who died yesterday told me the same thing."

The morning breeze blows and is not anxious how many and what sort of flowers bloom; it only blows in everything, and those buds that are full ripe to sprout open their eyes.

Beauty and pleasure are an accidental or momentary coincidence of the universal and the particular and an earnest of their complete reconciliation.

The sorrows and prosperity should fall on you as clearly and softly as the landscape falls on the eyes.

In music the symphony is not understood by examination

and comparison of the notes alone, but by experience of their relation to the deepest feelings; and nature is not explained by laws, but by its becoming—or rather being felt to be—the body of man which in turn is the marvelous interpreter and symbol of his inward being. We cannot say that one note is the cause of another, but we might say that each note stands in a causal subordination to the feeling which inspired the piece, which is the origin of the piece and the result of its performance, the alpha and omega.

When one looks out on a storm at night, he sees for an instant the landscape illumined by the lightning flash. All seems at rest. The branches in the wind, the flying clouds, the falling rain, and the running train are motionless in this instantaneous view.

Let us have at least the dignity of trees and rivers.

True religion is not belief in a God, but is a complete trust in the good in man.

Having created God in their own image, theologians find no difficulty in ascribing to Him their own motives.

To act by means of inaction is God.

The essence of prayer is to bring two things into unison—the will of God and the will of man. Superstition imagined, no doubt, that prayer would change the will of God, but the more spiritually minded have always understood that the will which must be modified in prayer was the will of man.

All the Vedantic way of life is typified by Arjuna giving the reins of his horses unto Krishna. To fight is your duty and not to bother about the circumstances.

Man's unhappiness, as I construe, comes of his greatness; it is because there is an infinite in him, which with all his cunning he cannot quite bury under the finite.

We are near awakening when we dream that we dream.

If thou art love's lover and seekest love, take a keen poniard and cut the throat of bashfulness.

Of the love that you poured forth, dear friend, in vain like a cup of water in the wide and thirsty desert, but it was all your life to you. Do you dream that it is lost? Perhaps it is; it may well seem so just now to you, yet indeed I do not think so. Think not that the love thou enterest into today is for a few months or years; the little seed set now must lie quiet before it will germinate, and many alternations of sunshine and shower descend upon it before it becomes even a small plant. When a thousand years have passed, come thou again, and behold! a mighty tree no storms can shake. Therefore, leave time; do not like a child pull thy flower up by the root to see if it is growing.

All this day we will go together. The sun shall circle overhead; our shadows swing round us on the road. The winter sunshine shall float wonderful promises to us from the hills; the evening see us in another land. The night ever insatiate of love we will sleep together and rise early and go forward in the morning. Wherever the road shall lead us, in solitary places or among the crowds, it shall be well. We shall not desire to come to the end of the journey nor consider what the end may be; the end of all things shall be with us. This is my trade. From this day it is not so much we that change, as the hours that glide past us. Each bends low as it passes with a gift.

I went to the woods because I wished to live deliberately to front only the essential facts of life, and I did not wish to live what was not life, living is so dear. I wanted to live deep and suck out all the marrow of life.

The soul opened out into the infinite, and there was a rushing together of the two worlds, the inner and the outer. It was deep calling unto deep, the deep within being answered by the unfathomable deep without, reaching beyond the stars. The ordinary sense of things around faded. Nothing but an ineffable joy and exaltation remained. No consciousness was left save that of being wafted upwards and almost bursting with emotion. Perfect equilibrium—"God surrounds me like the physical atmosphere. He is closer to me than my own breath. In him literally I live and move and have my being."

Why should I pray? Since all things far and near but answer to my spirit's inmost needs, I bring my joy, my gratitude, my love, I enter into life, fearless and confident. I cleanse myself from every hateful thought. I make my daily toil a song of praise. I love the earth and feel its very life is part of me. My only prayer is gladness which I love. Why should I make appeal for help from some far source, since life is mine, since I am one with Him who is the Life?

O world, you have been very gentle to me! Strangely, as to the dying, your beauty comes to me now.

O death, take me away. For I would be the dust; and I would be the silver rays of the moon and the stars and the washing sound of the midnight sea and nourishing sweet air and running water for the lips of them that I choose, to pass, to put on the invisible cap, to run round about the world unseen.

I am the light air on the hills . . . deny me not; my desire which was not satisfied is satisfied, and yet can never be satisfied. I pass and pass and pass.

From the hills I creep down into the great city . . . fresh and pervading through all the street I pass. Him I touch, and her I touch, and you I touch; I can never be satisfied. I who desired one give myself to all. I who would be the companion of one become the companion of all companions. The lowest and who knows me not, him I know best and love best. O air and elements break forth into singing! O arise.

Poems

I dance, I dance, I laugh and dance.
The stars I raise as dust in dance.
No jealousy, no fear,
I'm the dearest of the dear.
No sin, no sorrow,
No past, no morrow,
No rival, no foe,
No injury, no woe.
No, nothing could harm me,
No, nothing alarm me,
The soul of all,
The nectar fall,
The sweetest self,
Yea! health itself,
The prattling streams,
The happiest dreams,
All myrrh and balm,
Rawan and Rama,
So pure and calm
Is Rama, is Rama.

Then rise, awake.
Dost hear the palm trees sighing?
It is my heart that sighs
To hear thy lips replying
And gaze into thine yes.
Then wake! Awake!
Sweet love! See here, I bend to Thee,
Awake! Awake!
My loved one! Unfold thy heart to me,
Wake! Awake!
Dost see the Himalayan snows
That grow and never tire?
They cannot cool my burning love
Or quench my soul's desire.
Then wake! Awake!
Dost here the Ganga river,
Its sacred waters roll?
But deeper flows for ever,
The passion of my soul.
Then wake! Awake!

The garden of the world has nothing but roses;
Give up thy hallucination, the only thorn.

The wind, through fury, could achieve nothing;
Her hair looked beautiful, even when disarranged.*

* Translated from Urdu.

I saw a vision once, and it sometimes reappears;
I know not if 'twas real, for they said I was not well.
But often as the sun goes down, my eyes fill up with tears.
And then that vision comes, and I see my Florimel (India).
The day was going softly down, the breeze had died away;
The waters from the West came slowly rolling on.
The sky, the clouds, the ocean wave, one molten glory lay;
All kindled into crimson by the deep red sun.
As silently I stood and gazed before the glory past,
There rose a sad remembrance of days long gone;
My youth, my childhood came again, my mind was overcast
As I gazed upon the going down of that red sun.
The past upon my spirit rushed, the dead were standing near,
Their cheeks were warm again with life, their winding sheets were gone;
The voices rang like marriage bells once more upon my ear;
Their eyes were gazing there with mine on that red sun.
Many days have passed since then, many chequered years;
I have wandered far and wide, still I fear I am not well;
For often as the sun goes down, my eyes fill up with tears,
And then that vision comes, and I see my Florimel.

LOVE

I am the origin and end
Of all this changeful universe;
There is, oh mankind, naught beyond;
For all is strung on Me alone
As are the beads upon the thread.
I am the freshness of the waters,
The splendor of the sun and the moon,
The essence of the holy thought,
The sound of sounds, the man in men,
I am the life of life, oh man!

All true devotion's centered power,
All being's seed am I, the strength,
The wisdom of the strong and wise,
Lo, those who worship Me in truth,
Fulfilling in their acts my laws,
Regarding me their aim and end,
Their hearts, oh man, dwell then in love,
And I to them will always be a guide
From out the surging flood of wrong
and migratory life.

Passage to India!
O! We can wait no longer!
We too take ship, O soul!
To you, we too launch out on trackless seas!
Fearless for unknown shores, on waves of ecstasy
To sail. Amid the wafting winds
Carolling free, singing our song of God!
Chanting our chant of happy soothing Om!
Passage to India!
Sailing these seas or on the hills or walking in the night,
Thoughts, silent thoughts of time and space of death like waters flowing,
Bear me indeed as through the regions infinite
Whose air I breathe.
Bathe me, O God in Thee, mounting to Thee,
I and my soul to range in reach of Thee.
Passage to Mother India!
Reckoning ahead, O soul, when Thou the time achieved,
The seas all crossed, weathered the capes, the voyage done.
Surrendered, copest, frontest, God,
Yieldest the aim attained.
As filled with friendship, Love complete,
The Elder Brother fond,
The younger melts in fondness in his arms.
Passage to India!
Are thy wings plumed indeed for such far flight?
O soul, voyagest thou indeed on voyage like this?
Soundest below the Sanskrit and the Vedas?
Then have thy bent unabashed.

Passage to you, your shores, ye aged fierce enigmas,
Passage to you, to mastership of you,
You strangling problems.
Passage to Mother India!
O secret of earth and sky!
Of you, O waters of the sea!
O winding creeks and Ganga!
Of you, O woods and fields! Of you O mighty Himalayas,
Of morning red! O clouds! O rain and snows,
O day and night, passage to you!
O sun and moon and all ye stars, Sirius and Jupiter,
Passage to you!
Passage, immediate passage!
The blood burns in my veins!
Away, O soul, hoist instantly the anchor,
Cut the hawsers, haul out; shake out every sail.
Have we not stood here like trees in the ground long enough!
Sail forth, steer for the deep waters only,
For we are bound where mariner has not yet dared to go.
And we will risk the ship ourselves and all.
O my brave soul!
O farther, farther, sail,
O daring joy but safe,
O farther, farther, sail,
To your real Home.

LOVE'S CONSECRATION

Take my life and let it be consecrated, Lord, to
Thee.
Take my heart and let it be full saturated, Love,
with Thee.
Take my eyes and let them be intoxicated, God!
with Thee.
Take my hands and let them be engaged in sweating
Truth for Thee.
Beautiful eyes are those that show beautiful
thoughts that burn below.
Beautiful lips are those whose words
Leap from the heart like songs of birds.
Beautiful hands are those that do
Work that is earnest, brave and true,
I was not born, nor grow, nor die.
Dumb nature through the body works.
It is the Ego sows and reaps.
Not I the Self unchanging.

OLD AGE*

Wearing old age, I roam in the streets of man un-
afraid,
This old age is my cap, wearing of which makes me
invisible.
It is my disguise.

* Translated from the Urdu.

THE MISBEHAVIOR OF THE MOON*

In my wayward wanderings,
One evening on the edge of a lake,
I saw the cottage of a weaver,
And by the cottage stood a young maiden; she was the daughter of the weaver.
The breeze came blowing soft,
And the moonlight began its silver flow.
I saw the maiden standing motionless like a statue;
Her mouth was open wide,
And she was devouring the moon with her eyes!
The moon leapt from the windows of her eyes into the sacred temple of youth,
And there the moon melted away in the clear lake of her heart!
O Moon! Stop! You thief! What?
Entering without permission into other people's homes
Like this! O bold moon!
The waters of the lake have merely thy face reflected,
But thou hast made the maiden's heart thy home.
Ah! the secret that the scientist knows not,
The mystery that his telescope reveals not,
The solution that the mathematician finds not,
The riddle that astronomy unravels not,
Thou thus revealest that secret in the hut of a mere weaver.
O moon! What wayward wandering thine is this?
What is this calm luxury in that little heart?
And why strayest thou in the huts of the poor and the lowly like this?

* Translated from the Urdu.

No sin, no grief, no pain,
Safe in my blissful Self,
My fears are fled, my doubts are slain,
My day of triumph come.
O grave where is thy victory?
O death where is thy sting?
My Self to me my kingdom is,
Such perfect joy therein I find
My worldly waves my mind can toss,
To me no gain, to me no loss.
I fear no foe, I scorn no friend,
I dread no death, I fear no end.

As the light of the sun in the rain mist,
As the stars reflect in the sea,
So what to my wonder seems vastest
Is but a reflection from Me.
And all things that my spirit revereth,
All grandeurs my heart would enshrine,
By command of the silence that heareth
Already forever were mine.

THE SELF SUPREME

Break, break, break at the feet of thy crag, oh sea,
Break, break, break at my feet, O worlds that be.
O suns and storms, O earthquakes, wars,
Hail, welcome, come, try all your force on me!
Ye nice torpedoes, fire! My playthings, crack!
O shooting stars, my arrows, fly!
You burning fire! Can you consume?
O threatening one, you flame from me;
You flaming sword, you cannon ball,
My energy headlong drives forth thee!
The body dissolved is cast to winds;
Well doth infinity me enshrine!
All ears, my ears; all eyes, my eyes;
All hands, my hands; all minds, my minds!
I swallowed up death, all difference I drank up;
How sweet and strong a food I find!
No fear, no grief, no hankering pain;
All, all delight, or sun, or rain!
Ignorance, darkness, quaked and quivered,
Trembled, shivered, vanished forever;
My dazzling light did parch and scorch it,
Joy ineffable! Hurrah! Hurrah!

I am the mote in the sunbeam, and I am the burning sun.
"Rest here!" I whisper the atom, I call to the orb, "Roll on."
I am the blush of the morning, and I am the evening breeze.
I am the leaf's low murmur, the swell of the terrible seas.
I am the net, the fowler, the bird and its frightened cry;
The mirror, the form reflected, the sound and its echo I;
The lover's passionate pleading, the maiden's whispered fear;
The warrior, the blade that smites him, his mother's heart-wrung tear.
I am intoxication, grapes, winepress and musk and wine,
The guest, the host, the traveller, the goblet of crystal fine.
I am the breath of the flute, I am the mind of man;
Gold's glitter, the light of the diamond, the sea-pearl's lustre wan.
The rose, her poet nightingale, the songs from the throat that rise;
The flint, the sparks, the taper, the moth that about it flies.
I am both good and evil, the deed and the deed's intent;
Temptation, victim, sinner, crime, pardon and punishment.
I am what was, is, will be—creation's ascent and fall;
The link, the chain of existence; beginning and end of all.
Lo! the trees of the wood are my next of kin,
And the rocks are alive with what beats in me;
The clay is my flesh, and the fox my skin,
I am fierce with the gadfly, and sweet with the bee.
The flower is naught but the bloom of my love,
And the waters run down in the tune I dream.
The sun is my flower uphung above,
I flash with the lightning, with falcon's scream,

I was never born, yet my births of breath
Are as many as waves on the sleepless sea.
I cannot die though forever death
Weave back and fro in the warp of me.

Letters

Lehore, March 11, 1890, to Dhanna Bhakta

Thou, the absolute existence, the absolute knowledge, the infinite Brahma, the absolute bliss, the abode of peace, the embodiment of joy and blessedness, the one without a second, the matchless, the great lord, the pure and the holy!

I offer my all at your feet; continue to be merciful to me. Neither you come, nor do you send letters. I do not know what sins I have committed that you are so annoyed with me.

It is said God is merciful and peaceful. Then why are you angry? Why don't you forgive me? I fancy you have learned from the House of God that I have some defect which will stand in my way of seeing Him, and having learned that, you are disregarding me, for the world would laugh at you that Tirtha Rama being yours could not see God. But my attitude is—forgive me, and look not at my defects.

> If you call me in, I know but this one door;
> If you turn me out, I know but this one door.
> I know no other door.
> I know this head, and I know its one place, your door sill!

Lahore, 1894, to Dhanna Bhakta

I get up at about 5 a.m. and study up to 7 a.m. Having attended to nature's call and taken my bath and exercise, I go to Panditji reading all the way. I take my meal there after an hour and drive with him to the College. On my way back from the College I take milk. I stay for a few minutes at my residence, then proceed to the river bank where I walk for about half an hour. From the river I walk back home through the gardens surrounding the city. At home I stroll on the roof till it is dark, when I take exercise, light the lamp and study till 7 p.m. Be it remembered when I am on my legs I am always reading. After 7 p.m. I go out for my evening meal and tuition at Prem's; on return take exercise for 10 or 12 minutes and study up to 10 p.m. when I retire to bed. I have learned by experience that a healthy stomach gives a great bliss, keeps the mind pure and keeps one in constant remembrance of his Maker; intellect, memory and energy are alert. Firstly I take very little food, and secondly what I do eat I masticate thoroughly.

Lahore, 1894, to Dhanna Bhakta

Rama had taken at night the most abstruse problems in higher mathematics and had vowed within himself to solve them before sunrise; and if he could not solve them, then his head must be severed from his body. For the latter purpose, a sharp dagger was kept under Rama's seat. It was a very wrong thing to have done, but Rama tells you it was through such discipline, right or wrong, that he passed to get to the knowledge he gathered. Well, three out of the four problems were solved by midnight. But the fourth gave trouble. Rama had not solved it as the light of early dawn peeped through the window. True to his vow, Rama got up and took the sharp dagger and went on to the roof of the house and put the thin point of the dagger on his throat. As the dagger just began piercing --it actually caused a little abrasion and the blood drops oozed out and Rama was dazed—he saw the solution of the problem written in letters of light in air. Rama saw the solution and then took it down. It was the most original work ever done. Professor Mukerji of the Government College was astonished. Thus did Rama many times through sheer hard labor acquire the knowledge of mathematics.

Lahore, Spring, 1894, to Dhanna Bhakta

Nothing in this world is real and reliable. It is due to God's great mercy that one can have faith in Him and rely solely on Him and is an ascetic at heart. The whole creation dances at the feet of such truly great men.

Nothing in this world is ours. If we want peace we must consider even our body as not ours but His and pass our days doing His work.

In fact, everything in this world is impermanent. He who relies on things worldly and not on God certainly sells his soul. The rich are like those who roam about stark naked but claim to be in flowing robes. What relief can these naked paupers afford?

Good company, sacred books and prayer make one the king of the three worlds. Bad company annoys God and causes various troubles. God comes and keeps company of him who lives in solitude and takes frugal diet.

Maharaji! God is very good. I like Him immensely. He is so sweet. You ought to live on terms of peace with Him. He is never harsh. Only He is playful and at times what we consider our suffering is His humor. I know many things about Him now. I will tell you some day.

Lahore, September, 1894, to Dhanna Bhakta

God is extremely kind to all. It is the mischief of our mind that it reposes no confidence in God and makes us miserable. Mind comes under control by practice. One must study good books like *Yoga Vashishtha*. To take a little food or to fast is of supreme importance.

Lahore, Summer 1895, to Dhanna Bhakta

I offer everything at your feet, please continue to have mercy on me.

"God Himself is the house for storing the goods of reliance in. It is the door of bounty, don't sit here hopeless of its being opened. From every lock here its key grows like a seed."

By your grace I enjoy bliss.

"None (in reality) is poor and hungry; everyone has diamonds in his bundle, but knows not how to open it, hence finds himself a beggar."

Lahore, July, 1895, to Dhanna Bhakta

I am making some efforts, I visit Europeans; but my heart is not enchained by desires.

"I have passed beyond the stage of desire: desire is now at an end. Desires were a veil on the fair face of the Desired One."

Lahore, December, 1895, to Dhanna Bhakta

I have taken nothing for the last eight days. I live only on milk. But I have just been on a thirty miles' walk, and I do not feel tired.

Lahore, June, 1896, to Dhanna Bhakta

Got your letters. I am entirely yours. I don't consider anything as my own. It is no joy to me to gather the wealth of this world. It is no pleasure to me to get ornaments for my wife. I need no furniture either. For me I require the shade of a tree for a house, ashes for my wear, the bare earth for my bed and the bread begged from a few doors for my food—if I get these, I feel very happy. To offend you for the sake of money! Tell me to live like an ash-covered *sadhu*, and I start forthwith. I would at the same time keep on working in the College. Whatever I may get from there is wholly yours. Spend it as you please. Give to my wife out of it what you like. I am a poor slave; mine is to work, work and build a little sacred shrine for God in my heart. This inner peace gives me that joy which nothing of the outside world can give me. The peace I get by my work for God is enough salary for me. Let this College salary alone; do what you may like with it. I neither increase nor decrease by the addition or the subtraction of such things. I am joy absolute.

Lahore, August, 1897, to Dhanna Bhakta

If while going through our work and business, our mind is immersed in God, and our feeling cometh not down from those giddy heights celestial, then blessed is our life. Otherwise human life is certainly fruitless.

These days I have to devote myself entirely to Self contemplation *(vedanta vichar)*, prayer *(bhajan)* and solitude *(ekant sevan)*. I am so happy that I cannot give them up.

I have read many English books on Vedanta, but reading is not so interesting as contemplation in solitude and practice of Vedanta. Whatever by your blessings I acquire, I distribute among seekers in English speeches.

Thanks to your benedictions, I mostly reside now in my real Self.

I have read more than twenty books on Vedanta in English at Lahore and have read them with care. They generally contain the Upanishads and other authoritative Vedantic works. The society of books gives an impetus to practice; it is practice which yields real bliss. To stop desire and will leads to automatic fulfillment of desires just as a seed grows by being buried under ground. You have great experience in this line. Renounce Maya and the world and they become your slaves; if you turn your face against shadow and proceed towards the sun, the shadow follows you.

By your grace I have now attained fearlessness. There is utter absence of fear, and bliss reigns supreme.

My mind, thanks to your grace, is fixed in the Self and enjoys bliss. This is the true wealth. I am practicing this these days: "Know the *Atman* alone. Talk not of others. That alone is the bridge to immortality."

Lahore, October, 1897, to Hiranand Rama

My dear father! Salutations to you! Your letter came and with it great joy! The body of your son, Tirtha Rama, is now sold; it is sold to Lord Rama. It is no more his own. Today is Dewali. I have lost my body in the gamble, and I have won the Lord; I congratulate you. Now whatever you may need, ask of my Lord. He will provide you with it or will make me send it to you. But for once call upon Him with faith.

For the last 19 or 20 days He has come and taken upon Himself all my tasks, duties and debts. Why will He not do yours too? You must not lose heart. As He wills, so I must work. Maharaj, the Lord alone is the wealth of us Brahmans; it is not becoming of us to renounce our inner precious wealth and go after the worthless outer. Just enjoy once the pleasure of your inner and real Treasure.

Lahore, December, 1897, to Dhanna Bhakta

It is about 8 p.m. I have finished my exercise. My inside is quite pure and full of bliss. I remember you with love. Blessed are you, on account of whom I am bathing in the ocean of bliss. There is complete identity; this time there is no difference between you and me, not even of a hair's breadth:

> I became you, and you became me; I became the body, and you the soul, so that no one may say hereafter that you and I are different.
>
> Writer,
> You Yourself

Lahore, March, 1898, to Dhanna Bhakta

"Oh! How wonderful is my own Self who possesses nothing but to whom belongs all that comes within the range of the senses and the mind."

Says Bhagwan Shankaracharya, "How handsome and wonderful is my own Self in which exist the entire universe (of sight, hearing and thought), which owns all this, yet which possesses nothing, so wonderful is my Self." I salute to such a Self of mine.

Lahore, April, 1898, to Dhanna Bhakta

The lesson taught by the way to Katasraj is perfectly true. Happiness which one finds in solitude and Self concentration is found nowhere else.

> O deer, thy musk has filled the whole forest with sweet scent. Musk is within thyself; why dost thou run about in search of it?

One's own happiness reflects itself in outer objects. All the Vedas and sacred lore are within ourselves.

Near Rishikesh above Hardwar, August, 1898

You have tried to persuade me in your letter to come home. Your letter has been thrown into the running waters of the Ganga. Strange! You ask me whether I feel no pain for not keeping up to my duties! Pain of what?

> Unknown are the beginnings of these things,
> Unknown are the ends of these things,
> And just known is a little middle of the things that seem at present,
> And so unknown when all is,
> What pain is there?

What shall the people say?
My reply is in the Urdu couplet:
Wearing my own shroud as my turban,
I have come to the street of the Beloved!
Let them taunt me as they choose,
What care I for thousands such!

You talk of obeying you. From the Punjab of my body, I am going fast to the Home of God. I am mingling myself with Truth.

It is about midnight, not a man nor his ghost near by me. Within is the sound of ecstasy in tides, without me is the music of the glorious Ganga in flow! Within me is peace, peace, peace; without me is bliss. It is the night of my union; it is not dark night, only the night of union has thrown the black curtain on the face of the world for privacy.

I mean the night of union has effaced both from within and without the world. The eyes are the rivers of nectar. At least to remind me at such times of bliss of the world! Alas!

Tell my people to think of meeting me at the center where all meet and not at the circumference where no one can meet.

Where limpid waters flow like the moonlight silver
in flood
To be sitting on those banks of the river Ganga,
Where all sounds are hushed at night,
With my hair on end in joy of His name,
Freedom from the pain and presence of earthly life,
Saying "Shiva, Shiva" I may weep tears of ecstasy
And thus fulfil the being of my eyes!
When would such good days dawn for me!

Bhartri Hari

The kings renounce their thrones to realize this joy! The gods pine for the banks of the holy Ganga. And is the vessel of my luck alone so shattered to pieces that after having reached here, I should think of my duties and false things.

People come to Tirthas (holy places); Tirthas do not go to the people. Tell those of my household that they should seek the feet of Tirtha Ram (the God of holy places), who dwells in Tirthas (holy places), that very God. It is only then they can see the Lord Tirtha Ram! Otherwise not. Till Satya Ganga floweth not in my house, I cannot live there, my heart cannot beat there. I cannot stop there.

Nobody does send messages to the dead to return, but those who wish to see them die themselves. I am dead; I am dead while still in body. Let not my people try to call me back. But if they be like me, then meeting is quite easy.

If Murliwala of Murali (his own village) becomes Jurari—of God—then possibly the one who makes Tirthas (holy places) holy, might come there. Where the Ganga of peace floweth not, there my coming is difficult. After all, all dead bones have to come and rest in the Ganga. Why not bring them quite willingly when still alive?

Uttarakhand, Summer, 1898

O heart! This is the lane of thy Beloved; attach no importance to thy life.
In the presence of the Beloved, talk not of the world, the heart, aye, even life itself.
Life has no value. Don't talk much of it. Keep quiet if thy life is lost in the way of the Beloved.
If thou hast any pain from Him, talk not of its treatment; feel the pain better than its treatment.
When conviction appears, forget the story of doubts and suspicions. Don't argue any more when the Beloved has shown His face.

Put aside the knowledge of the irreligious and don't count ignorance as wisdom; talk not of the ideas (philosophy) and magic (mysticism) of the Greeks.
Before the wine-like red lips, beautiful face and attractive tresses of thy Beloved, talk not of wine, beautiful ones, candle and night chamber.
Before His face and tresses, set aside belief and disbelief, and talk not of them at all.

Ganga! Is it thy breast at which *Brahma Vidya* is nurtured? Himalayas! Is it thy bosom in which *Brahma Vidya* frolics? Do you remember the day when Rama, with a pale face, cold sigh and wet eye, first came under your protection? Lonely nights were passed on these stones. Hiccoughs would come in unbroken succession. Ah! Where is that perfect bliss, the intoxication of which obliterates all distinctions of the past and the present? Oh! When shall I reach that flood of happiness which will wash away, like dirt, the pleasures of the world? When will the sun of knowledge be at its zenith? When will the desires of the body and the perception of the senses disappear like darkness? Ganga's water never gets warm. When will the time come when through the intoxication of reality frowns and favors will become incapable of affecting Rama even in a dream? When will sin and sorrow disappear like the past? Is the state of Self-realization (turiya) only to be found mentioned in books? Where is it? Rama is roaming about in the hilly forest, bare headed, barefooted and naked like a lunatic, with the Upanishads in his hand.

To me wine is the blood of my liver, and the drizzling my wet eyes; my cup (of wine) is not indebted to the spring clouds.
To bewail in a small chamber gives me no relief; hence crying aloud in the wilderness gives satisfaction.

I shall go and write the condition of my heart on myrtle leaves, so that it might perhaps reach the hands of the Beloved.
Unforgettable is the sympathetic response (echo) of the mountain caves and valleys.
The day that the portfolio of love was allotted to me, I received sighs in cash (reward) and forests in jagir (land grant).

That is all! The throne or the bier! Parents! Your son is not to return now. Students! Your teacher is not to go back now to you. Wife! How long will your relation have to be put up with? The inevitable must happen. Either I shall rise above all relations, or all your hopes shall be blasted. Either time and space will be drowned in the waves of Rama's surging bliss, or Rama's body will be floating on Ganga's waves. After death everyone's bones are taken to the Ganges; if Self is not realized in all its nakedness, and the least smell of individuality persists, Rama's bones and flesh shall be offered alive to the fish of the Ganges.

As thy moth, I have come to Thee, O Self-effulgent Light (on Mount Sinai)!
But let not the talk between Thee and the Prophet Moses begin again, as here is a different sort of demand.
Why does not the sound sleep of bliss come to my eyes?
O astrologer! Open my horoscope and see why my eyes always throb for the sight of the Beloved!

If Ganga does not flow under Rama's feet, Rama's body shall float on Ganga. Eyes are showering rain; cold and deep breath is the high wind accompanying the rains. Inside there is a downpour; outside too it is raining heavily; Rama is disconsolate and crying:

Ganga! Hundreds of times will I sacrifice myself to thee.
My bones and flesh I cast as an offering—these are

the flowers and sweets I bring to Thee.
Ganga! Hundreds of times will I sacrifice myself to thee.
Mind I throw away before thy monkeys. Intellect I set afloat on thy waves.
Ganga! Hundreds of times will I sacrifice myself to thee.
Consciousness thy fish may devour; egoism I bury in thy cave.
Ganga! Hundreds of times will I sacrifice myself to thee.
Sin and merit I burn before thee. This is the candle light for thee.
Ganga! Hundreds of times I will sacrifice myself to thee.
As I fall in thee, I dive and become one with thee.
Ganga! Hundreds of times I will sacrifice myself to thee.
The priests, water and land, air and the ten directions I convert into my own form.
Ganga! Hundreds of times I will sacrifice myself to thee.
I shall play on the current of truth, or I shall cease to be called Rama.
Ganga! Hundreds of times I will sacrifice myself to thee.

This time the whole army of ignorance is dispersed; both darkness and ignorance are untraceable. What does the glory and joy of these mountains prove? What glad tidings do the coolness and bliss of the place bear? That Rama shall achieve his object; his desires shall attain heaven.

Be happy, O heart! That someone whose breath is like that of Jesus is coming. His sweet breath gives scent of someone.

How happily is Rama bathing, throwing up water and crying with joy!

O the queen of rivers, Ganga Rani, splashes of thy water give a strange pleasure, Ganga Rani!
Keep me ever with thee, O Ganga Rani!
On this bank or that, but always keep me with thee,

O Ganga Rani!
Let me dive deep hundreds of times in thee and always ride on thy waves, O Ganga Rani!

Sun is about to set. Rama is sitting on a projecting rock. His condition is queer. He is neither indifferent nor sad; nor is he happy, as the people of the world understand the term. He is neither awake nor alseep. Is he not intoxicated? But it is not the intoxication of the world. O! What a sweet and serene state of mind! Conches and tomtoms are sounded yonder behind the trees. Perhaps there is a temple; Arti is being performed. O look here, up above the peak in front peeps the moon, thirteen nights old. Is he coming to join the Arti? To join! No, he has lighted the candle of his own face to offer it as a sacrifice to Shiva. He looks himself like Arti. Hurrah! The whole of nature participates in Arti. How the sound of the conch reverberates from all sides! O, moon! Who art thou to excel me? Dear! Be not alone. Why shall not Rama light his whole body and like thee participate in the Arti?

Near Rishikesh, 1898

Thick forest. Brink of water. Wild orchard, blossoming. Solitude. A few Upanishads read through.

Tongue! Canst thou express that bliss? Blessed am I! Happy am I!

O my good luck! I have embraced that Beloved whose veil would hardly disclose now a foot, then a hand, now an eye, then an ear. Naked is He. So am I. Breast on breast. Get away you, heart and liver! Don't stand between us. Duality! Vanish. Distance! Perish. Separation! Be off. I; Beloved! Beloved, I! Is it joy? Or is it death in joy?

Tears! Why are you raining?

Is it the showers (of scented water) at the marriage, or is it the mourning at the mind's death? This is the last rite of rites. Desires are dead. Sorrow and poverty! They have vanished as darkness before light. Sunk is the fleet of actions, good and bad!

> The heart was creating a good deal of noise in my bosom! Not a drop of blood came out as it was cut open.
> Thanks! The good tidings of the Beloved's arrival has come. Now there is no room to remain in bereavement.
> I am myself the Beloved; where is the need for correspondence; I am the intoxication of wine itself; I need no tavern.

Turiya (self-realization) which, like the phoenix, was untraceable, I myself proved to be. The third person turned out to be the first one. Om! *Ham* (we). We. Om. No, neither we nor you. Entire record lost. Om. Om. Om!

String of tears? No. Showers of embrace!

Head! Fruitful is thy being today. Eyes! Blessed are you too. Ears! Your efforts, too, have succeeded. Blessed be these rejoicings! Blessed! Even the word blessed is blessed today.

> Hail to Thee, O divine madness! Thou art the remedy of all my ailments, my pride and honor. Thou art my Galileo and my Plato.

The dolls of egoism and intellect are burnt. Eyes! Congratulations on the constant showers of your black clouds. Auspicious or blessed is the rain of these intoxicated eyes.

> My Beloved prepared a garment; I put it on myself
> And thus embraced the Beloved fully.
> The inspiring rainy season set in
> To make me one with the Beloved.

Run away, run, O Beloved, if thou canst! Where wilt thou go? Up to the sky? I am there. To Kailas (the high and holy peak of the mountain)? There, too, am I. Into the ocean? I precede thee there. In the fire? It is my own mouth. In all the bodies, in all the forms, in all the shapes, in all the names, am I. Nay, these bodies, names and forms are verily I. Who to speak? Who to talk? Sweets in a dumb mouth. How can it be described?

Hurrah, hurrah, hurrah! How handsome am I? My beauty, my attractiveness, my lustre, my splendor, my charming face, no eye can see but mine.

I am intoxicated with my own grandeur. But alas! None is ready to pay for my beauty; none, to purchase my charms. Who can afford to have this priceless diamond?

> Who will appear to set the value of my Self.
> I see nothing but my own Self all around.
> I myself am the lover, myself the beloved.
> Lover or the beloved? I am love.

As I look out, each leaf, each flower, welcomes me with "Thou art that, Thou art that." The clouds of bliss within are drowning everything by their thunder. By and by, motionless become the limbs. Time and space, where are they? Distance, separation, in and out, what are they? Who can mention further?

> Many days and many nights thus passed away.
> But whose days and whose nights?
> Wherever I look, I see Thee and Thee alone.

It is afternoon. Rama is sitting naked in the middle of a hanging wooden bridge. Like Meghnad, he is thundering in the garb of clouds above. Like lightning, with his light, he is shining on stones and water. In the shape of rain, he is forcing every bird into its nest. Sky and hill and dale, none is visible; it is all a sheet of water as if the

Ganga has risen up to the skies to rest in her home, Rama. All these have found their home. Where should the homeless Rama take rest?

> No nest for me to rest, no feathers with which to fly.

Rama, the God resting in the deeps, is pervading the waters. He is moving in the clouds. He is decorating the ocean.

Sometimes it rains; sometimes rises the sun. But for Rama there is neither rising nor setting.

> When I knew the secret of the Beloved,
> I turned within and found Him there.
> Reside in bliss, in the temple (of the heart),
> where neither there is rise nor fall,
> But one cannot hold one's tongue.

World? No! Not the world, but Parvati, preparing drink. Shiva's eyes open. Here is the goblet. Consciousness regained is set afloat on wine. O my drunkard! Go on drinking; drink on without cares. Give me goblet after goblet, full to the brim. Go on drinking without cares.

Nature prepares no drink; it is itself wine and hemp. No, not wine and hemp but their intoxication. I myself am wine and hemp.

> I hope for nothing; I seek nothing; for in monism
> there is neither cup-bearer, nor cup, nor jar.
> Whenever the heart gets the discerning eyes,
> wherever it looks, it sees the beloved.
> I examined every flower in the garden; I found it
> of my color and my smell.
> Meum and tuum disappeared; we are one; no desires,
> no wants now remain.
> O fill up the goblet of wine!
> What is it that you feel shy of?

Uttarakhand, Summer, 1898

Is Rama All Alone?

There is neither any student nor any servant with Rama. There is no habitation near about. No man can be seen. It is mid starry night with absolute solitude, isolated retreat, complete seclusion and loneliness. But is Rama alone? No, never. The rains have just given a bath to Rama. The maid servant air is running about in his service. Just in front is Ganga, singing lullaby to Rama. Hundreds of servants are taking rest in the nearby shrubs and bushes. Here is a sound. Some wild animal is saying, "Yes sir. I am present." How can Rama be alone then? But the fact is that Rama is really one-without-a-second. There is none else besides him. There is neither servant, nor tree, nor air, nor Ganga, nor moon, nor any star. It is all Rama himself. There is no God besides me, no lover or beloved, no meeting and no union. It is all Rama and Rama alone. Even the thought of loneliness has left Rama alone.

A poet says:

I am alone, I am alone. Is it not strange
  that I am without a second?
There is no else besides me.
I am absolute oneness.
The sound in the jungle,
The jungle itself, the trees,
The mountains, day, or night
Air, stars, Ganga, clouds,
Shining moon, lover or beloved,
Union or separation, paper or pen,
The eyes or the subject matter and your own self
Are all Rama. There is nothing besides him.
It is all he and he alone.

Is Rama Without Any Work?

The lake, Mansarovar, of mind, is overflowing with

the nectar of ecstasy. The river of happiness is softly flowing through Rama's heart. The inner self is saturated with blissful delight. Just as virtues and purity overflow in the form of Ganga from the feet of Lord Vishnu, so too, Rama is over-saturated with permanent bliss. He is unable to contain the overflow of his ecstasy which is regularly being diverted for the good of the world. He is consistently distributing prosperity and cheerfulness for the benefit of the afflicted masses. Who can say that Rama is sitting idle and doing no work?

A Persian poem says:

> Be careful, O you wine supplier! Taste the wine of immortality from Me so that your love for God or Beloved increases day by day and your difficulties are made easy.
>
> My dazzling beauty is my own curtain, and the beauty of my love has created a commotion in the hearts of men.
>
> I am enjoying the moonlit night and the fragrant breeze at the banks of a refreshing river with my Beloved by my side. How can the persons drowned under the waves of worldly worries and miseries appreciate my feelings of ecstasy?
>
> I am very happy at my destination, the union with my Beloved. The bell is unnecessarily disturbing my peace. I cannot go anywhere else. Let them sermonize in any way they like.
>
> Through my union with my Beloved, all my mission has been completed. This fact is no more a secret. It is well known to everybody.
>
> Do you want the face-to-face presence of your Beloved? But He is omnipresent. Nothing is hidden from Him. He is this world, the other world, God and everything. He is all in all.

Rama orders you to say sincerely with all your heart and understanding that "You are God." If you realize this, you will immediately attain your unity with Him and reach your final destination of Self-realization.

No sin, no grief, no pain.
Safe in my blissful Self
My fears are fled, my doubts are slain,
My day of triumph come.
O grave where is thy victory?
O death where is thy sting?
My Self to me my kingdom is
Such perfect joy therein, I find
My worldly waves, my mind, can toss
To me no gain, to me no loss.
I fear no foe, I scorn no friend,
I dread no death, I fear no end.

Rama is never idle. All the work in this world is being done by Rama himself.

A Persian poet says:

The sun is worried, "Where is light?"
The rivers run around to inquire,
"Where is water?"
Last night my sleep was making inquiry
from my eyes, "Where is sleep?"
Intoxicated persons are in search of self-forgetfulness.
The cup of wine in circulation wants to know where wine is.
The Beloved is present without any veil,
yet the lover inquires the whereabouts of his Beloved.
When all men are working, I remain idle
because I am the source of their energy to work.
The whole world is in motion only due to Me.
How can I go beyond Me? I am everywhere.
Where and why am I to work? I am the spirit and the destination of the universe.

Is It Ego?

Who is proud, haughty or swollen? Only the one who is suffering from ignorance. He alone is egoistic who is proud of his status, family, wealth, knowledge, complexion, position, etc. All this is not his. He has got it from God. It means that the egoistic person is, as a matter of fact, a mere beggar but wrongly considers his real poverty and dependence to be something respectable. Faroon and

Namrood had declared themselves to be God. In spite of their ignorance and heresy, they were, in a way, blessed to the extent that at least once they uttered the great sacred sentence, "I am He." Their only fault was that they belittled their real Self and considered it to be limited. They did not know that they were one-without-a-second. They could not realize their supreme reality. They considered God to be separate from themselves and tried to copy Him in His greatness. They feigned that their little self was great instead of realizing their real sublimity. They trumped up their eulogy and glorified their body consciousness. They, therefore, harmed themselves by creating their own rival against themselves. But Rama is not like them. He, who is the life force in the fragrant roses, who infuses charm and attraction in the beauties of this world and who bestowed greatness upon Mansoor, has no business to take to the beggary of pride or egoism instead of enjoying his own supreme greatness and real dignity.

According to a Persian poet:

> Why was Namrood humiliated? Because of his narrow mindedness. Such pride or egoism does not become Me because I am all-pervading and interpenetrating like God Himself.
>
> Why should I indulge in pride when I am all in all and the greatest being?

Is It Madness?

It has come to the knowledge of Rama that certain so-called intellectuals opine that he (Rama) is suffering from melancholia and that he is developing madness. The king of the present day logicians, Mr. J. S. Mill, writes that only that man has a right to prefer either of the two happenings who is fully acquainted with each of them. One who knows about only one phase is incapable of comparing the two. You followers of Mill or David Hume!

O you intellectuals or logicians! Did you ever care to have any personal experience of this madness? Did you ever care to know what this madness is like? No, never. According to a poet:

> A so-called wise man cannot know how the heart is stolen away. Only that man can talk about it who has personally lost his own heart.

As such you have no right to say anything against this blessed madness. O you who are mad after the transitory pleasure or enjoyment! Go. The alcoholic liquors are calling you; and beautiful girls are waiting for you. Go there and enjoy them. But, please listen to Rama. What is it in these beautiful ladies, sweet tunes, alcoholic liquors and other attractive sense objects that have enslaved you? Dear friends, it is only a transitory glimpse of Rama's madness and nothing more. Are you not ashamed that you seek artificial enjoyment in liquor, that you are prepared to sacrifice your all on creamy flesh for a mere transitory pleasure and that you allow yourself to be enslaved by sex and other similar considerations? Come to Rama. He will bestow upon you that everlasting bliss which is not lotted even to emperors.

> He is no doubt mad, but
> Whatever he says is correct.

You collect money with great difficulty or efforts and then weep when it is no more with you. You are only after transitory pleasures. Why not take refuge in your own universal Self and enjoy the eternal happiness. Do not care for the opinion of the world. It is wrong to see things with the eyes of others or to depend upon the opinion of the unthinking masses without exercising your own discretion. Do away with duality and otherness, and make yourself free from any bondage. It is irksome madness to swing, like a pendulum of a clock, between pain and pleasure and to remain undecisive. Do away with this embarrassing situation. Realize your own godhood.

Yes, Rama is mad, in a way because he is beyond mind and intellect. He creates out of himself the seeming universe unnecessarily and is then lost into it. Is it not the work of madness to put up a show of illusions?

A Persian couplet says:

I am mad because I have nothing to do with wisdom.
I myself create the universe and then remain unattached to it.

Uttarakhand, August, 1898, to Dhanna Bhakta

I reveal the secret of Him whose address is unknown
So that His lovers may run mad after Him.

I received the letter in which you have persuaded me to return home. It was immediately dispatched to the Highest Abode, in other words consigned to the waves of the Ganges.

Mother! I can't turn the wheel (of a householder's life); condemn me not to it.
You have by force taken my very life out of me; Not an ounce of flesh, nor a drop of blood is now left in my body.
Color flies from my face at the very sight of the wheel (drudgery of the house). Tell me how to sit again in the midst of His lovers.
O Husain! The madness of love destroys all wisdom; those who advise them otherwise lose their heads too.

You threaten me with the taunts people level against me. But, Lord! What care I? It is now only the Ganges and I. Charges, like arrows, have no effect on me.

It is not the fault of the arrow if its blade does not rankle in my heart; for the fire burning therein has

> the nature to melt iron.
> Love shall forsake me not, till it has burned away egoism. Love, like fire, is furiously pursuing me.

Your Rama is now finished; he is good for nothing. You ask me if I do not grieve for my home! How strange! that you do not grieve for the real Home which you have forgotten.

You have tried to recall me, reminding me of everybody being busy with his worldly duties. Well, if the majority be the test of truth, tell me from Adam downward, who is in a majority—those who by their deeds declare the world to be real or those who from every particle of dust, proclaim the unreality of the world? Why weep for the things whose beginning and end are unknown and the mere middle is known?

My Lord! I am carrying out your behests; I am striving to meet you soon. From a physical point of view bodily separation is inevitable; two bodies can not simultaneously be in the same place. However near each other they may be, some space will always intervene; otherwise, interpenetration of bodies would have been possible. In fact, night and day is Rama striving to end separation; he shall not let a trace of it remain. Rama shall have no rest till he sees himself in your inner self, in your heart, in your eyes, yes, in the heart of everyone. Come, leave the mire of the five rivers (the Punjab, as also the body, is composed of blood, urine, sweat, semen and saliva) and return to your real Home (your own Self). You shall be dragged from this Punjab (the land of the five rivers) to the mountains of the Self. Now it is meet to meet only at the center where once we meet, we cannot separate. How long shall we play hide and seek on the circumference? If Rama does not see Ganga flowing out of his feet, people shall certainly see his body floating on Ganga's waters.

Of the martyrs of love, I stand at the top. I lost my head *(sar)* but remained on the top of the gallows *(sar-i-dar)*.

Pearl, having once come out of the shell, never goes back into it.

Zulekha never again had sound sleep after she had seen Joseph in dream.

Lahore, October, 1898

Writer: Shri Dhanna Rama, from "Nowhere."

Don't remember me at all. I have become memory itself, having lost the little self.

I prayed, "Please forget me not." He destroyed duality and became one and forgot the separation thus.

I wish to dance today.

I dance, the king of dancers! I dance, Maharaj!

I dance as sun! I dance as stars! I dance as the moon! I dance, the king of dancers!

I dance as atoms! I dance as ocean! I dance as clouds! I dance, the king of dancers!

In thy body I dance as breath! I dance as arteries and veins! I dance, the king of dancers!

I dance as clouds! I dance as winds! I dance as rivers and brooks! I dance, the king of dancers!

Music and singing go on every minute. I dance with all paraphernalia! I dance, the king of dancers!

My abode is in merriments, and in merriments is my abode. I dance a rhythmic dance! I dance, the king of dancers!

I dance today as drunkard, drinking again and again strong wine. I dance, the king of dancers!

Rama is dancing! Rama is singing! I dance without shame! I dance, the king of dancers!

Lahore, November, 1898

Catarrh still persists. There may perhaps soon be some change in the service of the Mission College. Inner (real) bliss is increasing day by day. "I have obtained that perfect bliss, which dies not, moves not, burns not nor is lost in darkness." Happiness or joy is filled within the heart; the guru has taught the *Shruti "Brahma Twameva"* (Thou art Brahma).

All are merged in me. *Baqi* (remainder) the Lord Vasudeo, alone has remained. "I am Vasudeva myself" have I thus realized.

The knot is cut; ignorance is destroyed.
Rama, the indestructible, is the reality.

Lahore, December, 1898

Bliss, bliss, bliss, excessive bliss I have. Night and day exist only for the earth. There is neither night nor day in the sun; there it is all light.

Pleasure and pain, satisfaction and dissatisfaction are for the people of the world. You are the store of perfect bliss, all-light.

Night and day are lost in the sun.
I am light! light! light!
Fire may feel cold and water thirsty.
But hope or desire can have nothing to do with
Rama, the store of bliss.

In the one-essence of mine, a million colors are produced. What fun I enjoy. Hurrah! Hurrah!

Lahore, December, 1898

I got your letter in which you write "I can't understand what you are always thinking about." Believe me, just as your body at Gujranwala cannot understand what Rama thinks about, your body at Lahore too does not understand it. I find no thought in Rama, for thought there is none. How can there be dust of thought in the perfect, pure essence and the clear sky of consciousness? "Dust can never fly in the clear sky of pure consciousness."

One of the causes of the delay in reply was that I had no stamp or post card; I found three postage stamps in a book today and found your card in front demanding a reply, so I wrote this letter.

The same is the condition of provisions. There is no oil in my lamp today. So I shall not stay at home tonight; I will walk round the city. I am ever happy.

Pray do not infer from this account that Rama is poor and in distress. No, he is not. This outer poverty and indigence are the cause of his extreme richness and kinghood. This lesson has been so fully learnt that I feel no need for the fulfillment of that for which materials are not available; in fact, a need which appears in the absence of its materials is a false need. Formerly I had to strive hard to meet my needs, but now, if after having been fulfilled, they happen to appear of themselves, Rama may cast a glance on them, else they are not fortunate enough to be noticed by Rama. *Prarabdha karma* and time, if like servants they need, may come to kiss Rama's feet a hundred times. Else what does emperor Rama care to remember whether that servant has or has not come to offer his respects.

> If a hundred times they so desire, they may wash thy feet and drink the water. Why shouldst thou incline towards the sky, the sun and the moon?
> Dagger dare not inflict a wound on thee.
> Thy own thought has wounded thee.

Kashmir, Summer, 1899

Rama is comfortably sitting on a peak near Kukarnag. Are there on the hillsides beds upon beds of flowers or are they chairs occupied by the gods of air, water, light, wealth, etc.? It is the court of emperor Rama. Below in the plains are beautifully arranged red, green and bright green carpets. On this stage dancing girls (rivers) are gaily dancing and are winning one's heart with their sweet songs. Bravo, your winning of the heart! Whosoever looks at you gets a place in your very heart (so clear is the water). These tall trees, wearing garlands of creepers and earrings of blue and yellow flowers, why are they waving to and fro? They are appreciating the beauty of the rivers.

My charming Beloved who steals my heart, puts on for me new ornaments and paints every moment.

I am wrong. Those rivers whom I thought to be playful dancing girls are really snakes and their consorts. They are biting (too cold) serpents that are darting forward, waving, coiling, curling and hissing. Shankar (Amarnath) has sent his snakes to dance before Rama.

Have a walk and from a distance see the flowers of this garden. Beware! Do not make garlands of them for your neck. The world is the children's playground in my eyes. Night and day the play goes on before me. The desert conceals itself in sand as I appear. The river rubs his head on the dust before me. The world is but a name to me; the being of things is but imagination.

Green hills on both sides. Thick shade. Rama going on the river bank. The eyes are pleased and the heart is happy at the sight of pretty little green leaves and fresh foliage. Waterfalls and zig-zag natural gardens at every step are intoxicating me with the wine of my own essence (Self). Luxuriant green trees in clusters, drowsy with the bloom of youth, are decorating themselves with flowers in their ears and garlands of creepers in their necks, as if they are to form a marriage procession.

My gracefully walking Beloved comes at every moment in fresh grandeur and strolls on the banks of the river of the world.

The beauties of nature's garden are standing in rows after rows in a fancy fair, waiting to sell their grace to one blandishing glance of Rama.

Tehri, Fall, 1900

Residence in Forest

> Let us go and take up our abode where there may be none else, neither foe nor friend.
> If we fall ill, none may be there to inquire about us, and if we die, none to lament.
> Farewell! O Prison! Madness is knocking at the door,
> Goodness, O thorns of the forest! The soles of my feet again are itching.
> Spring has returned to the garden, the wounds of the rose (heart) has become fresh.
> The scars of my madness are playing havoc with me.

Two years ago Rama's living bones were cast into the Ganges. About a year ago, he took a trip to Kashmir.

If one discovers a mirage, why will one go there to take water? If he is forced by someone to go, he will not go with zest.

The reality of sense objects is realized. Their charm is gone. How can I be interested in them? The potter, having put his wheel in motion, goes and sits on his comfortable seat; of mere inertia, the wheel goes on rotating, but how long? After all its speed slackens; without the master's fresh impetus, it would gradually stop.

When the *jiva*, the doer and enjoyer in a particular body, has taken his real seat, how long will that body revolve like the potter's wheel? Worldly relations will loosen, and gradually bodilessness will set in, and thus this couplet will be translated into action.

> How can the light ones (those relieved from worldly desire) remain captives in their native land (drudgery of worldly life)?
> The scent of the rose always jumps out of the walls of the garden.

It is night. I am in a forest in a valley amidst beautiful trees. How am I to describe the sky? It is a tray of sapphire full of pearls. The moon is a large ruby among pearls; clouds are a kerchief covering the tray. With this tray on her head is dancing happy nature. What a happy idea has occurred to the wind; he has discovered what Rama has in his heart. He is gently fanning Rama with sweet, cool breeze laden with the scented vapors of Gangaji flowing close by. The privilege of serving Rama had made the wind glad, and he has raised his head up to the clouds. He is now playing pranks with them; and is turning over the skirt of the clouds. Lo! He has made the kerchief fly and disclosed the blue tray full of wealth.

Nature is happy; she is glittering; her brilliant eyes

she is turning on all the four sides. Is it Ganga in the moonlight or milk colored with diamonds? Excellent! Forest is tonight in a happy mood. Come and see it, come, come, come. "O life of my life! Come, come, this is a different world, with different water, different air, and different place."

Gangotri, Winter, 1900

With a piece of cloth round his waist, Rama is going and singing. What? Om.

At one place, continually for ten miles, run two parallel walls of mountain ranges. In between them, on one side striking aginst the rocks, Ganga is winding her way; on the other side, on the steep hillside, is cut a narrow bridle path. It is about two or three o'clock in the night. Stillness prevails; clouds are hanging; not a bird flutters its wings. Lo! Lightning flashes; clouds thunder and try their strength with the mountains. Boulders and trees begin to fall on the bridle path with a crash. Rama has no umbrella over his head; bare are his feet; no stick in hand, no warm clothing.

Through the dampness of spirit I am grief incarnate;
  exertion causes blisters in the feet.
My dampness of spirit is like the dust storm of grief,
  and my walking is like tears of shame.
I have no nest to rest in, no feathers to fly with.
Tyranny! Rank tyranny! That thy blandishments
  give me no opportunity of getting free.
The forest is proud of being measured by my feet.
The thorns are proud of having kissed my feet.

This is the spot which even in midday man rarely happens to pass. Who is walking here at dead of night? Who else but he who keeps awake even in the darkest night of deep sleep.

Always I awake, always I awake.

Walking under these conditions, a broken path is met with; the way is blocked. But what obstacle can prevent Rama? Catching hold of thorny bushes and feeling his way among gravel and boulders, Rama is ascending the hill. Rama is present where even a goat cannot reach.

I have reached the world of realization, having
  torn three thousand curtains.
I am the fruit of the tree of reality, I am the garden
  of the spring of God.
The head of Kaaba burns with my magic, the heart of
  the temple is warm with the rush of my blood.
Pass not by the scene of my madness, for I am the
  omnipresent day of judgment.

How loud are the shouts of Om, Om, Om on the top of the mountain. O people who keep in bed in the latter part of the night, has not this clamor reached your ears yet? Your sleep is not yet broken? Clouds! Go and proclaim to the world with beat of drum, "Om." Lightning, run and write in letters of fire, "Om."

In response, the clouds roar and awaken the very stones, lightning flashes light on trees and animals. Light has gladly obeyed Rama's command. Sky has carried it on his head.

India awakens! Awakens! Awakens!
The sky said, "Well." The angels said, "Well done!"
Om! Om! Om!

Slavery! Weakness! It is the time for you to roll up your bed; take your goods and run for your life; leave the land of the emancipated. Clouds are weeping at your death. Flow away in the Ganges. Go and drown yourself in the ocean. Get yourself frozen on the Himalayas.

At this dangerous and dreadful spot, Rama is fearlessly warning death. Does he not fear for his life?

How can he, who is not absent from anywhere, entertain fear? Has death the power even to breathe without Rama's permission? This body of Rama shall not fall till India has risen!

Sacramento, May, 1903, Mrs. Florence Wellman

The President of the United States on his way to the north stopped at the Springs awhile. The representative lady of the Springs Company presented him with a basket of lovely flowers, and immediately after that he accepted from Rama most gracefully, lovingly and cheerfully the "Appeal on behalf of India." He kept the book in his right hand all the time, and while responding with his right hand to the salutations of the crowds, the book naturally and spontaneously rose up to his forehead at least a hundred times. When the train started, he was seen reading it attentively in his carriage, and once more he waved thanks to Rama from the leaving train.

But lo! Rama never invited the President to the luxury of enjoying a swing in the poetic hammock. Could you guess why not? Do guess, please. Well, as you don't speak, Rama will tell you. The reason is plain enough. The President of the so-called free Americans is not a thousandth part as free as Rama's birdies and the air.

Never mind the President. You can be free, ever free, as Rama, and have air and light as your faithful servants. Be Rama, and Rama will give you all—suns, stars, air, ocean, clouds, forests, mountains and what not? Everything will belong to you. Is not that a lovely bargain? Isn't it, dear? Do you have everything, please?

At four in the morning, waked by the kisses of

Aurora and tickled to laughter by free zephyrs, welcomed by the sweet songs of carolling birds, Rama goes out walking on the tops of mountains and the riverside.

Come, let us laugh together, laugh, laugh, laugh. Come soon, my child; look into the fearless smiling eyes of Rama and live close to nature and Rama. The ecstasy itself is I.

Denver, January, 1904

The object of this philosophy is to regulate the conduct of the present life. It has a plain, practical bearing upon the things of today. You may be disappointed, but there is nothing mystical, or occult about me, although I come from the deepest forests of the Himalayas. To minimize the waste of energy, to abolish wear and tear of body and mind, to secure freedom from all kinds of dissipation due to envy, vanity, distemper and blues, to cure mental dyspepsia and to remove intellectual pauperism and spiritual slavery, to attain the secret of successful work, to realize God through love, to keep in touch with the origin of knowledge, how to preserve our equilibrium and peace, these are the subjects I teach.

My religion is not Hinduism, Mohammedanism, Christianity, Catholicism or Protestantism, but it is antagonistic to none. The overlapping area covered by the light, the sun, the stars, the rivers' gravity; mind and body, this is the field of my religion. Are there any Presbyterian lilies? Are there any Methodist landscapes? So do I make no distinction of class, color, or creed in greeting, as my co-religionists, the rays of sun, the beams of stars, the leaves of trees, the blades of grass, the grains of sand, the hearts of tigers, elephants, lambs, ants, men, women and children. My religion is the religion without a nickname. It is the religion of nature. I label none, brand none, possess none, but serve all like light and sun. So I call it "The Common Path."

The central teaching of the "Common Path" I have put into verse:

> Dear little violet, with thy dewy eye,
> Look up and tell me truly
> When no one is nigh,
> What thou art?
>
> The violet answered with a gentle sigh:
> If that is to be told when alone,
> Then I must sadly own
> It will never be known
> What am I,
> For my brothers and sisters are all around
> In the air and on the ground
> And they are the same as I.

India, Early 1905

The land of India is my body; the rivers are my arteries; the mountains, my bones. As my hand goes of itself to scratch any part of my body, so nature comes to my help to fulfil the needs of my soul. The snowstorm on the heights of the Himalayas, a sure death for others, spreads for me only a soft white velvet making stepping on it so easy. It is a sacrilege to walk on the rocks with any socks or shoes on. The touch of the bare ground inspires omniscience in the bare foot; my flesh and the flesh of the rocks must touch each other fully to know each other fully. We talk and understand each other heart to heart, and our love goes silently all underground from breast to breast. Man is God only if he drops his dotted "i" and washes it in the flowing Ganges. Man is God if joy flows from him to heaven, blessed by heaven in a reflex current back. I am Shiva; the Malabar and Coromandel are my two legs; the deserts of Rajputana, my breast; the Vindhyachals are my loins, and I spread my arms to the West as well as to the East. The Himalayas are my tressed head, and in my curls winds the pure silver Ganga. I am India. I am man; I am bird, beast; I am God.

Darjeeling, Spring, 1905

Day passes into night, and night again turns into day, and here is your Rama having no time to do anything, very busy in doing nothing. Tears keep pouring, vying well with the continuous rains of this the most rainy district; the hairs stand on end, the eyes wide open seeing nothing of the things before them. Talk stopped; work stopped unfortunately (?). No, most fortunately. Oh, leave me alone. This continuous wave after wave of inarticulate ecstasy—O love! Let it go on. On the most delicious pain!

Away with writing.
Off with lecturing.
Out with fame and name.
Honors? Nonsense.
Disgrace? Meaningless.
Are these toys the end of life?

Logic and science, poor bunglers! Let them see me and get their blindness cured.

In dreams a sacred current flows.
In wakefulness, it grows and grows.
At times, it overflows the banks
Of senses and the mortal frame.
It spreads in all the world and flows,
It inundates in wild repose.

For this the sun, he daily rose.
For this the universe did roll.
All births and deaths for this.
Here comes rolling, surging, wonder, undulating bliss.
Here comes rolling laughter, silence.

Darjeeling side, Summer, 1905

Om, om, om! Peace! Blessings! Love! Joy! Joy!
Most Blessed Dear Divinity,

Perhaps you know already Rama is in the hills about a thousand miles from Mussoorie. Rama lives all alone in an old house belonging to the Bengal Forest authorities, away from the railway line, removed from the Post Office, beyond reach of visitors and callers, surrounded by a scenery among the richest in the world, with beautiful rills, and a spring running at short distance from it, and when the weather is fair, commanding a distant view of the world's highest mountain, Mt. Everest. Even here fresh milk is brought to Rama by the mountaineers living in the woods. Walks in the woods and study fill up Rama's time.

What are name, fame, ambitions, wealth, achievements and all when "man in the woods with God may meet?" Why should we catch and cherish the fever of doing?

Let us be divine. The morning breeze blows and is not anxious how many and what sort of flowers bloom. It simply blows on everything, and those buds that are full ripe to sprout open their eyes. The dens of lions, the burning jungles, the dingy dungeons, the earthquake shocks, the falling rocks, the storms, the battlefields and the gaping graves, if accompanied by God-consciousness in us, are far sweeter than pomp, honor, glory, thrones, luxuries, retinue and all when with these a man is not himself, in inner solitude one with the One without a second. Oh! the joy of the finished purpose, light steps going about making every step our goal, every night the bodily death and every day our new life.

Farewell, friends, and part.
The mansion-universe is too small.
I and my love alone will play.
Oh! The joys of swimming together!
Together? No.
The joy of swimmers dissolved rolling as the ocean!
Joy! Joy! Om! Your own Self, OM

Vashishtha Ashram, June, 1906

This evening it stopped raining. The clouds, assuming all sorts of fantastic shapes and different degrees of thickness, have somewhat parted in different directions. Light refracted and reflected from them makes the entire scene a blazing sphere of glory. Then the playful children of heaven put on fascinating colors of all varieties. What painter could paint? What observer could note all the passing shades and hues? Look where you will, the eyes are charmed by the orange, purple, violet and pink colors and their indescribable varieties, while between these the ever-welcome blue-black ground is out here and there. The effulgent glory brings on ecstasy, and tears of joy appear in Rama's eyes. The clouds dissolve but leave a permanent message behind. They brought a cup of nectar from the Lord and went back to Him. Such are, in fact, all attractive objects. They appear, reflect Rama's glory for a second and dissolve. Insane indeed must he be who falls in love with the passing clouds, and yet folks endeavor to hold fast to the unsteady clouds of seeming things and cry on like children finding them gone. How amusing! O! I cannot suppress a laughter.

Others again expend all their time in minutely observing and faithfully noting down the smallest details of transitory changes in clouds (phenomena). O me! What are these creatures! There is a flood of glory around them, and yet they care not to slake their raging thirst for light. These are what they call scientists and philosophers. Being too busy in splitting the hairs, they take no notice of the glorious head of the Beloved to which the hairs belong. O! I cannot suppress a laughter. Happy is he whose vision no clouds of names and forms could obstruct, who could always trace the attracting light to its true source, the *Atman* and whose affections reached the goal (God) not being lost in the way like streams dried up before reaching the sea. The pleasing relations must vanish. They are only postmen. Miss not the Lord's love-letter which they have brought for you. The matchstick must soon burn off, but blessed is he who has lighted his lamp permanently therewith. The steam and food supply must ere long be consumed, but fortunate is the boat which before the fatal loss reached the home, the harbor. He lives who could make of every object whatever a stepping stone to God or rather a mirror to see God. The world with all its stars, mountains, rivers, kings and scientists, etc. was made for him. Verily it is so; I tell you the truth.

The fields and landscapes, wherein lies their refreshing charms as contrasted with the sickening smoky streets of cities, by criticism or compliments, they excite not in man the sense of limitation, and they drive him not into the corner (bodyhood). Man, in their presence, can well occupy the position of a witness-light. Inwardly, the vegetable kingdom has as much, and perhaps more, of strife and struggle and unrest, etc., than the civilized societies but even their struggles become interesting in so far as a man among cedars, oaks and pines easily sees himself not one of them, but can keep himself the witness-light unconcerned. He who can live in busy streets as anybody might move in forest, feeling the Self as disinterested witness-light, not identifying himself with the body which in this case may be taken as a plant among plants, who could deny that the universe is a garden of Eden to him? Such people of god-life are the light of the world. The light which appears as unconcerned witness is the very life of all that it witnesses.

The river of life is flowing. None exists but God. Of whom shall I be afraid, of whom ashamed? All life is my God's life, nothing other. He and Me too is He. The whole world is my own Himalayan woods. When light dawns, flowers begin to laugh, birds sing, and streams dance with joy! O that light of lights! The sea of light of lights is flowing! The breeze of bliss is blowing!

In this beautiful forest, I laugh and sing, clap hands and dance.

Did they jeer? It was blowing of the breeze. Did they sneer? It was hissing of the leaves. Shall I be overshadowed by my own life pulsating in the streams, cedars, birds and breezes?

Sumeru Visited

While living in the Jamnotri cave, Rama's daily food

was marcha and potatoes once in twenty-four hours. This brought on indigestion. About seven motions every day for three successive days. On the fourth day of ill health, early in the morning after bathing in the hot springs, he started on his trip to Sumeru, wearing no clothes except a Kaupin (a rag around the loins), no shoes, no headdress, no umbrella. Five strong mountaineers, having warm clothes on accompany him. Narayana and Tularam were sent back down to Gharsali.

To begin with we had to cross the infant Jamuna three or four times. Then the Jamuna valley was found blocked up by an enormous avalanche about 45 yards in height and one furlong and a half in length. Steep mountains like two vertical walls stood proudly on both sides. Have they conspired to deter Rama Badshah from advancing further? Never mind! All obstructions must disappear before a strong adamantine will. We began to climb the western mountain wall. Now and again we could get absolutely no foothold and had to support our bodies partly by catching hold of the twigs of fragrant but thorny rose bushes, and partly by entangling our toes in the tender blades of the soft mountain grass called cha. At times we were within an inch of sure death. A deep abyss with the cold bed of snow filling the Jamuna valley was a grave wide agape, just ready to give too hospitable a reception to any one of the party whose foot might tremble ever so little. From beneath, the slow, faint, murmuring sound of the Jamuna was still reaching our ears like the death dirge of muffled drums. Thus we had to move along in the jaws of death, as it were, for three quarters of an hour. Strange situation indeed, death staring us in the face on one side and air redolent with sweet scent refreshing and animating on the other. By this circuitous, dangerous enterprise we reached at last beyond the awful avalanche. Here the Jamuna left, and the party ascended a steep mountain. There was no road, no foot-path, nothing of the kind. A thick dense forest was passed where we could not see the wood of the trees. Rama's body received several scratches. After a little more than an hour's struggle in this forest of oak and birch trees, we reached open ground covered all over with smaller growth. The atmosphere was charged, rather saturated, with delicious odors. The ascent put all the mountaineers out of breath. Even Rama felt it to be a good exercise. Inclines of 80° and even more had to be scaled. The ground was for the most part slippery. But all around, the stately vistas and charming flowerage and teeming foliage beguiled the hard journey. European gardeners, in general, get seeds of flowers from places like these to decorate Indian company gardens, where the ignorant English speaking young men call them English flowers. But the remarkable peculiarity of most of these flowers is that when planted elsewhere they yield no fragrance, although they retain their original color.

Young men puffed up with European education, while reading the re-echoes of the Vedanta through the writings of European professors become fond admirers of what they deem to be Western thought, not knowing that the flowers of thought for which they have taken a fancy have been transplanted from their own motherland, with this remarkable difference that in the hands of European teachers the wonderful flowers have lost their sweet fragrance of renunciation. Vedanta as presented by Europeans keeps the form and color of philosophy but loses the delicious scent of realization.

What about the health of Rama who had been ailing? He was all right that day, no disease, no fatigue, no complaint of any kind. No mountaineer could go ahead of him. We went on climbing and climbing till every one of the part felt very hungry. By this time we had reached a region where it never rains, but snow falls in gracious bounty. There was no trace of vegetation of any kind on these bald bleak heights. There had been a fresh snowfall before our arrival.

A red blanket was spread on a big slab of stone as a carpet for Rama. Potatoes that had been boiled the night before were given him to eat. The companions took their stale simple food most thankfully. There is no one in his company now.

For nearly three miles he walked over the snows. Sometimes the legs got immersed and were drawn out not without struggle. At last on a snowy mound, the red blanket was spread. Rama sits on it, all alone, above the noises and turmoils of the world, beyond the fumes and furies of the multitude. Perfect silence reigns here. What perfect peace prevails! No sound of any kind audible except the *ananda shanti*.* Most blessed serene solitude!

The veil of clouds became a little less thick. The rays of the sun sifted through the thin clouds fell on the scene and immediately turned the silver snows into burning gold. Very appropriately has this place been called Sumeru, the mountain of gold.

O ye men of the world! Mark it; no purple bloom on a lady's cheek, no bright jewelry or fine ornaments, no superb mansion can ever possess an iota of the transcendent

* blissful peace.

enchantment and fascination of this Sumeru. And numberless Sumerus like this you will find within you when once you realize your own real Self. All nature shall do you homage, "from cloud to cloud, from the blue sky to the green earth, all living creatures therein included, from the eagle to the mole." No god shall dare disobey!

Clear up, O sky! Disperse, ye clouds of ignorance that overhang India! No more shall ye hover over this blessed land. O Himalayan snows, your master orders you to keep fast to your purity and faithfulness to truth (light). Never shall ye send waters impregnated with dualism to the plains.

The clouds are rent asunder. The snows all assume ochre-colored appearance. Have the mountains embraced Sannyas? They have certainly put on Rama's livery; what a phenomenon! The mountain snows look up to Rama in submissive willingness to run his errands.

Hip Hip Hurrah! Hip Hip Hurrah!
The rounded world is fair to see,
Nine times folded in mystery:
Though baffled seers cannot impart
The secret of its laboring heart.
Throb time with nature's throbbing breast,
And all is clear from east to west.

"Well," says the American sage, "nature is the incarnation of a thought and turns to a thought again as ice become water and gas." The world is mind precipitated, and the volatile essence is forever escaping again into the state of free thought. Hence this virtue and pungency of the influence on the mind of natural objects, whether inorganic or organized. Man imprisoned, man crystallized, man vegetative, speaks to man impersonated.

Question: If the world is my own idea (mind precipitated) why do not the external objects change at my will?

Answer: Says Gaudapada Acharya, "Mere thought in the dreamland divides itself into external objects on the one hand and internal emotions, desires and so forth, on the other. Moreover, the internal thought in that state seems to be in one's control, changeable and comparatively unreal, whereas the external objects (as in a nightmare) appear to possess comparatively uncontrollable, stable reality of their own."

Now as a matter of fact, from the point of view of man in the wakeful state, both the real and the unreal, the external and the internal aspects of a dream are but idea, pure and simple, and they are besides one's own idea, one's own creation. Again, in the wakeful state, people distinguish between what they call stern, constant, external objects and the unreal, internal thought. But to the man of Self-realization the hard objects, no less than the variable thoughts in the long run, become non-entity like a dream, and so long as their appearance lasts, they affect him as his own; even though they cannot be altered at will, yet they are his own ideas. Your intellect cannot give an explanation of the growth of your hair or of the bloom of your face, still you regard the hair and the fair complexion your own. Just so, a *Jivana-Mukta* finding himself to be the soul of all must regard every object his own. He is all love. For him even the appearance of the real as well as the ideal is gradually relieved by the only One-without-a-second consciousness.

Maya

Torch-whirling *(mahratti jwala)* is not uncommon in certain parts of India. The glowing flame looks now like a broad circle of light, now appears to be an unbroken streak of fire, again assumes an elliptical form, goes up, comes down and manifests many amusing phenomena. Are these phenomena inherent in the flame? Do they come out of the torch or firebrand? Do they come from without? When the *mahratti* is not revolving do the phenomena enter into it or do they go elsewhere? To all these queries one has to answer in the negative. The torch in whirling motion exhibits straight and curved lines; when motion stops there is no trace of such appearances in the torch. Even when the torch was in rapid motion, the curves, though visible, were far from being real.

Just so absolute consciousness, like the firebrand at rest, has no trace of manifold names and forms (the phenomenal worlds), and even when the variety of names and forms makes an appearance, their appearance is illusory like that of the *mahratti* phenomena. Consciousness is always untouched and untainted by them. The one indivisible flame (light) is ever present in all the phenomena, and the phenomena never exist in the flame (light). Similarly, in all names and forms Rama is manifest, but in Rama names and forms are evanescent. As the *mahratti* phenomena owe their seeming existence to motion, so the multiplicity of names and forms that make up the world owe their seeming existence to the maya *shakti. Shakti* or power has not any existence of its own. It may be manifested; it may not be manifested. It cannot exist apart. This *maya shakti* in the case of the individual is revealed as what may be called consciousness, motion or activity, *manas* (mind). *Manas* in notion and the phenomenal world are the obverse and reverse of one and the same thing. *Manas* at rest is identical with consciousness.

The absolute *manas* (Brahman) purged of its dross (desires, attachments) loses its fickleness and tends to become steady. Perfect steadiness being attained, *manas* is one with Brahman. By this *sakshatkar maya* is overcome, and the world is converted into a garden of Eden; the Lost Paradise is immediately regained. Beauty breaks in everywhere. The sense of separateness is killed out; all cares and anxieties are merged in the supremely sublime existence, consciousness and bliss forever and ever.

A young man in the presence of Rama plucked a beautiful rose with a view to enjoy its smell. No sooner did he bring it in contact with his nose than a bee stung him just on the tip of the nose. The man cried with pain; the rose fell from his hand.

Do the petals of every rose enfold a bee? Certainly, there is not a rose of sensual pleasure which has not got the bee of injury concealed in it. Unbridled desires must be punished by inevitable pain.

Ye given to dreadful oblivion, forget not your own Self. Ye need not pluck the gaudy rose. Wherever the full blown rose lies, there you are; its vermillion or sweet scent is your own. King, his staff is yours; beauty, he her charms are yours; diamond or gold, its burning rays are yours. Why entertain vain desires, and what for? Realize your unity with the All, your oneness with God. You are that divine Krishna who danced hand in hand with every one of the hundreds of Gopis at one and the same time. In the sea as well as in the palace, in the garden as well as in the desert, in the battlefield or the private chamber, you are always equally present.

Rama cries from the tops of the highest mountains, "Ye who complain of weakness and poverty, verily ye are

Lord Almighty, ye are Rama himself. Imprison not yourself, shake off your sleep and this dream of a world." Why grovel in misery and helplessness when it is no other than your own Self which is all in all? O, rise up to Self-consciousness, and all sorrows shall vanish. Ye are the essence of all happiness; ye are the soul of all joy. Nothing can do you harm. For Rama's sake, know your *Atman*. Why delay? Know it; as it is , it ought to be known. Are ye not hunting after happiness day and night with unremitting zeal and unflagging efforts but with unfailing failure? Don't make fools of yourselves. Seek not happiness in the objects of the senses. Dupes of senses! Give up your vain search outside. The ocean of immortality is within you. The kingdom of heaven is within you. Ye are the nectar of nectars. Let both the mind and the world be melted down in God-consciousness. Just abandon your little selves to blessed madness. Ye dear ones, why care so much for the quarantine of a mortal body. Harbor not a single thought within you as to what shall become of this not-self. Banish the superstition of all relations. Let the eyes perish that do not see God. Woe unto the heart that cherishes the disease of desires! Wipe away all ungodliness. Hold fast to your true position. No praise or blame can come up there, no sorrow or petty joy can disturb then. Receive divinity into the ship and then let all go. Let go the shore; let go the little self; let go the sail! Yet the gale of divine love takes the poor flimsy dark cotton sail of this frail human bark and wafts it right out on the ocean of God-consciousness. Happy is he who is drowned in heavenly intoxication. Blessed is he who is dead-drunk in divine madness. Worshipful is he who is absorbed in deep *Atmananda* and supreme bliss, being lost to the world.

July, 1906

Visit to Sahasru-Tal

To travel on almost heaven-high ridges for miles and miles, viewing the waving forests of birch and juniper spreading far below, flowery precipices lying on the right as well as the left hand side; to walk barefooted on extensive fields covered with soft velvety grass where loving dainty flowers cling to your feet getting entangled in the toes; to enjoy the silvery sights of rushing waterfalls on distant Kailas-cliffs; to watch clever, little musk deer springing at lightning speed before you (well might the moon ride such a beautiful runner); to be startled now and then by *garuras* (royal eagles) fluttering their painted, large wings now on this side, then on the other; to stoop to pick every now and then Kailas lotuses which in their lovely petals combine gold and fragrance; to be amused at the coolies outdoing each other in digging *Masi, Lesar, Guggal*, the different kinds of incense which abound here in charming plenty and to sing hymns and chant OM, engaged our time. Far, far and above the din and bustle of worldly life, deep and vast blue lakes in their crystalline expanse, rippling under the pure and free Kailas air, surrounded by chaste, virgin snows, hold a mirror up to the very face of the blooming, blushing sun. In such lofty solitude, serenely does the sun enjoy his charming glory. On such heights, no hamlet or hut could be expected; the nights were passed in caves where breezes sleep. O, the joy of leaving behind the prosaic of plains of parching body consciousness! O, the joy of mingling with the sun and breezes! O, the joy of roaming in the heavenly infinite forest deeps of One-without-a-second!

the Himalayan Institute

GLOBAL HEADQUARTERS (USA)

The main building of the Himalayan Institute headquarters near Honesdale, Pennsylvania, USA.

FOUNDED IN 1971 BY SWAMI RAMA, the Himalayan Institute has been dedicated to helping people grow physically, mentally, and spiritually by combining the best knowledge of both the East and the West.

Our international headquarters is located on a beautiful 400-acre campus in the rolling hills of the Pocono Mountains of northeastern Pennsylvania, USA. The atmosphere here is one to foster growth, increase inner awareness, and promote calm. Our grounds provide a wonderfully peaceful and healthy setting for our seminars and extended programs. Students from all over the world join us here to attend programs in such diverse areas as hatha yoga, meditation, stress reduction, ayurveda, nutrition, Eastern philosophy, psychology, and other subjects. Whether the programs are for weekend meditation retreats, week-long seminars on spirituality, months-long residential programs, or holistic health services, the attempt here is to provide an environment of gentle inner progress. We invite you to join with us in the ongoing process of personal growth and development.

Programs and Services *include:*

The Institute is a nonprofit organization. Your membership in the Institute helps to support its programs. Please call or write for information on becoming a member.

Programs and Services Include:

- Himalayan Institute Press
- Seminars and Workshops
- Meditation Retreats
- Yoga Teacher Training
- Self-Transformation Program™
- Residential Programs
- Pancha Karma
- Himalayan Institute Total Health Products and Services
- Spiritual Excursions
- Humanitarian Projects and Community Centers in Africa, India and Mexico
- YogaInternational.com

For further information about our programs, humanitarian projects, and products,

call: +1 800-822-4547

e-mail: info@HimalayanInstitute.org

write: The Himalayan Institute
952 Bethany Turnpike
Honesdale, PA 18431

or visit: www.HimalayanInstitute.org

THE HIMALAYAN INSTITUTE INDIA is a beacon of practical wisdom and an indispensable guide for sincere spiritual seekers. Its main mission is to promote the wisdom of the Himalayan Tradition through publication of a wide range of titles on yoga, meditation, spirituality, and holistic health. Himalayan Institute India is headquartered in Allahabad (U.P.), at its 30-acre campus on the banks of the Ganga.

The Himalayan Institute Press has long been regarded as the resource for holistic living. We publish books that offer practical methods for living harmoniously and achieving inner balance. Our approach addresses the whole person—body, mind and spirit—integrating the latest scientific knowledge with ancient healing and self-development techniques. As such, we offer a wide array of titles on physical and psychological health and well-being, spiritual growth through meditation and other yogic practices, as well as translations of yogic scriptures.

Himalayan Institute Press Titles

Swami Rama

A Practical Guide to Holistic Health ₹250
Book of Wisdom (Ishopanishad) ₹250
Celestial Song: Gobind Geet ₹295
Choosing a Path ₹295
Creative Use of Emotion ₹295
Enlightenment without God (Mandukya Upanishad) ₹250
Exercises for Joints and Glands ₹250
Fearless Living: Yoga & Faith ₹295
Freedom from the Bondage of Karma ₹195
Happiness Is Your Creation ₹250
Indian Music ₹350
Inspired Thoughts of Swami Rama ₹395
Japji: Meditation in Sikhism ₹199
Living with the Himalayan Masters ₹425
Love and Family Life ₹250
Love Whispers ₹250
Life Here and Hereafter (Kathopanishad) ₹295
Meditation and Its Practice ₹250
Meditation in Christianity ₹250
Mystical Poems of Kabir ₹250
Path of Fire and Light ₹295
Path of Fire and Light, Volume-2 ₹295
Perennial Psychology of the Bhagavad Gita ₹695
Science of Breath ₹250
Spirituality: Transformation Within & Without ₹295
Swami Rama Gift Book Set ₹250
The Art of Joyful Living ₹295

The Royal Path: Practical Lessons on Yoga ₹295
Wisdom of the Ancient Sages (Mundaka Upanishad) ₹295
Yoga and Psychotherapy ₹495

Pandit Rajmani Tigunait, PhD

From Death To Birth (Understanding Karma and Reincarnation) ₹295
Inner Quest: Yoga's Answers to Life's Questions ₹350
Lighting the Flame of Compassion ₹250
Sakti Sadhana (Tripura Rahasya) ₹350
Sakti: The Power in Tantra ₹350
Seven Systems of Indian Philosophy ₹350
Swami Rama of the Himalayas (Photobiography) ₹2500
Tantra Unveiled (Seducing the Forces of Matter and Spirit) ₹295
The Himalayan Masters: A Living Tradition ₹295
The Official Biography of Swami Rama of the Himalayas ₹395
The Power of Mantra & The Mystery of Initiation ₹295
The Pursuit of Power and Freedom: Katha Upanishad ₹295
The Secret of the Yoga Sutra: Samadhi Pada ₹695
Touched By Fire ₹395
Why We Fight ₹195

Books by Other Authors

Anatomy of Hatha Yoga, David Coulter PhD ₹695
Freedom From Stress, Phil Nuernberger, PhD ₹350
God, Swami Veda Bharati ₹295
Happiness: The Real Medicine, Blair Lewis ₹295
Healing the Whole Person, Swami Ajaya, PhD ₹295
Moving Inward: The Journey to Meditation, Rolf Sovik, PsyD ₹395
Philosophy of Hatha Yoga, Swami Veda Bharati ₹250
Spirit on the Move, Yoga International ₹295
The Muscle Book, Paul Blakey ₹250
The Practical Vedanta of Swami Rama Tirtha, Edited by Brandt Dayton ₹495
The Theory and Practice of Meditation, Rudolph Ballentine, M.D., Swami Rama ₹295
Yoga: Mastering the Basics (Photobook), Sandra Anderson & Rolf Sovik ₹995
Yoga Psychology (A Practical Guide to Meditation), Swami Ajaya, PhD ₹250
Yoga Sutras of Patanjali, Swami Veda Bharati ₹895

Hindi Titles

Anandmaya Jeevan Ka Utsav, Swami Rama ₹150
Himalaye ke Siddha Yogi: Sri Swami Rama (Shiksha aur Sadhana), Pandit Rajmani Tigunait ₹150
Himalaye ke Santo ke Sang Niwas, Swami Rama ₹295
Janam Mrithyu ka Rahasya (Kathopanishad), Swami Rama ₹125
Karam Bandhan se Mukti, Swami Rama ₹95

HIMALAYAN
INSTITUTE®
INDIA